ISBN 978-1-331-88032-5
PIBN 10249068

This book is a reproduction of an important historical work. Forgotten Books uses
state-of-the-art technology to digitally reconstruct the work, preserving the original format
whilst repairing imperfections present in the aged copy. In rare cases, an imperfection in
the original, such as a blemish or missing page, may be replicated in our edition. We do,
however, repair the vast majority of imperfections successfully; any imperfections that
remain are intentionally left to preserve the state of such historical works.

1 MONTH OF
FREE
READING

at

www.ForgottenBooks.com

By purchasing this book you are eligible for one month membership to ForgottenBooks.com, giving you unlimited access to our entire collection of over 1,000,000 titles via our web site and mobile apps.

To claim your free month visit: www.forgottenbooks.com/free249068

THE

COMPLETE WORKS

IN

VERSE AND PROSE

OF

SAMUEL DANIEL.

VOL. III.—THE DRAMATIC WORKS.

THE
COMPLETE WORKS

IN

VERSE AND PROSE

OF

SAMUEL DANIEL.

Edited, with Memorial-Introduction and a Glossarial
Index embracing Notes and Illustrations.

BY THE
REV. ALEXANDER B. GROSART,

D.D., LL.D. (EDIN.), F.S.A. (SCOT.),

St. George's, Blackburn, Lancashire;

IN FOUR VOLUMES.

VOL. III.—THE DRAMATIC WORKS.

I. CLEOPATRA. 1594—1623.
II. PHILOTAS. 1607.
III. THE VISION OF THE TWELVE GODDESSES. 1604.
IV. THE QVEENES ARCADIA. 1606.
V. TETHYS FESTIVALL. 1610.
VI. HYMENS TRIUMPH. 1615.

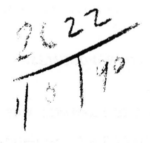

CONTENTS.

CONTENTS.

PRELIMINARY NOTE

ON THE POSITION OF DANIEL'S TRAGEDIES
IN ENGLISH LITERATURE.

[It gives me no little pleasure to avail myself of the following spontaneous 'Note' by my friend GEORGE SAINTSBURY, Esq. More on the subject may be looked for in the ' Memorial-Introduction II.—Critical ' on other lines of influence of the Senecan or Daniel form of plays. But meanwhile the present 'Note' is complete within its self-appointed limits.—A. B. G.]

THESE few words are not intended as a criticism of *Cleopatra* and *Philotas*: I have no intention of interfering with Dr. Grosart's province to that extent, or of abusing his good nature. It has, however, often struck me that the precise position of these tragedies in our literature, and the very interesting reflections which they present to any one who knows the sixteenth-century literature of France and Italy, especially of France, has been singularly overlooked. I have, I think, a tolerably fair acquaintance with Elizabethan drama; but except these two, and the translation of Garnier's *Cornelia* which Kyd executed, I cannot think of any English tragedies (written by dramatists at all well known, and belonging to the formative period of the drama) which are distinctly couched in the form of the Senecan model. No doubt some earlier plays show traces (more or less) of the influence of that model, and some later show traces of the influence of the French dramatists who adopted it ; but these only follow it exactly. The fact is, of course, in no sense a discovery ; but I need only quote two well-known books of different kinds to show that the inferences from it have, as a rule, concerned English dramatic critics very slightly. In Professor Morley's big book on " English Plays," I can find (and the index at least does not convict me of carelessness) no mention whatever of Daniel's dramas, nor is *Cornelia* mentioned in the notice of Kyd. W. C. Hazlitt, in reprinting this last play in his " Dodsley," makes a kind of apology for letting it appear, and alleges the fact of his predecessor's printing it as an only if not a sufficient excuse.

And yet if the commonwealth of English letters (as Charles Kingsley pleasantly expressed it) was exposed to a severe danger from that assault on rhyme which our poet himself repelled so vigorously, it was most assuredly exposed to a danger still greater by the popularity of the dramatic model which Daniel, by a very odd contrast, himself adopted. Comparatively few people read Seneca's tragedies now. They are of the classics that are no classics—that is to say, that enter into no school or university curriculum, and that are read, if they are read at all, for love, and not for duty or for money or for fame. But they had an extraordinary influence on the world of the Renaissance. I do not know that I am quite a fair judge of them, for I read them as a boy, with the interest that some ill-regulated boys are wont to bestow on anything that does not " pay." A friend gave me the pretty little " Regent Classics " edition some five-and-twenty years ago, and I read it without, I confess, the remotest knowledge or idea of Garnier or Kyd, of Jodelle or Daniel. It has been said that no man is a fair judge of literature that he reads under such circumstances. I think, however, that it is not very difficult to judge Seneca judicially, and that it is certainly not difficult to understand his effect on the Renaissance. How great that effect was, no literary historian of the countries in which it had free course has failed to notice; though in France, at any rate, the abundant dramatic production to which it gave rise has only recently met with much attention, and the French themselves have left it to Germany to produce Garnier and promise Montchrestien in modern editions.

The peculiarity of the Senecan tragedy is to be found, first, in its exact and careful form ; secondly, in the prominence which it gives to moral over romantic interest ; thirdly, in the simplicity of its plot and situations. The precepts which Horace drew from the Greek drama seem to have been worked out in it almost without reference to the original material, except in points of form. It is entirely a school drama, an exercise in literature. It knew no sort of condescension to the audience : the audience were expected to make all the advances. Hardly any more words are needed to show how utterly opposed it is to our own form of play, in which at all times, more or less, but most of all between 1575 and 1630, the tastes of the audience were consulted first of all, and splendid literature was offered them as a kind of bonus—a thing into the bargain. It may be said, of course, that the scanty following of this academic style of dramatic performance

in England is sufficient in itself to show that it was
alien from the English genius, and could never have
done much harm. I am not so sure of that. It ought
to be remembered that a form not much worse, and
certainly not any better—the rhymed heroic drama—
held England a little later for a quarter of a century,
and left traditions which coloured English tragedy for
a century more. The attitude of contempt seems to me
by no means so appropriate as the attitude of thank-
fulness in reference to these decorous and scholarly
exercitations, with their choruses and their monologues,
their unities and their decencies of action. When these
identical plays took the French stage by storm, in the
middle of the sixteenth century, and held it in their
simple form till the first quarter of the seventeenth,
in a very slightly changed form till the first quarter of
the nineteenth, they had to deal with a people at least
as fond of dramatic shows as the English, and even
more generally accustomed to a rough but lively variety
of them. Why was one people taken   he other
left ? Why did Seneca take captive the whole drama
of France, from Jodelle, through Garnier and Mont-
chrestien and even Hardy, through Corneille and
Racine and Voltaire, leaving his traces even on Victor
Hugo? Why in England do *Cleopatra* and *Philotas*
stand practically alone, with a lawless multitude, a
hopelessly irregular and incomparably delightful crowd
of quite different productions, surrounding them ? It
is not my business to answer these questions, for which
of course I or any one else could give not one but
half a dozen elaborate and more or less unsatisfactory
answers. I only wish to point to the fact, to the

curious fact, of these two or three plays standing by themselves, as high-water marks of the utmost range of the Senecan tide in literary Europe. " *Tu me crois la marée, et je suis le déluge*," says the great French poet. It was exactly reversed in this case. A deluge of dramatic correctness seemed to menace Europe, and lo ! it was, as far as England was concerned, only a tide, and such an exceptional tide, that literary historians themselves hardly record its farthest. That farthest the reader has now before him, as far as England is concerned, in works (for, as has been said, *Cornelia* is a mere translation, though in parts a pretty free one) almost unique of their kind· No one who knows Daniel's almost unsurpassed faculty of ethical verse-writing will be surprised at his personal adoption of the Senecan tragedy ; but what is really curious is that he stands in that adoption almost alone, amidst a generation of learned persons, all like himself prone to moralise, most eager to write, many enamoured of the dramatic manner of writing. Here, if anywhere, the genius of the nation seems to have exerted its saving force.

X.

DRAMATIC WORKS.

I. CLEOPATRA.
1594—1623.

NOTE.

'Cleopatra' was first published in the 1594 edition of 'Delia' (see title-page of this volume in Vol. I., p. 22), and had this separate title within an architectural (woodcut) design—

THE

Tragedie of

Cleopatra.

(∵)

Ætas prima ca-
nat veneres poſtre-
ma tumul-
tus.

1594.

It was reprinted in the 'Poeticall Eſſayes' of 1599 (see its title-page, Vol. I., p. 3) with this separate title-page within a broad-bordered woodcut design that occurs in various contemporary books—

THE

TRAGEDIE OF

CLEOPATRA

(***)

Aetas prima canat veneres po-
ſtrema tumultus.

SAM. DANYELL.

AT LONDON
Printed by P. S. for Symon
Waterſon.   1599.

The next edition was in the folios of 'Workes' (see Vol. I., p. xix.), 1601, 1602, with no separate title-page. Following this came the successive editions of "Certaine Small Workes Heretofore Divulged by Samuel Daniel" of 1605, 1607, 1609, 1611 ; and in the last year (1611) a distinct impression of the Tragedy by itself (British Museum, b. 19). This brings us to the Quarto of 1623.

Returning on these, the text of 1594 offers noticeable readings, that on revision were deleted in part and in part modified. We record the whole in their places. 1599, 1601 (= 1602), and 1605, except in orthographical and very slight verbal changes, correspond with the text of 1623. But the texts of 1607 and 1611, and the other of 1611, agree in recasting the Play, and in introducing various minor alterations. We have intimation of these changes on the *verso* of the general title-page of 1607 thus—

'The tragedy of Cleopatra newly altred,'

albeit this is (stupidly) repeated similarly in 1609 and 1611 (not in the separate edition of 1611). The editions of 1605, 1607, and 1609 omit the verse epistle-dedicatory to

"The Subject of all verfe
Sidney's fifter, Pembroke's mother,"

except that in the title and half-title respectively they have this—

"To the Ladie Marie Coun-
teffe of Pembrooke."

In 1611 (both editions) the full Dedication is restored ; and so in the 4to of 1623.

In 1607, 1609 and 1611 (both) 'Actus I. Scæna I.' opens with 'Cleopatra, Cæfario, and Rodon,' and commences—

"Come *Rodon*, here, conuey from out this coaft
This precious iem, the chiefeft I haue left . . ."

In the original and all other editions this 'Scene' forms part of 'Actus IV.,' and 'Rodon' speaks it substantially to 'Seleucus' in giving account of his own treachery (ll. 875-89). These various readings occur—

l. 875, 'Come Rodon, here,' for 'Here Rodon, take.'
l. 876, 'I haue left' for 'that I haue.'
A new line 'My deare *Cæfario:* Saue him, faue my theft.'
l. 879, 'Conceale' for 'Safeguard.'
l. 885, 'fhattered' for 'broken.'

Then comes this speech of Rodon—

> *Ro.* No doubt he may, deare Soueraigne, when the rage
> Of this confufed ftorme is ouerpaft,
> That furioufly now beates vpon this age,
> And, may be, is too violent to laft.
> And *Cæfars* fortune which now feems to gròw
> Into th'Afcendent of felicitie,
> And makes the round and full of glory read,
> May come to warne, like others wretchednes :
> No tyrant can prefcribe to iniurie :
> Kings Rights may oft be ficke, but neuer die.

Cleopatra answers (in a new speech)—

> *Cle. Rodon,* my felfe, thofe turnés of *Chance* haue feen
> And known both fides of fortune, worft & beft,
> And therefore he, whofe birth, whofe fexe hath beene
> Worthier then mine, why fhould not he rebleft
> Turne backe to rule the fcepter of this land ?
> Which ah, how well it would become thy hand !

She continues, much as in ll. 890—915. These various readings may be noted :—

l. 891, 'Now die,' for 'O hòw.'

l. 895, 'And had he not, ay me, bin borné fo late' for 'And O if he had not beene borne fo late.'

l. 898, 'But O deare fonne, the time yields no delaies' for 'Then vnto him, O my deere fonne (fhe faies,)'

l. 907, 'Thee in the way' for 'Thee and thy wayes.'

l. 910, 'tender well' for 'looke well to.'

l. 913, 'But mothers caft' for 'Mothers will caft.'

ll. 914-15 in " ".

l. 917, 'ominous' for 'luckleffe bad.'

l. 918, 'And yet perhaps my love' for 'But yet it may 'tis but.'

l. 919, 'On . . . which' for 'Or . . . with'—the former accepted in its place.

l. 922, 'in time regaine his' for 'recouer better.'

l. 923, 'with greater glory' for 'may come in pompe.'

l. 924, 'feare' for 'doubt.'

l. 925, 'more powerful' for 'malignant.'

l. 926, 'And Egypt haue' for 'Egypt muft haue.'

l. 929, 'If' for 'Sith.'

l. 956, 'perhaps it is' for 'it may be 'tis,'
l. 961, 'me and thee' for 'thee and me.'
After l. 964 this new line—'Though I haue made an ende, I haue no done.' A new speech by Cæsario succeeds :—

    Cæl. Deare foueraigne mother, fuffer not your care
        To tumult thus with th'honor of your ftate :
        Thefe miferies of ours no ftrangers are,
        Nor is it new to be vnfortunate.
        And this good, let your many forrows paft
        Worke on your heart t'ipharden it at laft.
        Looke but on all the neighbour States befide,
        Of *Europe, Afrique,* Afia, and but note
        What Kings ? what States ? hath not the Roman pride
        Ranfackt, confounded, or els feruile brought ?
        And fince we are fo borne that by our fate,
        Againft thefe ftormes we cannot now beare faile,
        And that the boiftrous current of their ftate
        Will beare downe all our fortunes, and preuaile :
        Let vs yet temper with the time : and thinke
        The windes may change, and all thefe States oppreft,
        Colleagu'd in one, may turne again to fmoke
        Their Greatneffe, who now holds them all diftreft :
        And I may lead their troupes, and at the walles
        Of greedie *Rome,* reuenge the wrongèd blood
        Of th'innocent, which now for vengeance calls,
        And doe th'inthralled Prouinces this good.
        And therefore my deare mother doe not leaue
        To hope the beft. I doubt not my returne.
        I fhall doe well. Let not your griefe bereaue
        Your eyes of feeing thofe comforts when they turne.

This is followed up with a wholly new paffage :—

    Cleop. Well, worthy fonne, and worthely the fonne
        Of fuch a father. And in this thou fhewft
        From whence thou camft ; I fay no more : be gone,
        Grow in thy virtue, as in yeares thou growft.
                          Exeunt.

           Cleopatra folus.
    Poore comforts can they giue, whom our diftreffe
    Makes miferable, and like comfortleffe,

NOTE.

Alas, fuch forcèd cheering from our owne,
Vpon our griefes doe more affliction lay.
To thinke, that by our meanes they are vndone,
On whom we fought our glory to conuay.
Well then, here is a fad daies work begun :
For firft, betweene thefe armes, my *Antony*
Expir'd this day : and whilft I did vphold
His ftruggling limmes in his laft extafie
The yet vnclofèd wound, which his owne fword
Had made before, burft out, imbru'd my wombe,
And here with thefe faire collours of my Lord
Which now I weare, I come from out a tombe,
To fend away this deereft part of me
Vnto diftreffe, and now whilft time I haue,
I goe t'interre my fpoufe : So fhall I fee
My fonne difpatcht for death, my loue t'his graue.

                             Exit.

Succeeding this is ' Scena II.,' which is entirely new, as thus :—

       Octauius.   Dircetus.   Gallus.   Proculeius.

       What newes brings now *Dircetus* from our foe,
       Will *Antony* yet ftruggle beeing vndone ?
Dir. Noe, *Cæfar*, he will neuer vexe thee more :
       His worke is ended.   *Anthony* hath done.
       Here is the fword that hath cut off the knot
       Of his intangled fortunes, and hath freed
       His grieued life from his difhonor'd blot.
Oct. Who is the man that did effect this deed ?
Dir. His owne hand, and this fword hath done the deed.
Oct. Relate *Dircetus* of the manner how.
Dir. My Lord when *Anthony* had made this laft
       And defperate triall of his fortunes, and
       With all the forces which he had amaft
       From out each coaft and corner of the Land,
       Had brought them to their worke, perceiuing how
       His fhip in ftead of blowes fhooke hands with yours,
       And that his powers by land were vanquifht now,
       Backe to the citty he with griefe retires,
       Confounded with his fortunes, crying out
       That *Cleopatra* had betraid his truft.

NOTE.

She all amaz'd, and fearing left he mought
In this conceipt to farther rages burft,
Haftes to the tombe which fhee erected had
(A ftately vault to *Ifis* temple ioynd)
And thence cauf'd word be fent how fhe was dead,
And had difpatcht her felfe, through griefe of minde.
　　Which whē *Antonius* heard, he ftraight burft forth
Into this paffion: what? and haft thou then
Preuented me, braue Queene by thy great worth?
Hath *Cleopatra* taught the worke of men?
Hath fhee outgone me in the greateft part
Of refolution, to die worthely?
And muft I follow? doth fhee difapoint
Me, of th'example to teach her to die?
　　Come *Eros*, doe this feruice for thy Lord,
The beft and greateft pleafure thou canft doe:
Imploy this weapon here; come, make this fword
That wone me glory, *Eros*, this:
For thefe drie deaths are womanifh and bafe.
It is for an vnfinewed feeblenesse
T'expire in feathers, and t'attend difgrace.
Ther's nothing eafier *Eros* then to die,
For when men cannot ftand, thus they may flie.
　　Eros, his late infranchif'd feruant takes
The fword, as if he would haue done the deed,
And on it falles himfelfe: and thereby makes
Antonius more confuf'd to fee him bleed,
Who fhould haue firft euented out his breath:
O *Eros*, faid he, and hath Fortune quite
Forfaken me? muft I b'outgone in all?
What? can I not by loofing get a right?
Shall I not haue the vpper hand to fall
In death? muft both a woman, and a flaue
The ftart before me of this glory haue?
With this he takes his fword, and down he falls
Vpon the difmall point, which makes a gate
Spacious enough for Death, but that the walles
Of Nature, fkornd to let it in thereat.
And he furuiues his death. Which when his loue,
His royall *Cleopatra* vnderftood,
Shee fends with fpeed his body to remoue,
The body of her loue imbru'd with bloud.

Which brought vnto her tombe, (left that the preafe
Which came with him, might violate her vow)
She drawes him vp in rowles of taffatie
T'a window at the top, which did allow
A little light vnto her monument.

    There Charimon, and poore Eras, two weake maids
Foretir'd with watching, and their miftreffe care,
Tug'd at the pulley, hauing n'other ayds,
And vp they hoife the fwounding body there
Of pale *Antonius*, fhowring out his bloud
On th'vnder lookers, which there gazing ftood.

    And when they had now wrought him vp half way
(Their feeble powers vnable more to doe)
The frame ftood ftill, the body at a ftay,
When *Cleopatra* all her ftrength thereto
Puts, with what vigor loue and care could vfe,
So that it mooues againe, and then againe
It comes to ftay.   When fhee afrefh renewes
Her hold, and with r'inforced power doth ftraine,
And all the weight of her weake bodie laies,
Whofe furcharg'd heart more then her body wayes.
At length fhee wrought him vp, and takes him in,
Laies his yet breathing body on her bed,
Applies all meanes his fences to rewinne,
Stops vp his wound againe that frefhly bled,
Calles him her Lord, her fpoufe, her Emperor,
Forgets her owne diftreffe, to comfort his,
And interpoints each comfort with a kiffe.

    He after fome fmall reft and cherifhing
Raifes himfelfe, and frames a forcèd cheere,
Wils *Cleopatra* leaue her languifhing,
And like herfelfe thefe accidents to beare,
Confidering they had had fo full a part
Of glory in this world ; and that the turne
Of Change was come, and Fortune would depart.
'Twas now in vaine for her to ftand and mourne :
But rather ought fhe feeke her race to free,
By all the meanes (her honor fau'd) fhee can ;
And none about *Octauius* truft, faid he,
But *Proculeius* ; he's an honeft man.

    And for myfelfe, fuffize I haue not fail'd
In any acte of worth : and now in this,

A Roman hath but here a Roman quayld,
And onely but by Fortune's varioufnes.
And yet herein I may this glory take,
That he who me vndoes, my fword did make.
    This faid, he calles for wine, which he requires
Perhaps not for his thirft, but t'end his breath :
Which hauing taken, forthwith he expires :
And thus haue I declar'd *Antonius* death,

Octa.   I grieue to heare this much.   And I proteft
.By all the gods, I am no caufe of this :
He fought his ruine, wrought his owne vnreft ;
And here thefe letters are my witneffes,
How oft I labourd to recall him home,
And woo'd his friendfhip, fu'd to him for loue :
And how he ftill contemnd me, fkornèd Rome,
Your felues my fellow cittizens can proue.
    But *Gallus* you, and *Proculeius* hafte
With fpeed vnto the cittie to preuent
Left *Cleopatra* defperat now at laft,
Bereaue vs of the onely ornament,
Which is herfelfe, that can our triumphs grace.
Or fire the treafure which fhee hath amaft
Within that vault, of all the precious ftuffe
That Egypt yieldes, and difappoint at laft
Our trauels of the benefit thereof.
Supple her heart with hopes of kind reliefe,
Giue words of oyle, vnto her wounds of griefe.

ll. 197—257 (Chorus) follow, with two misprints—l. 205, ' muft ' for
' moft,' which is repeated in 4to of 1623, and l. 252, ' graue ' for ' gaue.'

The next Act (' Actus ii. Scena I.') is the first Scene of the original and
other editions named, but following the later not '94 text. It is headed—

            ' *Cleopatra. Charmion. Eras,*'

These various readings may be noted, leaving the reader to compare
them with our text (ll. 1 onward) :—

    l. 1, ' can breath.'
    l. 15, ' and the Champion of my pride.'
    ll. 20—24 omitted,
    l. 41, ' The.'
    l. 42, ' other.'
    l. 52, ' extreamities.'

After l. 54 the following speeches are inserted—

> *Char.* Come *Eras*, fhall we goe and interrupt
>   With fome perfwading words, this ftreame of mone?
> *Eras*, No *Charmion*, ftay, the current that is ftopt
>   Will but fwell vp the more : let her alone.
>   Time hath not brought this hot difeafe of griefe,
>   T'a *Crifis* fit to take a medicine yet ;
>   'Tis out of feafon to apply reliefe,
>   To forrows late begun, and in the fit,
>   Calamitie is ftubborne in the prime
>   Of new afflictions ; we muft giue it time.

ll. 55—66 are omitted ; but Cleopatra resumes at l. 67—

> 'Shall Rome behold my fcepter-bearing hand, etc.'

These variations are again noted—

l. 69, 'Shall I paffe by.'
ll. 83—98 omitted.
l. 105, 'And my luxurioufnes fhould end the date.'
l. 109, 'Why fhould I not but make.'
l. 110, 'mine.'
l. 111, 'And leaue ingrau'd.'

After l. 115 Charmion resumes—

> 'Deare madam, do not thus afflict your heart,
> No doubt you may worke out a meane to liue,
> And hold your ftate, and haue as great a part
> In *Cæfars* grace, as *Anthony* could giue :
> He that in this fort doth follicit you,
> And treats by all the gentle meanes he can,
> Why fhould you doubt that he fhould proue vntrue,
> Or thinke him fo difnaturèd a man,
> To wrong your royall truft or dignity?'

Cleopatra replies—

> 'Charmion, becaufe that now I am not I,
> My fortune, with my beauty, and my youth,
> Hath left me vnto mifery and thrall,
> And *Cæfar* cares not now by wayes of truth,
> But cunning, to get honor by my fall.'

The interview-dialogue is continued—

> *Ch.* You know not *Cæsars* dealing till you try.
> *Cle.* To try, were to be loft, and then difcry.
> *Ch.* You to *Antonius* did commit yourfelfe,
> And why might not *Antonius* fo haue done ?
> *Cl.* I woone *Antonius,* *Cæsar* hath me woone.
> *Er.* But madame, you might haue articuled
> With *Cæsar,* when by *Thyrius* he of late
> Did offer you fo kindly as he did,
> Vpon conditions to haue held your ftate.
> *Cl.* 'Tis true, I know I might haue held my ftate,
> If I would then haue *Anthony* betraid.
> *Er.* And why not now, fince *Anthony* is dead,
> And that *Octauius* hath the end he fought,
> May not you haue what then was offered ?
> On fairer tearmes, if things were fitly wrought
> And that you would not teach how to deny,
> By doubting him, or afking fearefully.
> *Cleop.* Fearefully? *Eras* peace, I fkorne to feare ;
> Who now am got out of the reach of wrath,
> Aboue the power of pride.   What fhould I feare
> The might of men, that aim at one with death ?
> Speake ye no more to me I charge you here.
> What ? will you two who ftill haue tooke my part
> In all my fortunes, now confpire with feare
> To make me mutinie againft my heart ?

Then at l. 115 our text is returned to, with these various readings :—
l. 115, 'No.'
l. 116, ' That t'was my weakenes that hath.'
l. 118 is followed by these new lines—

> ' My conftancy fhall vndeceiue their mindes,
> And I will bring the witneffe of my blood
> To teftifie my fortitude, that binds
> My equall loue, to fall with him I ftood ' (cf. ll. 123-6).

ll. 119-20 (see in the place in our text).
l. 121, ' And my condemnd.'
After l. 126 is this couplet—

> ' Defects I grant I had, but this was worft
> That beeing the firft to fall, I di'd not firft.'

After l. 138 is this—

> ' And I confeſſe me bound to ſacrifice
> To death and thee the life that doth reproue me.

ll. 139—148 omitted.
l. 150, ' now.'
ll. 151-8 omitted.
l. 159, ' When heretofore my vaine.'
l. 165, ' When thou bred in.'
l. 166, ' The ryotous pompe of Monarches neuer learnedſt.'
Our ' Act ii., Scene I.,' forms ' Scena II.' of ' Act 2,' commencing with
l. 260 ; but Gallus is added as an interlocutor. These various readings
again are noted—
l. 267 inadvertently drops ' keepes the.'
ll. 280-1, ' . . . tell me what y'haue done.
> Will yet this womans ſtubborne heart be wonne?'

After l. 281 the speech varies—

> My Lord, we haue all gentle meanes impli'd (=employ'd)
> According to th'inſtructions which you gaue,
> And hope in time ſhee will be pacified
> And theſe are all the likelihoods we haue.
> Firſt when we came into her archèd vault,
> I *Gallus* ſent to entertaine the time
> Below with her, confering at a grate,
> Whilſt I found meanes vp to the top to clime :
> He there perſwaded her to leaue that place,
> And come to *Cæſar*, and to ſue for grace.

It will be observed the last is our l. 289 ; and so on to l. 293.

ll. 294-7 omitted.
l. 298, ' I now deſcending.'
l. 301, ' forc'd.'
l. 302, ' raught.'
l. 306, ' ſhould you.'
l. 307, ' your.'
l. 328, ' As words of rule.'
l. 339, ' that.'
l. 340, ' thus muſt ſeeke to.'
l. 341, ' On th'wofull . . . wretched.'
l. 352, ' th'woefull.'
l. 353, ' A mixed.'

l. 365, 'your.'

l. 366, 'And wight.'

l. 370, 'Wherewith at laft fhee feem'd.'

l. 371, 'And gaue great fhewes to be.'

l. 372, 'And faw . . . your.'

l. 374, 'wherewithall.'

ll. 375-7—'Some obfequies vnto the coarfe
      Of her dead loue, according to her rite
      And in the meane time might be free from force.'

l. 379, 'well in reft.'

l. 380, '*Oct.* But doe you.'

ll. 382-3—'Ah priuate thoughts, aime wide from princes hearts,
      Whofe ftate allows them not t'act their owne parts.'

l. 385, 'die,' as in [1].

l. 386, 'She may by yielding work.'

l. 396, 'feare fh'will not.'

ll. 400-1—'And well obferue with whom fhee doth,
      And fhortly will myfelfe.'

There succeeds then the Chorus (ll. 773 onward), but it opens—

    'Sterne and imperious Nemefis';

and l. 808, 'naught' for 'nought.' Act III. answers to ours substantially
I note these various readings—

l. 474 has added '2. Philofophers.'

l. 484, 'And that we liue in.'

l. 501, 'For when this fhip of life pale terror boords.'

l. 509, 'Wherein I my profeffion.'

l. 513, 'No priuiledge Philofophy doth giue.'

l. 519, 'For neuer age could better teftifie.'

· ll. 521-2—'How foone improuident profperitie
      Comes caught, and ruin'd.'

l. 540, 'would.'

ll. 541-2—'S'ingulph this ftate in th'end, that no deuice
      Our vtter ouerwhelming could withhold.'

l. 544, 'Of mighty lands.'

l. 560, 'our loofe felicitie.'

l. 561, 'doth' (*bad*).

l. 562, 'confufd with miferie.'

ll. 577-8—'T'extinguifh thus the race of *Antony*
      And *Cleopatra*, to confirme his owne.'

l. 579, 'their iffue be extinguifhed?'

After l. 579 comes this—

>   *Ar.* It muſt: *Antillus* is already dead.
>
>   *Th.* And what? *Cæſario* ſprung of *Cæſars* bloud?

l. 586, 'Men feeke to quench.'

ll. 589-92—'They thinke his death will farther tumults ceaſe :

>   Competitors are ſubiects miſeries,
>
>   And to the end to purchaſe publike peace,
>
>   Great men are . . .'

l. 595, 'emptie.'

l. 597, 'Though I thinke Rome ſhall neuer.'

l. 603, 'Or thinke you, your.'

l. 604, 'As.'

l. 607, 'm'oppreſſed ſoule.'

l. 608, 'Likes.'

l. 609, 'in.'

l. 611, 'I thought not euer Roman.'

l. 612, 'diſtreſſed.'

l. 614, 'A capture.'

l. 617, 'madame riſe your ſelfe was.'

l. 618, 'your,' and so l. 619.

ll. 621-4, 'For you diſſolu'd that . . .

>   Which makes my winning ioy a gaine vnto
>
>   Who cannot now looke out . . .
>
>   But through the horror.'

l. 625, 'you.'

And so to the close in trivial changes, but which in noting it seems inexpedient to record further, except a few put in their places in our text from this point. Act III. closes with our Chorus (ll. 402-72). Act IV. is also our Act IV. A few various readings are given in the places in our text, not mere trivialities. After l. 1097 forward to l. 1430 is omitted, and thus reading—

>   'Come Diomedes, thou who haſt bin one
>
>   In all my fortunes, and art ſtill all one ;
>
>   Whom the amazing ruine of my fall,
>
>   Neuer deterd to leaue calamitie,
>
>   As did, etc.'

After l. 1456 there are these new passages—

>   *Diom.* I who am ſworne of the ſocietie
>
>   Of death, and haue indur'd the worſt of ill,
>
>   Prepar'd for all euents, muſt not deny
>
>   What you cōmand me, come there what there will.

And I fhall vfe the aptest fkill I may
To cloake my worke, and long I will not ftay.   *Exit.*
Cleop. But hauing leaue I muft goe take my leaue,
And laft farewell of my dead *Antony,*
Whofe dearely honord tombe muft here receiue
This facrifice, the laft before I die.
Then the scene goes back to l. 1102, being headed—
' *Cleopatra at the tombe of Antonius.'*

See in the place in our text various readings.   After l. 1191 comes this
new speech—

Eras. Good madame, if that worthy heart you beare
Doe hold it fit, it were a finne in vs
To contradict your will ; but yet we feare
The world will cenfure that your doing thus,
Did iffue rather out of your defpaire
Then refolution, and thereby you loofe
Much of your glory, which would be more faire
In fuffring, then efcaping thus your foes.
For when *Pandora* b[r]ought the boxe from heauen
Of all the good and ill that men befall,
And them immixt vnto the world had giuen,
Hope in the bottom lay, quite vnder all.
To fhew that we muft ftill vnto the laft
Attend our fortune ; for no doubt there may
Euen at the bottom of afflictions paft
Be found fome happier turne if we but ftay.
Cl. Eras, that hope is honors enemie,
A traytor vnto worth, lies on the ground,
In the bafe bottom of feruilitie :
The beggars wealth, a treafure neuer found,
The dreame of them that wake, a ghoft of th'aire,
That leads men out of knowledge to their graues,
A fpirit of groffer fubftance then defpaire ;
And let them, *Eras* hope, that can be flaues . . .'

Then takes up at l. 1191, which see for various readings in our text in
the place.   After l. 1199 comes in ' ' Scena iii,' opening thus new—

*Cefario, with a Guard conueying him
to Execution.*

Now gentle Guard, let me in curtefie
Reft me a little here, and eafe my bands,

> You fhall not need to hold me, for your eye
> May now as well fecure you, as your hands.
>
> *Gu.* Doe, take your eafe *Cefario*, but not long,
> . We haue a charge, which we muft needs performe.
>
> *Cef.* Loe here brought backe, by fubtile traine to death,
> Betraid by Tutors faith, or traitors rather,
> My fault my blood, and mine offence my birth ;
> For beeing the fonne of fuch a mighty father,
> I now am made th'oblation for his feares
> Who doubts the poore reuenge thofe hands may doe him,
> Refpecting neither blood, nor youth, nor yeares,
> Or how fmall fafétie can my death be to him.
>   And is this, etc.—

taking now up from l. 1000, which place in our text see for various readings.

After l. 1052 the scene thus concludes—

> ' But yet *Cefario*, thou muft die content,
> God will reuenge, and men bewaile the innocent.
> Well now along ; I refted haue ynow,
> Performe the charge, my friĕds, you haue to doe.'
>
>   *Exeunt.*

Then follows the ' Chorus,' ll. 1200—1270. Act V. is same as our Act V. See various readings in our text in the places. After l. 1328 are these lines—

> ' And what my power and praiers may preuaile,
> Ile ioyne them both, to hinder thy difgrace :
> And euen this prefent day, I will not faile
> To do my beft with *Cæfar* in this cafe.'

ll. 1329-48 omitted in ⁴. Scene II. thus opens in ⁴—

> *Cleopatra. Eras. Charmion. Diomedes.*
> *The Guard, and Cæfars meffengers.*
>
> Now *Eras*, come, what newes haft thou lookt out,
> Is *Diomedes* comming yet or not ?
>
> *Eras.* Madame, I haue from off the turret top,
> View'd euery way, he is not comming yet.
>
> *Cl.* Didft thou fee no man tending hitherward ?
>
> *Er.* None truly madame, but one countriman
> Carrying a bafket as I could difcerne.

Cle. Alas then *Eras* I doe feare th'euent
Of my defigne. For fure he would not ftay
Thus long I know, did not fome force preuent
His forward faith, and hold him by the way.

Char. Madame, there may be many hindrances
To counterchecke and interupt his fpeed.
He hath a wary worke to doe in this,
He muft take time.

Cl. *Charmion* tis true indeed :
And yet in all this time me thinkes he might
Effected haue his worke, had all gone right.

Er. Alas we euer thinke the ftay is more,
When our defire is run t'our wifh before.

Cle. *Eras* I know my will to haue it done,
Rides poft, and feare in doing to b'vndone,
Puts fpurs thereto : whilft that for which we long
Creepes but a foote. Yet fure he ftaies too long.
Good *Eras* goe and looke out once againe—
Yet ftay awhile, I know it is in vaine.
O gods, I craue no other fortune I
Of heauen and you, but onely lucke to die.
And fhall I not haue that? Well I will yet
Write my difpatch to *Cefar*, and when that
Is done, I will difpatch my felfe ; what way
So euer, I muft vfe no more delay.

Enter the Guard with Diomedes.

Gua. And whither now fir, ftay, what haue you there?

Diom. Good firs, I haue a fimple prefent here,
Which I would faine deliuer to our queene.

Gu. What ift? lets fee.

Can fuch poore robes beguile a Princes power?
Why then I fee, it is our outfides moft
Doe mocke the world.   But tell me are they here ?
Speake Diomedes.

Diod.   Madame, they are there.

Cl. O good ill-lucke, moft fortunate diftreffe,
Deare *Diomedes*, thou haft bleft me now :
And here, goe take thefe letters, and difmafke
Thyfelfe againe, returne to thine owne fhape
Good *Diomedes*, and giue *Cæfar* thefe.
Goe, leaue me here alone, I need no more ::
I haue but thefe to keepe a death in ftore.
I will not vfe their helpe till needes I muft,
(And that is now) goe *Diomedes* goe.

Diom. Good madame, I know well this furniture
Of death, is farre more requifite, then that
Of life, where fuch as you cannot endure
To lie beneath your felues, debaf'd in ftate.
I goe t'effect your will as well in this
As I haue done in that, and onely pray
Our tutelarie gods to giue fucceffe
Vnto the fame, and be it what it may.

Cl. Come fweet heart, etc.

Then takes up from l. 1509 onward.   See our text for various readings.
After l. 1626 comes this —

Eras. Come *Charmion*, come, wee muft not onely be
Spectators in this Scene, but Actors too.
Now comes our part ; you know we did agree
The fellowfhip of death to vnder goe,
And though our meaner fortunes cannot claime
A glory by this acte, they fhall haue fame.

Ch. *Eras* I am prepar'd, and here is that
Will doe the deed.

Er. And here is of the fame.

Cl. But *Eras* Ile begin, it is my place.

Er. Nay *Charmion*, here I drinke a death to thee ;
I muft be firft.

Ch. Indeed thou haft preuented me ;
Yet will I haue this honor to be laft
Which fhall adorne this head, which muft be feene

To weare that crowne in death, her life held faſt ;
That all the world may ſee ſhee di'd a queene.
O ſee this face, etc.,

returning to l. 1639 from 1662.   After l. 1645 the close runs—

Ces. meſſ. See, we are come too late, this is diſpatcht :
   Cæſar is diſappointed of this grace.—
   Why how now *Charmion*, what? is this well done ?
Ch. Yea very well ; and ſhee that from the race
   Of ſo great kings defcends doth beſt become.

Our ' Chorus ' (ll. 1687—1771) also concludes [4].

I am not aware that these remarkable ' alterings ' of this tragedy of ' Cleopatra ' have been before noted ; and certainly it is singular that John Daniel should have ignored the text of 1607, especially as it was repeated in 1609 and 1611 (both). Unquestionably some of the finest work of Daniel has thus been lost hitherto to literature.

My signs for the various readings placed below each page are these—
1594 = [1].

$$\left.\begin{matrix}1599 \\ 1601 \\ 1602 \\ 1605\end{matrix}\right\} = \text{our text of '23.} = {}^{2} \text{—only a few from 1599, 1602, and 1605.}$$

$$\left.\begin{matrix}1607 \\ 1609 \\ 1611 \text{ (two)}\end{matrix}\right\} = {}^{4}.$$

1623 = our text (substantially).

On this ' Tragedie of Cleopatra ' see our ' Memorial-Introduction II.— Critical.' I have collated all the above editions in exemplars in the British Museum and the Bodleian.   On other side is the title-page of 1623

A. B. G.

THE
TRAGEDIE

OF CLEOPATRA.

Aetas prima canat veneres poſtrema tumultus.

LONDON,
Printed by Nicholas Okes,
for Simon Waterson.

* The Scæne fuppofed *Alexandria.*

The Actors.

Cleopatra. Octauius Cæfar.
Proculeius. Dolabella.
Titius, feruant to Dolabella.
Arius, ⎱
Philoftratus, ⎰ two Philofophers.
Seleucus, fecretarie to Cleopatra.
Rodon, Tutor to Cæfario.
Nuntius.
The Chorus, all Egyptians.

* In ¹ afte the ' Argument.'

To the right honourable, the
Lady Mary, *Counteſſe of*
PEMBROOKE.

Loe heere the labour which ſhe did
    impoſe,   [Muſe :
Whoſe influence did predominate my
The ſtarre of wonder my deſires firſt
    choſe   [I vſe :
To guide their trauels in the courſe
She, whoſe cleare brightneſſe had
    the powre t'infuſe   [came,
Strength to my thoughts, from whence theſe motions
Call'd vp my ſpirits from out their low repoſe,
To ſing of State, and tragicke notes to frame.

I, who (contented with an humble ſong,)
Made muſique to my ſelfe that pleaſd me beſt,   10
And onely told of DELIA, and her wrong,
And praiſd her eyes, and plaind mine owne vnreſt :
(A text from whence my Muſe had not digreſt)

l. 1, 'worke the' ¹, ²: l. 2, 'Who onely doth' ¹, ²: l. 3, 'which my labours' ¹, ²: l. 4, 'way in all' ¹, ²: l. 5, 'doth alone' ¹, ²: l. 6, 'and makes me what I am' ¹, ².

Madam, had not thy well grac'd *Antony* ;
(Who all alone, hauing remained long,)
Requir'd his *Cleopatras* company.

Who if fhe here doe fo appeare in Act,
That he can fcarce difcerne her for his Queene,
Finding how much fhe of her felfe hath lackt,
And miff'd that grace wherein fhe fhould be feene,   20
Her worth obfcur'd, her fpirit embafed cleene ;
Yet lightning thou by thy fweete chearefulnes,
My darke defects, which from her powres detract,
He may her geffe by fome refemblances.

And I hereafter in another kinde,
More futing to the nature of my vaine,
May peraduenture raife my humble minde
To other mufique in this higher ftraine ;
Since I perceiue the world and thou doft daigne
To countenance my Song, and cherifh me,   30
I muft fo worke Pofteritie may finde,
My loue to verfe, my gratitude to thee.

Now when fo many Pennes (like Speares) are charg'd,
To chafe away this tyrant of the North ;
Groffe Barbarifme, whofe powre grown far inlarg'd
Was lately by thy valiant brothers worth

---

l. 14, '*Anthony*'[1]: l. 17, MS. 'Fact'[1,2]: l. 18, 'for his Queene and
Loue he fcarce will know her'[1,2]: l. 20, 'I fhould fhew her'[1,2]: l. 21,
'In maieftie debaf'd, in courage lower'[1,2]: l. 22, 'fauouring eyes'[1,2]:
l. 23, 'fp'rit'[1,2]: l. 24, 'yet may geffe it's fhee; which will fuffife'[1,2]:
l. 27, 'better pleafe thy'[1,2]: l. 28, 'And higher notes in fweeter mufique-
ftraine'[1,2]: l. 29, 'feeing that thou fo gracioufly dooft daine'[1,2]: l. 32,
'How much I did contend to honour thee'[1,2]: l. 36, 'thy'[1,2], for 'the'
of our text accepted.

Firft found, encountred, and prouoked forth :
Whofe onfet made the reft audacious,
Whereby they likewife haue fo well difcharg'd
Vpon that hideous Beaft incroching thus.   40

And now muft I with that poore ftrength I haue,
Refift fo foule a foe in what I may :
And arme againft Obliuion and the Graue,
That elfe in darkeneffe carries all away,
And makes of all an vniuerfall pray ;
So that if by my Penne procure I fhall
But to defend me, and my name to faue,
Then though I die, I cannot yet die all ;

But ftill the better part of me will liue,
And in that part will liue thy reuerent name,   50
Although thy felfe doft farre more glory giue
Vnto thy felfe, then I can by the fame.
Who doft with thine owne hand a bulwark frame
Againft thefe monfters, (enemies of honour)
Which euermore fhall fo defend thy Fame,
As Time, or they fhall neuer prey vpon her.

Thofe Hymnes which thou doft confecrate to heauen,
Which Ifraels Singer to his God did frame :
Vnto thy voyce Eternitie hath giuen,
And makes thee deare to him from whence they came.
In them muft reft thy venerable name,   61
So long as Sions God remaineth honoured ;

l. 40, cap. 'B' accepted from [1], [2] : l. 45, 'our honours but a'[1] : l. 50,
'Deckt and adorned with thy facred' [1], [2] : l. 56, 'nor' [1], [2] : l. 61, 'euer
reuerent' [1], [2].

And till confufion hath all zeale bereauen,
And murthered Faith, and Temples ruined.

By this (great Lady) thou muft then be knowne,
When *Wilton* lies low leuell'd with the ground :
And this is that which thou maift call thine owne,
Which facrilegious Time cannot confound ;
Heere thou furuiu'ft thy felfe, heere thou art found
Of late fucceeding ages, frefh in fame :
This monument cannot be ouerthrowne,
Where, in eternall Braffe remaines thy Name.

O that the Ocean did not bound our ftile
Within thefe ftrict and narrow limites fo :
But that the melodie of our fweete Ile,
Might now be heard to *Tyber, Arne,* and *Po* :
That they might know how far Thames doth out-go
The Mufike of declined *Italy* :
And liftning to our Songs another while,
Might learne of thee, their notes to purifie.

O why may not fome after-comming hand
Vnlocke thefe limites, open our confines,
And breake afunder this imprifoning band,
T'inlarge our fpirits, and publifh our defignes ;
Planting our Rofes on the *Apenines?*
And teach to *Rheyne,* to *Loyre,* and *Rhodanus.*
Our accents, and the wonders of our Land,
That they might all admire and honour vs.

Whereby great *Sydney* and our *Spencer* might,
With thofe *Po*-fingers being equalled,

l. 86, ' teach to ' ¹, ², accepted from ³ for ' to teach ' of our text.

Enchaunt the world with fuch a fweet delight,
That their eternall Songs (for euer read)
May fhew what great *Elizaes* raigne hath bred.
What muficke in the kingdome of her peace
Hath now beene made to her, and by her might,
Whereby her glorious fame fhall neuer ceafe.

But if that Fortune doth denie vs this,
Then *Neptune*, locke vp with the Ocean key
This treafure to our felues, and let them miffe
Of fo fweet riches : as vnworthy they   100
To taft the great delights that we inioy.
And let our harmony fo pleafing growne,
Content our felues, whofe errour euer is
Strange notes to like, and difefteeme our owne.

But, whither doe my vowes tranfport me now,
Without the compaffe of my courfe enioynd ?
Alas, what honour can a voyce fo low
As this of mine, expect hereby to find ?
But, (Madam,) this doth animate my mind,
That yet I fhall be read among the reft,   110
And though I doe not to perfection grow,
Yet fomething fhall I be, though not the beft.

l. 94-6—
  'That fauored by the Worthies of our Land,
     My lynes are lik'd ; the which may make me grow,
     In time to take a greater tafke in hand ' [1], [2].
  97, cap. 'F' from [1], [2], accepted.

The Argument.

Fter the death of *Antonius, Cleopatra,* (liuing ftill in the Monument fhee had caufed to be built,) could not, by any meanes be drawne foorth, although *Octauius Cæfar* very earneftly laboured it: and fent *Proculeius,*[1] to vfe all diligence to bring her vnto him: for that hee thought it would be a great Ornament to his Triumphes, to get her aliue to Rome. But neuer would fhee put her felfe into the hands of 10 *Proculeius,* although on a time he found the means, (by a window that was at the toppe of the Monument,) to come down vnto her: where he perfwaded her (all he might) to yeeld her felfe to *Cæfars* mercy. Which fhe, (to be ridde of him,) cunningly feemed to grant vnto. After that, *Octauius* in perfon went to vifite her, to whom fhe excufed her offence, laying all the fault vpon the greatnes, and feare fhe had, of *Antonius,* and withall, feemed very tractable, and willing to be difpofed of by him. 20

Whereupon *Octauius,* (thinking himfelfe fure) refolued

[1] Mifprinted 't' in our text.

prefently to fend her away to Rome: Whereof, *Dola-bella*, a fauorite of *Cæfars*, (and one that was growne into fome good liking of her) hauing certified her, fhee makes her humble petition to *Cæfar*, that he would fuffer her to facrifice to the ghoft of *Antonius*: which being granted her, fhe was brought vnto his fepulchre, where, after her rites performed, fhe returned to the Monument, and there dined with great magnificence. And in dinner time, came there one in the habite of a 30 countrey man, with a bafket of Figs vnto her, who (unfufpected) was fuffered to carry them in. And in that bafket (among the Figs) were conueyed the Afpickes wherewith fhe did her felfe to death. Dinner being ended, fhe difpatched Letters to *Cæfar*, con-tayning great lamentations, with an earneft fupplication, that fhe might be intombed with *Antonius*. Where-vpon *Cæfar* knowing what fhe intended, fent prefently with all fpeed, Meffengers to haue preuented her death; which notwithftanding, before they came, was dis- 40 patched.

Cæfario her fonne, which fhe had by *Iulius Cæfar* (conueyed before vnto *India*, out of the danger of the warres) was about the fame time of her death, mur-thered at *Rhodes:* trained thither by the falfehood of his Tutor, corrupted by *Cæfar*. And fo, hereby came the race of the *Ptolomies* to be wholly extinct, and the flourifhing rich Kingdome of *Egypt* vtterly ouerthrowne and fubdued.

49

THE TRAGEDIE
Of CLEOPATRA.

ACTVS PRIMVS.

Cleopatra.

ET doe I liue, and yet doth breath
    extend   [graue
My life beyond my life? nor can my
Shut vp my griefes, to make my end
    my end?   [I haue?
Will yet confufion haue more then
Is th'honor, wonder, glory, pompe,
    and all

Of *Cleopatra* dead, and fhe not dead?
Haue I out-liu'd my felfe, and feene the fall
Of all vpon me, and not ruined?
Can yet thefe eyes endure the ghaftly looke
Of Defolations darke and ougly face,   10

Wont but on Fortunes faireſt ſide to looke,
Where nought vvas but applauſe, but ſmiles, and
          grace ?
Whiles on his ſhoulders all my reſt relide,
On whom the burthen of m'ambition lay,
My _Atlas_, and ſupporter of my pride,
That did the world of all my glory ſway,
Who now throwne downe, diſgrac'd, confounded lies
Cruſht vvith the weight of Shame and Infamy,

l. 15, addition here from '—
                              ' poſſeſſe
          This hatefull priſon of a loathſome ſoule :
          Can no calamitie, nor no diſtreſſe
          Breake hart and all, and end a life ſo foule?
          Can *Cleopatra* liue, and with theſe eyes
          Behold the deereſt of her life bereft her ?
          Ah, can ſhee entertaine the leaſt ſurmiſe
          Of any hope, that hath but horror left her?
          Why ſhould I linger longer griefes to try?
          Theſe eyes that ſawe what honor earth could giue mee,
          Doe now behold the worſt of miſery :
          The greateſt wrack wherto Fortune could driue mee.
          Hee on whoſe ſhoulders all my reſt relyde,
          On whom the burthen of my'ambition lay :
          The *Atlas* and the Champion of my pride.'
l. 16, ' my whole fortune ' ¹ : l. 17, addition here—
          'Lyes falne, confounded, dead in ſhame and dolors,
          Following th'vnlucky party of my loue.
          Th'Enſigne of mine eyes, th'vnhappy collours,
          That him to miſchiefe, mee to ruine droue.
          And now the modell made of miſery,
          Scorne to the world, borne but for Fortunes foile,
          My luſts haue fram'd a Tombe for mee to lie,
          Euen in the aſhes of my Countries ſpoyle.
          Ah, who would think that I were ſhee who late,
          Clad with the glory of the worlds chiefe ritches,
          Admir'd of all the earth, and wondred at,
          Glittring in pompe that hart and eye bewitches.'

Following th'vnlucky party of mine eyes,
The traines of luft and imbecility,   20
Whereby my diffolution is become
The graue of Egypt, and the wracke of all ;
My vnforefeeing weakeneffe muft intoome
My Countries fame and glory with my fall.
Now who vvould thinke that I were fhe vvho late
With all the ornaments on earth inrich'd,
Enuiron'd vvith delights, compaft with ftate,
Glittering in pomp that hearts and eyes bewitch'd ;
Should thus diftreft, caft down from off that heigth
Leuell'd vvith low difgrac'd calamity,   30
Vnder the weight of fuch affliction figh,
Reduc'd vnto th'extreameft mifery ?
Am I the woman whofe inuentiue pride,
Adorn'd like *Ifis*, fcorn'd mortality ?
Is't I would haue my frailety fo belide,
That flattery could perfwade I vvas not I ?
Well, now I fee, they but delude that praife vs,
Greatneffe is mockt, profperity betrayes vs.
And vve are but our felues, although this cloud
Of interpofed fmoake make vs feeme-more :   40
Thefe fpreading parts of pomp wherof w'are proud
Are not our parts, but parts of others ftore :
Witneffe thefe gallant fortune-following traines,
Thefe Summer Swallowes of felicity

l. 34, (Adorn'd . . . Ifis) [1]: l. 35, 'that left my fence fo without guide' [1] :
l. 36, 'would not let him know twas' [1]: l. 37, 'Ah . . . fcarce tell
truth' [1]: l. 38, 'Crownes are beguild' [1]: l. 40, 'fmoake' accepted from '
for 'fmoakes' of other texts : ll. 43-6—
          ' What is become of all that ftatelie traine,
            Thofe troopes that wont attend profperitie?

Gone vvith the heate : of all, fee vvhat remaines,
This monument, two maydes, and vvretched I.
And I, t'adorne their triumphs am referu'd
A captiue, kept to honour others fpoyles,
Whom *Cæfar* labours fo to haue preferu'd,
And feekes to entertaine my life vvith wiles.   50
But *Cæfar*, it is more then thou canft do,
Promife, flatter, threaten extreamity,
Imploy thy wits and all thy force thereto,
I haue both hands, and vvill, and I can die.
Though thou, of both my country and my crowne,
Of powre, of meanes and all doft quite bereaue me ;
Though thou haft wholy Egypt made thine owne,
Yet haft thou left me that which vvill deceiue thee.
That courage vvith my blood and birth innated,
Admir'd of all the earth, as thou art now ;   60
Can neuer be fo abiectly abated
To be thy flaue, that rul'd as good as thou.
Thinke *Cæfar*, I that liu'd and raign'd a Queene,   .
Do fcorne to buy my life at fuch a rate,
That I fhould vnderneath my felfe be feene,
Bafely induring to furuiue my ftate :·
That Rome fhould fee my fcepter-bearing hands
Behind me bound, and glory in my teares ;

'See what is left, what number doth remaine,
        A tombe, two maydes, and miferable I ?'
l. 48, 'beautifie their '¹: l. 51, 'No *Cæfar* no, it is not thou canft doe
it'¹: l. 53, 'vnto it'¹: l. 55, 'of Country, kingdom'¹: l. 56, 'Though
thou of all my glory doft'¹: l. 57, 'all my . . . as'¹: l. 61, 'Cannot by
threates be vulgarly'¹: l. 63, 'Confider . . . that I am'¹: ll. 64-6—
        'And fcorne the bafenes of a feruile thought :
        The world and thou, doft know what I haue heene,
        And neuer thinke I can be fo low brought.'¹

No, I difdaine that head vvhich wore a crowne,
Should ftoope to take vp that which others giue ;
I muft not be, vnleffe I be mine owne,
Tis fweet to die vvhen we are forc'd to liue.
Nor had I ftayd behind my felfe this fpace,
Nor payd fuch int'reft for this borrow'd breath,
But that hereby I feeke to purchafe grace
For my diftreffed feede after my death.
It's that vvhich doth my deareft blood controule,
That's it alas detaines me from my tombe,   80
Whiles Nature brings to contradict my foule
The argument of mine vnhappy wombe.
     You luckleffe iffue of an vvofull mother,
The vvretched pledges of a vvanton bed,
You Kings defigned, muft fubiects liue to other ;
Or elfe, I feare, fcarce liue, vvhen I am dead.
It is for you I temporize with *Cæfar*,
And ftay this vvhile to mediate your fafety :
For you I faine content, and foothe his pleafure,
Calamity herein hath made me crafty.   90
But this is but to try what may be done,
For come what vvill, this ftands, I muft die free.
And die my felfe vncaptiu'd, and vnwonne :
Blood, Children, Nature, all muft pardon me,
My foule yeelds Honor vp the victory,

l. 71, 'that' [1]: l. 75, 'troubled now the world thus long' [1]: l. 76, ' And
beene indebted . . . little' [1]: l. 77, ' I feare, Cæfar would offer wrong ' [1] :
l. 78, ' To' [1]: l. 80, 'Tis that' [1]: l. 83, 'O . . . a' [1]: l. 84, 'Th'vngodly' [1] :
l. 85, 'now be flaues' [1]: l. 86, 'not bee (I feare)' [1]: l. 88, 'liue . . .
for to procure' [1]: l. 91, 'tis not long, Ile fee' [1]: l o3, 'Ile be my felfe,
my thoughts doe reft thereon ' [1].

And I muſt be a Queene, forget a mother;
Though mother vvould I be, were I not I;
And Queene would not be now, could I be other.
    But vvhat know I if th'heauens haue decreed,
And that the ſinnes of Egypt haue deſeru'd   100
The *Ptolomies* ſhould faile, and none ſucceed,
And that my weakenes vvas thereto referu'd,
That I ſhould bring confuſion to my ſtate,
And fill the meaſure of iniquity;
Luxurioufneſſe in me ſhould raiſe the rate
Of looſe and ill-diſpenſèd liberty.
If it be ſo, then what neede theſe delaies?
Since I was made the meanes of miſery:
Why ſhould I ſtriue but to make death my praiſe,
That had my life but for my infamy?   110
And let me vvrite in letters of my blood
A fit memoriall for the times to come:
To be example to ſuch Princes good
As pleaſe themſelues, and care not what become.
    And *Antony*, becauſe the world takes note
That my defe&ts haue onely ruin'd thee;
And my ambitious pra&tiſes are thought
The motiue and the cauſe of all to be;

l. 97, 'Yet'[1]: l. 98, 'I not now be, were'[1]: l. 105, 'Licentioufnes
. . . end her date'[1]: l. 106, 'Begunne in ill-diſpenſed libertie'[1]: l. 107--
        'If ſo it be, and that my heedles waies,
        Haue thus ſo great a deſolation raiſd,
        Yet let a glorious end conclude my dayes;
        Though life were bad, my death may yet be praiſ'd'[1].
l. 111, 'That I may'[1]: l. 115, 'although'[3]: addition here—
        'And Anthony, becauſe the world doth know,
        That my miſ-fortune hath procured thine,
        And my improuidence brought thee ſo low,
        To loſe thy glory, and to ruine mine:

Though God thou know'ſt, how iuſt this ſtaine is layd
Vpon my foule, vvhom ill ſucceſſe makes ill :   120
Yet ſince condemn'd misfortune hath no ayde
Againſt proud lucke that argues what it will,
I haue no meanes to vndeceiue their mindes,
But to bring in the witneſſe of my blood,
To teſtifie the faith and loue that bindes
My equall ſhame, to fall vvith whom I ſtood.
Defeᶜts I grant I had, but this vvas worſt,
That being the firſt to fall I di'd not firſt.
Though I perhaps could lighten mine owne ſide
With ſome excuſe of my conſtrained caſe   130
Drawne down with povvre : but that were to deuide
My ſhame : to ſtand alone in my diſgrace.
To cleere me ſo, vvould ſhew m'affeᶜtions naught,
And make th'excuſe more hainous then the fault.

> By grapling in the Ocean of our pride,
> To ſinke each others greatnes both together,
> Both equall ſhipwrack of our ſtates t'abide,
> And like deſtruᶜtion to procure to eyther :
> If I ſhould now (our common faulte) ſuruiue,
> . Then all the world muſt hate mee if I doe it,
> Sith both our errors did occaſion giue,
> And both our faults haue brought vs both vnto it.
> I being firſt inamour'd with thy greatnes,
> Thou with my vanity bewitched wholy ;
> And both betrayd with th'outward pleaſant ſweetnes,
> The one ambition ſpoyld, th'other folly.
> For which, thou haſt already duly paid
> The ſtatute of thy errors deareſt forfeit :
> Wherby thy gotten credite was decayd,
> Procur'd thee by thy wanton deadly ſurfeit.
> And next is my turne now to ſacrifize.'

ll. 119-20 in ⁴ read—
> ' Though God thou knowſt, this ſtaine is wrongly laid
> Vpon my ſoule, whom ' etc.

Since if I ſhould our errours diſunite,
I ſhould confound afflictions onely reſt,
That from ſterne death euen ſteales a ſad delight
To die vvith friends or vvith the like diſtreſt ;
And ſince vve tooke of either ſuch firme hold
In th'ouerwhelming ſeas of fortune caſt,   140
What powre ſhould be of powre to revnfold
The armes of our affections lockt ſo faſt ?
For grapling in the Ocean of our pride,
We ſuncke others greatneſſe both together ;
And both made ſhipwracke of our fame beſide,
Both vvrought a like deſtruction vnto either :
And therefore I am bound to ſacrifice
To Death and thee, the life that doth reproue me :
Our like diſtreſſe I feele doth ſimpathize,
And euen affliction makes me truely loue thee.   150
Which *Antony,* I much confeſſe my fault
I neuer did ſincerely vntill now :
Now I proteſt I do, now am I taught
In death to loue, in life that knew not how.
For vvhilſt my glory in her greatneſſe ſtood,
And that I ſaw my ſtate, and knew my beauty ;
Saw how the vvorld admir'd me, how they woo'd,
I then thought all men muſt loue me of duety,
And I loue none : for my laſciuious Court,
Fertile in euer freſh and new-choyſe pleaſure,   160
Affoorded me ſo bountifull diſport,
That I to ſtay on Loue had neuer leiſure :
My vagabond deſires no limites found,
For luſt is endleſſe, pleaſure hath no bound.

---

l. 148, cap. 'D' accepted from ' : l. 151, 'I . ./. fault' within ( ) in ' :
l. 162, 'think ' '.

Thou comming from the ftrictneffe of thy City,
And neuer this loofe pomp of monarchs learneft,
Inur'd to vvarres, in womens vviles vnwitty,
Whilft others faind, thou fell'ft to loue in earneft;
Not knowing how vve like them beft that houer;
And make leaft reckoning of a doting louer.   170
    And yet thou cam'ft but in my beauties vvaine,
When nevv appearing vvrinckles of declining
Wrought vvith the hand of yeares, feem'd to detaine
My graces light, as now but dimly fhining,
Euen in the confines of mine age, vvhen I
Failing of vvhat I was, and vvas but thus :
When fuch as we do deeme in iealoufie
That men loue for themfelues, and not for vs ;
Then, and but thus, thou didft loue moft fincerely,
O *Antony*, that beft deferu'[d]ft it better,   180
This Autumne of my beauty bought fo dearely,
For which in more-then death, I ftand thy debter,
Which I vvill pay thee vvith fo true a minde,
(Cafting vp all thefe deepe accompts of mine)
That both our foules, and all the world fhall find
All reckoning cleer'd, betwixt my loue and thine.
    But to the [end] I may preuent proud *Cæfar*,
Who doth fo eagerly my life importune,
I muft preuaile me of this little leafure,
Seeming to fute my mind vnto my fortune ;   190

l. 166, 'The wanton pompe of Courts yet neuer [learnedft]' : l. 167,
'womans'' : l. 169, 'women'' : ll. 183-6—
                         'moft faithfull zeale
        'And that ere long ; no Cæfar fhall detaine me :
        My death, my loue and courage fhall reueale,
        The which is all the world hath left t'vnftaine me '' :
l. 187, 'And to the end I may deceiue beft ''.

Thereby vvith more conuenience to prouide
For vvhat my death and honor beſt ſhall fit :
And yeelding baſe content muſt vvary hide
My laſt diſſigne till I accompliſh it,
That hereby yet the vvorld ſhall ſee that I,
Although vnwiſe to liue, had vvitt to die.   *Exit.*

CHORVS.

B Ehold what furies ſtill
      Torment their tortur'd breſt,
Who by their doing ill,   200
Haue wrought the worlds vnreſt.
Which when being moſt diſtreſt,
Yet more to vexe their ſprite,
The hideous face of ſinne,
(In formes they moſt deteſt)
Stands euer in their ſight.
Their conſcience ſtill within
Th' eternall larum is
That euer-barking dog that calles vpon their miſſe.

No meanes at all to hide   210
Man from himſelfe can finde :
No way to ſtart aſide
Out from the hell of minde.
But in himſelfe confin'd,
He ſtill ſee ſinne before ;
And wingèd-footed paine,
That ſwiftly comes behind,

l. 191, ' Whereby I may the better end ' [1]: l. 192, ' Of ' [1]: l. 193, ' A
ſeeming ' [1] : l. 205, ' moſt ' of [1] corrects ' muſt ' of our text.

The which is euer-more,
The sure and certaine gaine
Impiety doth get, 220
And wanton loose respect, that doth it selfe forget.

And Cleopatra *now,*
Well sees the dangerous way
She tooke, and car'd not how,
Which led her to decay.
And likewise makes vs pay
For her disordred lust,
The int'rest of our blood :
Or liue a seruile pray,
Vnder a hand vniust, 230
As others shall thinke good.
This hath her riot wonne :
And thus she hath her state, herselfe and vs vndone.

Now euery mouth can tell,
What close was muttered :
How that she did not well,
To take the course she did.
For now is nothing hid,
Of what feare did restraine ;
No secret closely done, 240
But now is vttered.
The text is made most plaine
That flattry glos'd vpon,
The bed of sinne reueal'd,
And all the luxury that shame would haue conceal'd.

The scene is broken downe
And all vncou'red lyes,

The purple actors knowne
Scarce men, whom men defpife.
   The complots of the wife,   250
Proue imperfections fmoakt :
And all what wonder gaue
To pleafure-gazing eyes,
Lyes fcattred, dafht, all broke.
Thus much beguiled haue
Poore vnconfiderate wights,
Thefe momentary pleafures, fugitiue delights.

ACT II.

      Cæfar.   *Proculeius.*   259

K Ingdomes I fee we winne, vve conquer Climates,
    Yet cannot vanquifh hearts, nor force obedience ;
Affections kept in clofe-concealed limits,
Stand farre without the reach of fword or violence,
Who forc'd do pay vs duty, pay not loue :   •
Free is the heart, the temple of the minde,
The Sanctuary facred from aboue,
Where nature keepes the keies that loofe and bind.
No mortall hand force open can that doore,
So clofe fhut vp, and lockt to all mankind :
I fee mens bodies onely ours, no more,   270
The reft, anothers right, that rules the minde.
    Behold, my forces vanquifht haue this Land,
Subdu'd that ftrong Competitor of mine :
All Egypt yeelds to my all-conqu'ring hand,
And all their treafure and themfelues refigne.

l. 258, 'Actvs Secvndvs': our text mifprinted 'iii.': l. 267, 'and' ac-
cepted from ¹ : l. 272, cap. 'L' accepted from ¹.

Onely this Queene, that hath loft all this all,
To whom is nothing left except a minde :
Cannot into a·thought of yeelding fall,
To be difpof'd as Chance hath her affign'd.
, But *Proculeius* what hope doth fhe now giue,   280
  Will fhe be brought to condifcend to liue ?
Pro. My Lord, what time being fent from you to try
  To win her forth aliue (if that I might)
From out the Monument ; where wofully
She liues inclof'd in moft afflicted plight :
No way I found, no meanes how to furprize her,
But through a grate at the entry of the place
Standing to treate, I labour'd to aduife her,
To come to *Cæfar*, and to fue for grace.
She faid, " fhe crau'd not life, but leaue to die,   290
Yet for her children, pray'd they might inherite ;
That *Cæfar* would vouchfafe (in clemencie)
To pittie them, though fhe deferu'd no merite."
So leauing her for then ; and fince of late,
With *Gallus* fent to trie an other time,
The whilft he entertaines her at the grate,
I found the meanes vp to the Tombe to clime.
Where, in defcending in the clofeft wife,
And filent manner as I could contriue ;
Her woman me defcri'd, and out fhe cries,   300
Poore *Cleopatra*, thou art tane aliue.
With that the Queene caught from her fide her knife,
And euen in act to ftab her martred breft,
I ftept with fpeede, and held, and fau'd her life,
And forth her trembling hand the blade did wreft,

l. 280, mifprints ' Proculei ' : l. 300, mifprinted '23 ' defiri'd ' : l. 302,
' raught ' ¹.

Ah *Cleopatra*, why fhouldft thou, (faid I)
Both iniury thy felfe and *Cæfar* fo?
Barre him the honour of his victory,
Who euer deales moft mildely with his foe?
Liue, and relie on him, whofe mercy will   310
To thy fubmiffion alwayes ready be.
   With that (as all amaz'd) fhe held her ftill,
Twixt maieftie confuz'd and miferie.
Her proud grieu'd eyes, held forrow and difdaine,
State and diftreffe warring within her foule:
Dying ambition difpoffeft her raigne,
So bafe affliction feemèd to controule.
Like as a bur[n]ing Lampe, whofe liquor fpent
With intermitted flames, when dead you deeme it,
Sends forth a dying flafh, as difcontent,   320
That fo the matter failes that fhould redeeme it:
So fhe (in fpight to fee her low-brought ftate,
When all her hopes were now confum'd to noght)
Scornes yet to make an abiect league with Fate, •
Or once defcend into a feruile thought:
Th'imperious tongue vnufed to befeech,
Authoritie confounds with prayers, fo
Words of cõmand conioyn'd with humble fpeech,
Shew'd fhe would liue, yet fcorn'd to pray her foe.
   "Ah, what hath *Cæfar* here to doe," faid fhee,   330
"In confines of the dead, in darkeneffe lying?
Will he not grant our fepulchres be free,
But violate the priuiledge of dying?
What, muft he ftretch foorth his ambitious hand
Into the right of Death, and force vs heere?

    • 331, 'liuing' [1] (bad).

Hath Mifery no couert where to ftand
Free from the ftorme of Pride ? is't fafe no where ?
Cannot my land, my gold, my crowne fuffice,
And all what I held deare, to him made common,
But that he muft in this fort tyrannize,   340
Th'afflicted body of an woefull woman ?
Tell him, my frailetie, and the gods haue giuen
Sufficient glory, could he be content :
And let him now with his defires make euen,
And leaue me to this horror, to lament.
Now he hath taken all away from mee,
What muft he take me from my felfe by force ?
Ah, let him yet (in mercy) leaue me free
The Kingdome of this poore diftreffed corfe :
No other crowne I feeke, no other good.   350
Yet wifh that *Cæfar* would vouchfafe this grace,
To fauour the poore of-fpring of my blood ;
Confufèd iffue, yet of Roman race
If blood and name be linckes of loue in Princes,
Not fpurres of hate ; my poore *Cæfario* may
Finde fauour notwithftanding mine offences,
And *Cæfars* blood, may *Cæfars* raging ftay.
But if that with the torrent of my fall,
All muft be rapt with furious violence,
And no refpect, nor no regard at all,   360
Can ought with nature or with blood difpence :
Then be it fo, if needes it muft be fo."
There ftaies and fhrinkes in horror of her ftate :
When I beganne to mittigate her woe,

l. 339, 'that'⁴ : l. 343, 'if hee could content him''¹ : l. 345, 'lamenting''¹ :
l. 362, " " put at beginning (l. 290), and at ll. 329-30 here, to mark out
Proculeius' narrative of her fpeech.

And thy great mercies vnto her relate ;
Wiſhing her not deſpaire, but rather come
And ſue for grace, and ſhake off all vaine feares :
No doubt ſhe ſhould obtaine as gentle doome
As ſhe deſir'd, both for her ſelfe and hers.
And ſo with much adoe, (well pacifide   370
Seeming to be) ſhe ſhew'd content to liue,
Saying ſhe was reſolu'd thy doome t'abide,
And to accept what fauour thou would'ſt giue ;
And herewithall, crau'd alſo that ſhee might
Performe her laſt rites to her loſt belou'd.
To ſacrifice to him that wroght her plight :
And that ſhe might not be by force remou'd.
   I granting from thy part this her requeſt,
   Left her for then, ſeeming in better reſt. 379
Cæſ. But doſt thou thinke ſhe will remaine ſo ſtill ?
Pro. I thinke, and doe aſſure my ſelfe ſhe will.
Cæſ. Ah, priuate men found not the harts of Princes,
   Whoſe actions oft beare contrary pretences. •
Pro. Why, tis her ſafetie to come yeeld to thee.
Cæſ. But tis more honour for her to goe free.
Pro. She may thereby procure her childrens good.
Cæſ. Princes reſpect their honour more then blood.
Pro. Can Princes powre diſpence with nature than ?
Cæſ. To be a Prince, is more then be a Man. 389
Pro. There's none but haue in time perſwaded beene.
Cæſ. And ſo might ſhe too, were ſhe not a Queene.
Pro. Diuers reſpects will force her be reclaim'd.
Cæſ. Princes (like Lions) neuer will be tam'd.
   A priuate man may yeeld and care not how,
   But greater hear[t]es will break before they bow.
   l. 385, 'die' ¹ : l. 392, '23 miſprints ' relaim'd.'

And fure I thinke fh'will neuer condifcend,
To liue to grace our fpoiles with her difgrace :
But yet let ftill a wary troupe attend,
To guard her perfon, and to watch the place.
And looke that none with her come to confer ;
Shortly my felfe will goe to vifite her.   401

CHORVS.

O Pinion, how do'ft thou moleft |
*   Th'affected mind of reftleffe man ?*
Who following thee neuer can,
Nor euer fhall attaine to reft,
For getting what thou faift is beft,
*   Yet loe, that beft he findes far wide*
*   Of what thou promifedft before :*
*   For in the fame he lookt for more,*   410
*   Which proues but fmall when once tis tride*
Then fomething elfe thou find'ft befide,
*   To draw him ftill from though[t] to thought :*
*   When in the end all prooues but nought.*
*   Farther from reft he findes him than,*
*   Then at the firft when he began.*
O malecontent feducing gueft,
*   Contriuer of our greateft woes :*
*   Which borne of winde, and fed with fhowes,*
*   Dooft nurfe thy felfe in thine vnreft,*   420
Iudging vngotten things the beft,
*   Or what thou in conceit defign'ft ;*
*   And all things in the world doft deeme, |*
*   Not as they are, but as they feeme : |*

1. 398, ' watch ' [1].

Which ſhewes, their ſtate thou ill defin'ſt :
And liu'ſt to come, in preſent pin'ſt.
  For what thou haſt, thou ſtill doſt lacke :
  O mindes tormentor, bodies wracke,
  Vaine promiſer of that ſweete reſt,
  Which neuer any yet poſſeſt.   430

If we vnto ambition tend,
  Then dooſt thou drawe our weakeneſſe on,
  With vaine imagination ⊦
  Of that which neuer hath an end.
Or if that luſt we apprehend,
  How doth that pleaſant plague infeſt ?
  O what ſtrange formes of luxurie,
  Thou ſtrait doſt caſt t'intice vs by ?
  And tell'ſt vs that is euer beſt,
Which we haue neuer yet poſſeſt.   440
  And that more pleaſure reſts beſide,
  In ſomething that we haue not tride.
  And when the ſame likewiſe is had,
  Then all is one, and all is bad.

This Antony *can ſay is true,*
  And Cleopatra *knowes tis ſo,*
  By th'experience of their woe.
She can ſay, ſhe neuer knew
But that luſt found pleaſures new,
  And was neuer ſatisfide :   450
  He can ſay by proofe of toyle,
  Ambition is a Vulture vile,
  That feedes vpon the heart of pride :
And findes no reſt when all is tride.

For worlds cannot confine the one,
Th'other, lifts and bounds hath none ;
And both fubuert the minde, the ftate,
Procure deftruction, enuy, hate.

And now when all this is prou'd vaine,
    Yet Opinion leaues not heere,   /   460
But ftickes to Cleopatra *neere ;*
  Perfwading now, how fhe fhall gaine
Honour by death, and fame attaine,
    And what a fhame it was to liue,
    Her Kingdome loft, her Louer dead :
    And fo with this perfwafion led,
    Defpaire doth fuch a courage giue,
That nought elfe can her minde relieue,
    Nor yet diuert her from that thought :
    To this conclufion all is brought.   470
    This is that reft this vaine world lends,
    To end in death that all things ends.   /

ACT. III.

Philoftratus.   *Arius.*

HOw deepely *Arius* am I bound to thee,
    That fau'dft from death this wretched life of
Obtaining *Cæfars* gentle grace for mee,   [mine :
When I of all helpes elfe defpaird but thine ?
Although I fee in fuch a wofull ftate,
Life is not that which fhould be much defir'd :   480
Sith all our glories come to end their date,
Our Countries honour and our own expir'd,

1. 460, cap. 'O' accepted from [1] : 1. 473, 'Actvs Tertivs' [1].
III.   4

Now that the hand of wrath hath ouer-gone vs,
Liuing (as 'twere) in th'armes of our dead mother,
With blood vnder our feete, ruine vpon vs,
And in a Land moft wretched of all other,
When yet we reckon life our deareft good.
And fo we liue, we care not how we liue :
So deepe we feele impreffed in our blood,
That touch which nature without breath did giue. 490
And yet what blafts of words hath Learning found,
To blow againft the feare of death and dying ?
What comforts vnficke eloquence can found,
And yet all faile vs in the point of trying.
For whilft we reafon with the breath of fafety,
Without the compaffe of deftruction liuing :
What precepts fhew we then, what courage lofty
In taxing others feares in councell giuing ?
When all this ayre of fweet-contriued words
Proues but weake armour to defend the heart.   500
For when this life, pale Feare and Terrour boords,
Where are our precepts then, where is our art ?
O who is he that from himfelfe can turne,
That beare about the body of a man ?
VVho doth not toyle and labour to adiorne
The day of death, by any meanes he can ?
All this I fpeake to th'end my felfe t'excufe,
For my bafe begging of a feruile breath,
VVherein I grant my felfe much to abufe,
So fhamefully to feeke t'auoide my death.   510
  Arius. Philoftratus, that felfe fame care to liue,
Poffeffeth all alike, and grieue not then

l. 494, 'fayles' ¹ : l. 501, ' For when this fhip of life pale Terror boords ' ' :
l. 504, ' beares ' ¹.

Nature doth vs no more then others giue :
Though we fpeake more then men, we are but men :
And yet (in truth) thefe miferies to fee,
Wherein we ftand in moft extreame diftreffe ;
Might to our felues fufficient motiues be
To loath this life, and weigh our death the leffe :
For neuer any age hath better taught,
What feeble footing pride and greatneffe hath.   520
How'improuident profperitie is caught,
And cleane confounded in the day of wrath.
See how difmaid Confufion keepes thofe ftreetes,
That nought but mirth & mufique late refounded,
How nothing with our eye but horror meetes,
Our ftate, our wealth, our pride, and al confounded.
Yet what weake fight did not difcerne from farre
This blacke-arifing tempeft, all confounding ?
Who did not fee we fhould be what we are,
When pride and ryot grew to fuch abounding.   530
When diffolute impietie poffeft
Th'vnrefpe&tiue mindes of Prince, and People :
When infolent Securitie found reft
In wanton thoughts, with luft and eafe made feeble.
Then when vnwary peace with fat-fed pleafure,
New-frefh inuented ryots ftill dete&ted,
Purchaf'd with all the *Ptolomies* rich treafure,
Our Lawes, our Gods, our myfteries negle&ted
Who faw not how this confluence of vice,
This inundation of diforders, muft   540
At length, of force pay backe the bloody price
Of fad deftru&tion, (a reward for luft.)

l. 532, 'fuch a people' l.

O thou and I haue heard, and read, and knowne
Of like proude ftates, as wofully incombred,
And fram'd by them, examples for our owne :
Which now among examples muſt be numbred.
For this decree a law from high is giuen,
An ancient Canon, of eternall date,
In Confiſtory of the ſtarres of heauen,
Entred the Booke of vnauoyded Fate ;   550
That no ſtate can in height of happineſſe,
In th'exaltation of their glory ſtand :
But thither once arriu'd, declining leſſe,
Ruine themſelues, or fall by others hand.
Thus doth the euer-changing courſe of things
Runne a perpetuall circle, euer turning :
And that ſame day that hieſt glory brings,
Brings vs vnto the point of backe-returning.
For fenceleſſe fenſuality, doth euer
Accompany felicity and greatneſſe.   560
A fatall vvitch, whoſe charmes do leaue vs neuer,
Till vve leaue all in forrow for our ſweetneſſe ;
When yet our felues muſt be the cauſe we fall,
Although the ſame be firſt decreed on hie :
Our errors ſtill muſt beare the blame of all,
This muſt it be ; earth, aſke not heauen why.
    Yet mighty-men vvith wary iealous hand,
Striue to cut off all obſtacles of feare :
All whatfoeuer feemes but to withſtand
Their leaſt conceit of quiet, held ſo deare ;   570
And fo intrench themſelues with blood, with crimes,
With all iniuſtice as their feares difpofe :
Yet for all this we fee, how oftentimes
The meanes they worke to keepe, are meanes to lofe.

And fure I cannot fee, how this can ftand
With great *Augustus* fafety and his honor,
To cut off all fucceffion from our land,
For her offence that pull'd the warres vpon her.

    Phi. Why muft her iffue pay the price of that ?
    Ari. The price is life that they are rated at.   580
    Phi. Cæfario too, iffued of *Cæfars* blood ?
    Ari. Plurality of *Cæfars* are not good.
    Phi. Alas, what hurt procures his feeble arme ?
    Ari. Not for it doth, but that it may do harme
    Phi. Then when it offers hurt, repreffe the fame.
    Ari. Tis beft to quench a fparke before it flame.
    Phi. Tis inhumane, an innocent to kill.
    Ari. Such innocents feldome remaine fo ftill.

And fure his death may beft procure our peace ;
Competitors the fubiect deerely buies :   590
And fo that our affliction may furceaffe,
Let great men be the peoples facrifice.

    But fee where *Cæfar* comes himfelfe, to try
And worke the mind of our diftreffèd Queene,
To apprehend fome falfed hope, whereby
She might be drawne to haue her fortune feene.

    But yet I thinke, Rome will not fee that face
    (That queld her champions) blufh in bafe difgrace.

                           [*Exeunt.*

SCENA. II.

Cæfar. Cleopatra. Seleucus. Dolabella.   600

VV Hat *Cleopatra*, doeft thou doubt fo much
        Of *Cæfars* mercy, that thou hid'ft thy face ?

l. 587, ' an ' accepted from ' for ' and ' of the other texts : l. 598, ' quel '¹.
l. 599, ' Secvnda '¹.

Or doeſt thou thinke, thy offences can be ſuch,
That they ſurmount the meaſure of our grace?
   Cle. O *Cæſar*, not for that I flie thy ſight
My ſoule this ſad retire of ſorrow choſe:
But that m'oppreſſed thoughts abhorring light
Like beſt in darkenes, my diſgrace t'incloſe.
And here to theſe cloſe limites of deſpaire, .
This ſolitary horror where I bide: 610
Cæſar, I thought no Roman ſhould repaire,
More after him, who here oppreſſèd dyde.
Yet now, here at thy conquering feete I lie,
Poore captiue ſoule, that neuer thought to bow:
Whoſe happy foote of rule and Maieſty
Stood late on the ſame ground thou ſtandeſt now.
   Cæſ. Riſe Queene, none but thy ſelfe is cauſe of all;
And yet, would all vvere but thyne owne alone;
That others ruine had not vvith thy fall,   619
Brought Rome her ſorrowes, to my triumphs mone.
For breaking off the league of loue and blood,
Thou mak'ſt my winning ioy a gaine vnpleaſing:
Sith th'eye of griefe muſt looke into our good,
Thorow the horror of our owne bloodſhedding:
And all, we muſt attribute vnto thee.
   Cle. To me? *Cæſar*, vvhat ſhould a woman doe
Oppreſt with greatnes? vvhat, was it for me
To contradi� my Lord, being bent thereto?
I vvas by loue, by feare, by weakeneſſe, made
An inſtrument to ſuch diſſeignes as theſe.   630
For vvhen the Lord of all the Orient bade,

---

   l. 616, 'yᵗ'¹: l. 617, '23 misprints 'mine': l. 622, accepted from ' for
' a gaine ' of the other texts: l. 630, ' to euery enterpriſe '⁴.

Who but obey'd ? vvho was not glad to pleafe ?
And how could I vvithdraw my fuccouring hand
From him that had my heart, and vvhat vvas mine ?
The int'reft of my faith in ftreighteft band,
My loue to his moft firmely did combine.

   Cæf. Loue ? alas no, it vvas th'innated hatred
That thou and thine haft euer borne our people :
That made thee feek all meanes to haue vs fcattred,
To difunite our ftrength, and make vs feeble.   640
And therefore did that breaft nurfe our diffention,
With hope t'exalt thy felfe, t'augment thy ftate :
To pray vpon the vvracke of our contention,
And (with the reft our foes,) to ioy thereat.

   Cleo. O *Cæfar,* fee how eafie tis t'accufe
Whom Fortune hath made faulty by their fall ;
The wretched conquered may not refufe
The titles of reproch he's charg'd vvithall.

    The conquering caufe hath right, wherein thou art,
    The vanquifht ftill is iudged the worfer part.   650
Which part is mine, becaufe I loft my part.
No.leffer then the portion of a Crowne.
Enough for me, alas vvhat needed Art
To gaine by others, but to keepe mine owne ?
But here let vveaker powers note vvhat it is,
To neighbour great Competitors too neere ;
If vve take part, vve oft do perifh thus,
If neutrall bide, both parties we muft feare.

l. 632, ' who then his helpe denies ' ⁴: l. 645, ' How eafie Cæfar is it ' ⁴ :
l. 647, ' They who are vanquifhed ' ⁴: l. 648, ' th'are ' ⁴; l. 650, ' The ouer-
throwne muft be ' ⁴: l. 653, '23 mifprinted ' need ' ; ' Ah what need I vfe ' ⁴ :
l. 655, ' may here fee what it is ' ⁴ : l. 656, ' fo ' ⁴ : l. 657, ' either part we ' ⁴ :
l. 658, ' ftand ' ⁴.

Alas, vvhat fhall the forft partakers do,
When following none, yet muft they perifh too ?　660
But *Cæfar*, fith thy right and caufe is fuch,
Be not a heauy vveight vpon calamity :
Depreffe not the afflicted ouer-much,
The chiefeft glory is the Victors lenity.
Th'inheritance of mercy from him take,
Of vvhom thou haft thy fortune and thy name :
Great *Cæfar*, me a Queene at firft did make,
And let not *Cæfar* now confound the fame.
Reade here thefe lines which ftill I keepe with me,
The witnes of his loue and fauours euer :　670
And God forbid this fhould be fayd of thee,
That *Cæfar* vvrong'd the fauourèd of *Cæfar*.
For looke vvhat I haue beene to *Antony*,
Thinke thou the fame I might haue beene to thee.
And here I do prefent thee vvith the note
Of all the treafure, all the iewels rare
That Egypt hath in many ages got ;
And looke what *Cleopatra* hath, is there.

　　Seleu. Nay there's not all fet downe within that roule,
I know fome things fhe hath referu'd apart.　680

　　Cle. What, vile vngratefull wretch, dar'ft thou con-
　　　　troule
Thy Queene and foueraigne, caitife as thou art ?

　　Cæf. Hold, hold ; a poore reuenge can worke fo
　　　　feeble hands.

　　Cle. Ah *Cæfar*, vvhat a great indignity
Is this, that here my vaffall fubiect ftands
T'accufe me to my Lord of trechery ?

---

l. 660, ' When they muft aid and yet muft ' ': l. 685, '23 misprints
' vaftall.'

If I referu'd fome certaine vvomens toyes,
Alas it vvas not for my felfe (God knowes),
Poore miferable foule, that little ioyes
In trifling ornaments, in outward fhowes.   690
But what I kept, I kept to make my vvay
Vnto thy *Liuia* and *Octauias* grace,
That thereby in compaffion moouèd, they
Might mediate thy fauour in my cafe.

    Cæf. Well *Cleopatra*, feare not ; thou fhalt finde
What fauour thou defir'ft, or canft expect :
For *Cæfar* neuer yet was found but kinde
To fuch as yeeld, and can themfelues fubiect.
And therefore giue thou comfort to thy mind,
Relieue thy foule thus ouercharg'd with care ;   700
How well I vvill intreate thee thou fhalt finde
So foone as fome affaires difpatchèd are.
Till then farewell.

    Cle.   Thanks thrife renowned *Cæfar*,
Poore *Cleopatra* refts thine owne for euer.

    Dol. No maruell *Cæfar* though our greateft fp'rits
Haue to the powre of fuch a charming beauty
Been brought to yeeld the honor of their merits :
Forgetting all refpect of other duty.
Then vvhilft the glory of her youth remain'd
The wondring obiect to each wanton eye :   710
Before her full of fweet (with forrow vvain'd,)
Came to the period of this mifery.
If ftill, euen in the midft of death and horror
Such beauty fhines, thorow clouds of age and forrow,
If euen thofe fweet decayes feeme to pleade for
    her,
Which from affliction mouing graces borrow :

If in calamity fhe could thus moue,
What could fhe do adorn'd vvith youth and loue ?
What could fhe do then, whenas fpreading wide
The pompe of beauty, in her glory dight ?   720
When arm'd with wonder, fhe could vfe befide,
Th'ingines of her loue, Hope, and Delight ?
    Beauty, daughter of Meruaile, O fee how
Thou canft difgracing forrowes fweetly grace.
What power thou fhew'ft in a diftreffèd brow,
That mak'ft affliction faire, giu'ft teares their grace.
What can vntreffèd lockes, can torne rent haire,
A weeping eye, a wailing face be faire ?
    I fee then, artleffe feature can content,
    And that true beauty needes no ornament.   730
    Cæf. What in a paffion *Dolabella*? what? take heed :
Let others frefh examples be thy warning ;
VVhat mifchiefes thefe, fo idle humors breed,
VVhilft error keepes vs from a true difcerning.
Indeed I faw fhe labour'd to impart
Her fweeteft graces in her faddeft cheere :
Prefuming on the face that knew the arte
To moue, with vvhat afpect fo eu'r it were.
But all in vaine ; fhe takes her ayme amiffe,
The ground and marke, her leuell much deceiues;   740
Time now hath altred all, for neither is
She as fhe was, nor we as fhe conceiues.
And therefore now, twere beft fhe left fuch badnes ;
Folly in youth is finne, in age, tis madnes.

ll. 723-4, 'Daughter of meruaile, Beautie how doft thou
       Vnto difgracing forrowes giue fuch grace ' ⁴:
l. 726, ' To make affliction faire and teares to grace ' ⁴: l. 727, 'difpoyled ' :
l. 732, ' charme this heate ' ⁴: l. 733, ' You fee what mifchiefes thefe vaine
humors breed ' ⁴: l. 734, ' When as they come our judgements to defeat ' ⁴.

And for my part, I feeke but t'entertaine
In her fome feeding hope to draw her forth ;
The greateſt Trophey that my trauailes gaine,
Is, to bring home a prizall of fuch worth.
And now, fith that fhe feemes fo well content
To be difpofd by vs, without more ftay　　　　750
She with her children fhall to Rome be fent,
VVhilſt I by *Syria* thither take my way.

CHORVS.

O *Fearefull-frowning* Nemeſis,
　　Daughter of Iuſtice, moſt ſeuere ;
　That art the worlds great Arbitreſſe
　And Queene of cauſes raigning here :
Whoſe ſwift-ſure hand is euer neere
　Eternall iuſtice, righting wrong :
　Who neuer yet deferreſt long　　　　760
　The prouds decay, the weakes redreſſe :
But through thy power euery where,
　Doſt raze the great, and raiſe the leſſe.
　The leſſe made great, doſt ruine too,　'
　To ſhew the earth what heauen can do.

Thou from darke-cloſ'd eternity,
　From thy blacke cloudy hidden ſeate,
　The worlds diſorders doſt deſcry :
　Which when they ſwell ſo proudly great,
Reuerſing th'order nature ſet,　　　　770
　Thou giu'ſt thy all confounding doome,

1. 754, - inferted : l. 756, cap. ' A ' accepted.

Which none can know before it come :
Th'ineuitable destiny,
Which neither wit nor strength can let,
　　Fast chain'd vnto necessity,
　　In mortall things doth order so,
　　Th'alternate course of weale or woe.

O how the powers of heauen doe play
　　With trauailèd mortality :
　　And doth their weakenesse still betray,　　　780
　　In their best prosperity ?
When being lifted vp so hie,
　　They looke beyond themselues so farre,
　　That to themselues they take no care ;
　　Whilst swift confusion downe doth lay,
Their late proud mounting vanity :
　　Bringing their glory to decay,
　　And with the ruine of their fall,
　　Extinguish people, state and all.

But is it Iustice that all we　　　　　　　790
　　The innocent poore multitude,
　　For great mens faults should punisht be,
　　And to destruction thus pursude ?
O why should th'heauens vs include,
　　Within the compasse of their fall,
　　Who of themselues procurèd all ?
　　Or do the gods (in close) decree,
Occasion take how to extrude
　　Man from the earth with cruelty ?
　　Ah no, the gods are euer iust,　　　　　800
　　Our faults excuse their rigor must.

This is the period Fate fet downe,
  To Egypts fat profperity :
  Which now vnto her greateft growne,
Muft perifh thus, by courfe muft die,
And fome muft be the caufers why
  This reuolution muft be wrought :
  As borne to bring their ftate to nought :
  To change the people and the crowne,
And purge the worlds iniquity :   810
  Which vice fo farre hath ouer growne.
  As we, fo they that treate vs thus,
Muft one day perifh like to vs.

ACTVS IIII.

Seleucus.   Rodon.

N Euer friend *Rodon* in a better houre,
      Could I haue met thee then eu'n now I do,
Hauing affliction in the greateft powre
Vpon my foule, and none to tell it to.
For tis fome eafe our forrowes to reueale,   820
If they to whom we fhall impart our woes
Seeme but to feele a part of what we feele,
And meete vs with a figh but at a cloze.
  Rod. And neuer (friend *Seleucus*) found'ft thou one
That better could beare fuch a part with thee :
Who by his owne, knowes others cares to mone,
And can, in like accord of griefe, agree.
And therefore tell th'oppreffion of thy heart,
Tell to an eare prepar'd and tun'd to care :

l. 814, 'Qvartvs' [1].

And I will likewife vnto thee impart   ˜830
As fad a tale as what thou fhalt declare.
So fhall vve both our mournefull plaints combine
Ile vvaile thy ftate, and thou fhalt pitty mine.
    Sel. Well then thou know'ft how I haue liu'd in grace
With *Cleopatra*, and efteem'd in Court
As one of Councell, and of chiefeft place,
And euer held my credite in that fort.
Till now in this confufion of our ftate,
VVhen thinking to haue vf'd a meane to climbe,
And fled the wretched, flowne vnto the great,   840
(Following the fortune of the prefent time,)
Am come to be caft downe and ruin'd cleane ;
And in the courfe of mine owne plot vndon.
For hauing all the fecrets of the Queene
Reueald to *Cæfar*, to haue fauour won,
My treachery is quitted vvith difgrace,
My falfhood loath'd, and not without great reafon
Though good for him ; yet Princes in this cafe
Doe hate the Traitor, though they loue the treafon.
For how could he imagine I would be   850
Faithfull to him, being falfe vnto mine owne ?
And falfe to fuch a bounteous Queene as fhe,
That had me raif'd and made mine honor knowne.
He faw twas not for zeale to him I bare,
But for bafe feare, or mine owne ftate to fettle.
Weakeneffe is falfe, and faith in Cowards rare,
ˋ Feare findes out fhifts, timiditie is fubtle.

l. 838, 'late fhifting' ⁴: l. 842, 'I come to be difgrac'd' ⁴: l. 843 dropped
in ⁴: l. 846, 'hath purchaf'd': l. 848, 'For Princes though they get
yet' ⁴: l. 849, 'They' ⁴: l. 851, 'Entire' ⁴: l. 852, 'worthy' ⁴: l. 853, 'As
. . . by whom my ftate was grown' ⁴.

And therfore fcorn'd of him, fcorn'd of mine owne.
Hatefull to all that looke into my ftate :
Defpif'd *Seleucus* now is onely growne   860
The marke of infamy, that's pointed at.

   Rod. Tis much thou faift, and O too much to feele,
And I doe grieue and doe lament thy fall :
But yet all this which thou dooft heere reueale,
Compar'd with mine will make thine feeme but fmall.
Although my fault be in the felfe-fame kind,
Yet in degree farre greater, farre more hatefull ;
Mine fprong of mifchiefe, thine from feeble mind,
₇ I ftaind with blood, thou onely but vngratefull.
For vnto me did *Cleopatra* giue   870
The beft and deareft treafure of her blood,
Louely *Cæfario* ; whom fhe would fhould liue
Free from the dangers wherein *Egypt* ftood.
And vnto me with him this charge fhe gaue,
Here *Rodon*, take, conuey from out this coaft,
This precious Gem, the chiefeft that I haue,
This iewell of my foule I value moft ;
Guide him to *India*, leade him farre from hence,
Safeguard him where fecure he may remaine,
Till better fortune call him backe from thence,   880

l. 860, in '23 mifprinted 'odely' : l. 869, 'Mine' ⁴ : l. 870, 'For *Cleopatra*
did commit to me' ⁴: l. 872, 'Her fon *Cæfario* with a hope to free' ⁴ :
l. 873, 'Him' ⁴ : ll. 874-5—
       ' And charg'd my faith, that I fhould fafely guide
        And clofe, to India fhould convey him hence ' ⁴.
Then follow thefe lines in ⁴—
       ' Which faith, I moft vnkindly falfifi'd,
       And with my faith and confcience did difpence.
       For fcarce were we arriu'd vnto the fhore,
       But *Cæfar* hauing knowledge of our way,
       Had fent,' etc. (see l. 977 onward).

And *Egypts* peace be reconcil'd againe.
For this is he that may our hopes bring backe ;
(The rifing Sunne of our declyning ftate :)
Thefe be the hands that may reftore our wracke,
And raife the broken ruines made of late.
He may giue limits to the boundleffe pride
Of fierce *Octauius*, and abate his might :
Great *Iulius* of-fpring, he may come to guide
The Empire of the world, as his by right.
   O how he feemes the modell of his Syre ?   890
O how I gaze my *Cæfar* in his face ?
Such was his gate, fo did his lookes afpire ;
Such was his threatning brow, fuch was his grace,
High fhouldred, and his forehead euen as hie.
And O, (if he had not beene borne fo late,)
He might haue rul'd the worlds great Monarchy,
And now haue beene the Champion of our ftate.
   Then vnto him, O my deere Sonne (fhe faies,)
Sonne of my youth, flie hence, O flie, be gone,
Referue thy felfe, ordain'd for better daies,   900
For much thou haft to ground thy hopes vpon.
Leaue me (thy wofull Mother) to endure
The fury of this tempeft heere alone :
Who cares not for her felfe, fo thou be fure ;
Thou mayft reuenge, when others can but mone.
Rodon will fee thee fafe, *Rodon* will guide
Thee and thy wayes, thou fhalt not need to feare.
Rodon (my faithfull feruant) will prouide
What fhall be beft for thee, take thou no care.
And O good *Rodon,* looke well to his youth,   910
The waies are long, and dangers eu'ry where.

l. 902, '23 ' thy ' (bad).

I vrge it not that I doe doubt thy truth,
Mothers will caſt the worſt, and alwaies feare.
  The abſent danger greater ſtill appeares,
  Leſſe feares he, who is neere the thing he feares.
And O, I know not what preſaging thought
My ſprite ſuggeſts of luckleſſe bad euent :
But yet it may be tis but Loue doth doat,
On ydle ſhadowes which my feares preſent ;
But yet the memory of mine owne fate   920
Makes me feare his.   And yet why ſhould I feare ?
His fortune may recouer better ſtate,
And he may come in pompe to gouerne heere.
But yet I doubt the *Genius* of our race
By ſome malignant ſpirite comes ouerthrowne :
Our bloud muſt be extinct, in my diſgrace,
Egypt muſt haue no more Kings of their owne.
Then let him ſtay, and let vs fall together,
Sith it is fore-decreed that we muſt fall.   929
Yet who knowes what may come ? let him goe thither.
What Merchaunt in one veſſell venters all ?
Let vs diuide our ſtarres.   Go, go my ſonne,
Let not the fate of *Egypt* finde thee here :
Try if ſo be thy deſtiny can ſhunne
The common wracke of vs, by being there.
But who is he found euer yet defence
Againſt the heauens, or hid him any where ?
Then what need I to ſend thee ſo farre hence
To ſeeke thy death that mayſt as well die here ?
And here die with thy mother, die in reſt,   940
Not trauelling to what will come to thee.

. l. 919, ' On ' for ' Or ' and ' which ' for ' with ' accepted from ⁴.

Why fhould we leaue our blood vnto the Eaft,
When *Egypt* may a tombe fufficient be ?
 O my diuided foule, what fhall I do ?
Whereon fhall now my refolution reft ?
What were I beft refolue to yeeld vnto ?
When both are bad, how fhall I know the beft ?
Stay : I may hap fo worke with *Cæfar* now,
That he may yeeld him to reftore thy right.
Goe : *Cæfar* neuer will confent that thou   950
So neare in blood, fhalt be fo great in might.
Then take him *Rodon*, goe my fonne, farewell.
But ftay : there's fomething elfe that I would fay :
Yet nothing now. But O God fpeed thee well,
Left faying more, that more may make thee ftay.
Yet let me fpeake : It may be tis the laft
That euer I fhall fpeake to thee my fonne.
Doe Mothers vfe to part in fuch poft haft ?
What, muft I end when I haue fcarce begunne ?
Ah no (deare heart) tis no fuch flender twine 960
Wherewith the knot is tide twixt thee and me ;
That blood within thy veins came out of mine,
Parting from thee, I part from part of me :
And therefore I muft fpeake. Yet what ? O fonne.
 Here more fhe would, when more fhe could not fay :
Sorrow rebounding backe whence it begunne,
Fill'd vp the paffage, and quite ftopt the way :
When fweete *Cæfario* with a princely fp'rite,
(Though comfortleffe himfelfe) did comfort giue ;
With mildeft words, perfwading her to beare it ; 970
And as for him, fhe fhould not neede to grieue.
And I (with proteftations of my part,)

Swore by that faith, (vvhich fworne I did deceiue)
That I vvould vfe all care, all vvit and art
To fee him fafe ; And fo vve tooke our leaue.
Scarce had vve trauell'd to our iourneys end,
When *Cæfar* hauing knowledge of our vvay,
His Agents after vs vvith fpeed doth fend
To labour me, *Cæfario* to betray.
Who vvith rewards and promifes fo large,   980
Affail'd me then, that I grew foone content ;
And backe to *Rhodes* did reconuay my charge,
Pretending that *Octauius* for him fent,
To make him King of *Egypt* prefently.
　　And thither come, feeing himfelfe betray'd,
And in the hands of death through trechery,
Wailing his ftate, thus to himfelfe he faid.
　　Loe here brought backe by fubtile traine to death
Betrai'd by tutors faith, or traitors rather :
My fault my blood, and mine offence my birth,   990
For being fonne of fuch a mighty Father.
　　From *India*, (vvhither fent by mothers care,
To be referu'd from *Egypts* common wracke,)
To *Rhodes*, (fo long the armes of tyrants are,)
I am by *Cæfars* fubtile reach brought backe :
Here to be made th'oblation for his feares,
Who doubts the poore reuenge thefe hands may doe him :
Refpecting neither blood, nor youth, nor yeares,
Or how fmall fafety can my death be to him.
　　And is this all the good of being borne great?   1000
Then vvretched greatneffe, proud rich mifery,
Pompous diftreffe, glittering calamitie.

　　l. 984, in ‘ this line is added—‘ And in their hands haue left him now to
die ’ ; then it passes to l. 1064 : l. 1001, ‘ golden ’ ’.

Is it for this th'ambitious Fathers fweat,
To purchafe blood and death for them and theirs ?
Is this the iffue that their glories get,
To leaue a fure deftruction to their heires ?
O how much better had it beene for me,
From low defcent, deriu'd of humble birth,
T'haue eat the fweet-fowre bread of pouertie,
And drunke of *Nylus* ftreames in *Nylus* earth ?   1010
Vnder the cou'ring of fome quiet Cottage,
Free from the wrath of heauen, fecure in minde,
Vntoucht when fad euents of Princes dotage
Confounds vvhat euer mighty it doth finde.
And not t'haue ftood in their way, whofe condition
Is to haue all made cleare, and all thing plaine
Betweene them and the marke of their ambition,
That nothing let, the full fight of their raigne.
VVhere nothing ftands, that ftands not in fubmiffion ;
Whofe greatneffe muft all in it felfe containe.   1020
Kings will be alone, Competitors muft downe,
Neare death he ftands, that ftands too neare a Crowne.
  Such is my cafe, for *Cæfar* vvill haue all.
My blood muft feale th'affurance of his ftate :
Yet ah weake ftate that blood affure him fhall,
Whofe wrongfull fhedding, gods and men do hate.
Iniuftice neuer fcapes vnpunifht ftill ;
Though men reuenge not, yet the heauens will.

---

l. 1005, 'th'inheritance' ⁴: l. 1006, 'th'eftate of ruine' ⁴: l. 1007,
'farre': 'Then' ⁴: l. 1008, 'from' ⁴: l. 1013, 'prowd attempts' ⁴:
l. 1014, 'Imbroyle the world, and ruinate mankind' ⁴: l. 1015, 'So had I
not impeach'd their line' ⁴: l. 1016, 'Who muft haue all things cleere' ⁴:
l. 1018, 'profpect' ⁴: l. 1020, 'Whofe' ⁴ accepted for 'Where' of other
texts : l. 1023, 'Auguftus' : l. 1027, 'cannot fcape and flourifh' ⁴: l. 1028,
'doe not reuenge it th'' ⁴.

And thou *Auguſtus* that with bloody hand,
Cutt'ſt off fucceſſion from anothers race, 1030
Maiſt find the heauens thy vowes ſo to withſtand,
That others may depriue thine in like cafe
When thou maiſt fee thy prowd contentious bed
Yeelding thee none of thine that may inherite :
Subuert thy blood, place others in their ſted,
To pay this thy iniuſtice her due merite.

If it be true (as who can that deny
VVhich facred Prieſts of *Memphis* doe fore-fay)
Some of the of-fpring yet of *Antony*,
Shall all the rule of this whole Empire fway ; 1040
And then *Auguſtus*, what is it thou gaineſt
By poore *Antillus* blood, or this of mine ?
Nothing but this, thy victory thou ſtaineſt,
And pull'ſt the wrath of heauen on thee and thine.

In vaine doth man contend againſt the ſtarr's,
For that he feekes to make, his wifedome marr's.

Yet in the meane time we whom Fates referue,
The bloody facrifices of ambition,
VVe feele the fmart, what euer they deferue,
And we indure the prefent times condition. 1050

The iuſtice of the heauens reuenging thus,
Doth onely fatisfie it felfe, not vs.

Yet tis a pleafing comfort that doth eafe
Affliction in fo great extremitie,
To thinke their like deſtruction ſhall appeafe

---

l. 1029, 'And he that thus doth feeke' ⁴: l. 1030, '23 mifprints 'curſt'
(bad) ; in ⁴ 'T'extinguiſh the ofspring of': l. 1032, 'his' ⁴: l. 1033, 'he
ſhall fee his' ⁴: l. 1034, 'him . . . his,' l. 1035, 'his,' l. 1036, 'his' ⁴:
l. 1042, '23 'Antillius': l. 1047, 'But': l. 1052, 'facrififfe' ¹, altered in
MS. to 'fatisfie.'

Our ghofts, who did procure our mifery.
But dead we are, vncertaine what fhall be,
And liuing, we are fure to feele the wrong;
Our certaine ruine we our felues doe fee.
They ioy the while, and we know not how long.   1060
But yet *Cæfario*, thou muft die content,
For men will mone, and God reuenge th'innocent.
Thus he complain'd, and thus thou hear'ft my fhame.
      Sel. But how hath *Cæfar* now rewarded thee?
      Rod. As he hath thee.   And I expect the fame
As fell to *Theodor* to fall to mee:
For he (one of my coate) hauing betraid
The yong *Antillus* fonne of *Anthony*,
And at his death from off his necke conuaid
A iewell: which being afkt, he did denie: 1070
Cæfar occafion tooke to hang him ftrait.
Such inftruments with Princes liue not long:
Although they need fuch actors of deceit,
Yet ftill our fight feemes to vpbraid their wrong;
And therefore we muft needes this danger runne,
And in the net of our owne guile be caught:
We muft not liue to brag what we haue done,
For what is done, muft not appeare their fault.
      But here comes *Cleopatra*, wofull Queene,   1079
And our fhame will not that we fhould be feene.
                                                Exeunt.

ll. 1066-8, ' As *Theodorus* had to . . .
              And with a great extreamitie of fhame
              For *Theodorus* when he had ' [4].
l. 1073, ' vfe thofe ' [4] : l. 1074, ' their . . . obraid ' [4].

Cleopatra.

VVHat hath my face yet powre to win a Louer?
 Can this torne remnant ferue to grace me fo,
That it can *Cæfars* fecret plots difcouer,
What he intends with me and mine to do?
Why then poore beauty thou haft done thy laft,
And beft good feruice thou could'ft doe vnto me;
For now the time of death reueal'd thou haft,
Which in my life didft ferue but to vndoe me.

  Heere *Dolabella* farre forfooth in loue,   1090
VVrites, how that *Cæfar* meanes forthwith, to fend
Both me and mine, th'ayre of *Rome* to proue:
There [h]is Triumphant Chariot to attend.
I thanke the man, both for his loue and letter;
The one comes fit to warne me thus before,
But for th'other I muft die his debter,
For *Cleopatra* now can loue no more.

  But hauing leaue, I muft goe take my leaue
And laft farewell of my dead *Anthony*:
Whofe dearely honour'd tombe muft here receiue 1100
This facrifice, the laft before I die.
  O facred euer-memorable ftone,
That haft without my teares, within my flame;
Receiue th'oblation of the wofull'ft mone
That euer yet from fad affliction came.
And you deare reliques of my Lord and Loue.
(The fweeteft parcels of the faithfull'ft liuer,)
O let no impious hand dare to remoue
You out from hence, but reft you here for euer.

l. 1081, in ⁴ on margin 'Cleopatra reading Dolabella's letter': l. 1097,
see our Note before this Play on this passage: l. 1105, 'fad' accepted
from ⁴: l. 1107, 'worthieft.'

Let *Egypt* now giue peace vnto you dead,   1110
That liuing, gaue you trouble and turmoile :
Sleepe quiet in this euer-lafting bed,
In forraine land preferr'd before your foile.
And O, if that the fp'rits of men remaine
After their bodies, and do neuer die,
Then heare thy ghoft, thy captiue fpoufe complaine
And be attentiue to her mifery.
But if that labourfome mortality
Found this fweete error, onely to confine
The curious fearch of idle vanity,   1120
That would the deapth of darknes vndermine :
Or rather, to giue reft vnto the thought
Of wretched man, with th'after-comming ioy
Of thofe conceiuèd fields, whereon we dote,
To pacifie the prefent worlds annoy.
If it be fo, why fpeake I then to th'ayre ?
But tis not fo, my *Antony* doth heare :
His euer-liuing ghoft attends my prayer,
And I do know his houering fprite is neere.
And I will fpeake, and pray, and mourne to thee. 1130
O pure immortall foule that daign'ft to heare,
I feele thou anfwer'ft my credulity
With touch of comfort, finding none elfewhere.
Thou know'ft thefe hands intomb'd thee here of late,
Free and vnforc'd, which now muft feruile be,
Referu'd for bands to grace proud *Cæfars* ftate,
Who feekes in me to triumph ouer thee.
O if in life we could not feuerd be,

---

l. 1122, ' a ' not accepted from ' : l. 1126, ' Then why doe I complaine
me ' : l. 1131, ' foule ' accepted for ' loue ' of other texts, from .

Shall Death diuide our bodies now afunder?
Muft thine in Egypt, mine in Italy,   1140
Be kept the Monuments of Fortunes vvonder?
If any powres be there whereas thou art,
(Sith our country gods betray our cafe,)
O worke they may their gracious helpe impart,
To faue thy wofull wife from fuch difgrace.
Do not permit fhe fhould in triumph fhew
The blufh of her reproach, ioyn'd vvith thy fhame:
But (rather) let that hatefull tyrant know,
That thou and I had powre t'auoyde the fame.
But what do I fpend breath and idle winde,   1150
In vaine inuoking a conceiuèd aide?
Why do I not my felfe occafion finde
To breake the bounds wherein my felfe am ftayd?
Words are for them that can complaine and liue,
Whofe melting hearts compof'd of bafer frame,
Can to their forrowes, time and leafure giue,
But *Cleopatra* may not do the fame.
No *Antony*, thy loue requireth more:
A lingring death, with thee deferues no merite;
I muft my felfe force open wide a dore   1160
To let out life, and fo vnhoufe my fpirit.
Thefe hands muft breake the prifon of my foule
To come to thee, there to enioy like ftate,
As doth the long-pent folitary Foule,
That hath efcapt her cage, and found her mate.
This facrifice to facrifice my life,
Is that true incenfe that doth beft befeeme:
Thefe rites may ferue a life-defiring wife,

l. 1139, cap. 'D' accepted: l. 1143, 'caufe' ⁴: l. 1157, 'muft' ⁴:
l. 1167, 'befeemes,' and l. 1169, 'fufficient deemes' ⁴.

Who doing them, t'haue done enough doth deeme.

My hart bloud fhould the purple flowers haue bin, 1170

Which here vpon thy tombe to thee are offred,

No fmoake but dying breath fhould here bin feene,

And this it had bin too, had I bin fuffred.

But what haue I faue thefe bare hands to do it?

And thefe weake fingers are not yron-poynted:

They cannot pierce the flefh being put vnto it,

And I of all meanes elfe am difappointed.

But yet I muft a way and meanes feeke, how

To come vnto thee, whatfoere I do.

O Death, art thou fo hard to come by now,   1180

That we muft pray, intreate, and feeke thee too?

But I will finde thee wherefoere thou lie,

For who can ftay a minde refolu'd to die?

And now I go to worke th'effe&t indeed,

Ile neuer fend more words or fighes to thee:

Ile bring my foule my felfe, and that with fpeede,

My felfe will bring my foule to *Antony*.

Come, go my Maydes, my fortunes fole attenders, •

That minifter to mifery and forrow:

Your Miftris you vnto your freedome renders,   1190

And will difcharge your charge yet ere to morrow.

And now by this, I thinke the man I fent,

Is neere return'd that brings me my difpatch.

God grant his cunning fort to good euent,

And that his fkill may well beguile my watch:

So ſhall I aɛ the laſt of life with glory,
Die like a Queene, and reſt without controule. , *Exit.*

CHORVS. 1200

*M*Iſterious Egypt, wonder breeder,
    ſtriɛ Religions ſtrange obſeruer,
State-ordrer zeale, the beſt rule-keeper,
    foſtring ſtill in temp'rate feruor :
O how cam'ſt thou to loſe ſo wholy
    all religion, law and order ?
And thus become the moſt vnholy
    of all Lands, that Nylus border ?
How could confuſ'd Diſorder enter
    where ſterne Law ſate ſo ſeuerely ?   1210
How durſt weake luſt and riot venter
    th'eye of Iuſtice looking neerely ?
Could not thoſe means that made thee great
Be ſtill the meanes to keepe thy ſtate ?

Ah no, the courſe of things requireth
    change and alteration euer :
That ſame continuance man deſireth,
    th'vnconſtant world yeeldeth neuer.
We in our counſels muſt be blinded,
    and not ſee what doth import vs :   1220
And often-times the things leaſt minded
    is the thing that moſt muſt hurt vs.

l. 1199, 'Exeunt' 4.

Yet they that haue the fterne in guiding,
  tis their fault that fhould preuent it ;
For oft they feeing their Country fliding,
  take their eafe, as though contented.
We imitate the greater powres,
The Princes manners fafhion ours.

Th'example of their light regarding,
  vulgar loofeneffe much incences :   1230
Vice vncontrold, growes wide inlarging,
  Kings fmall faults, be great offences,
And this hath fet the window open
  vnto licence, luft, and riot :
This way confufion firft found broken,
  whereby entred our difquiet.
Thofe lawes that old Sefoftris *founded,*
  and the Ptolomies *obferued,*
Hereby firft came to be confounded,
  which our ftate fo long preferued.   1240
The wanton luxury of Court,
Did forme the people of like fort.

For all (refpecting priuate pleafure,)
  vniuerfally confenting
To abufe their time, their treafure,
  in their owne delights contenting :
And future dangers nought refpecting,
  whereby, (O how eafie matter
Made this fo generall neglecting,
  confuf'd weakeneffe to difcatter ?)   1250

l. 1226, ' for their printe are ' ⁴.

Cæſar *found th'effeɛt true tried,*
in his eaſie entrance making :
Who at the ſight of armes, deſcried
all our people, all forſaking.
For ryot (worſe then warre,) ſo ſore
Had waſted all our ſtrength before.

And thus is Egypt ſeruile rendred
to the inſolent deſtroyer :
And all their ſumptuous treaſure tendred,
all her wealth that did betray her.   1260
Which poyſon (O if heauen be rightfull,)
may ſo farre infeɛt their ſences,
That Egypts pleaſure ſo delightfull,
may breed them the like offences.
And Romans learne our way of weakenes,
be inſtraɛted in our vices :
That our ſpoyles may ſpoyle your greatnes,
ouercome with our deuiſes.
Fill full your hands, and carry home,
Enough from vs to ruine Rome.   1270

ACT V.

Dolabella. Titius.

Ome tell me. *Titius* eu'ry circumſtance
How·*Cleopatra* did receiue my newes :
Tell eu'ry looke, each geſture, countenance,
That ſhe did in my Letter's reading, vſe.
  Tit. I ſhall my Lord, ſo farre as I could note,

l. 1271, 'Quintvs' ¹ : '23 misprinted 'iiii.'

Or my conceit obferue in any wife.
It was the time when as fhe hauing got
Leaue to her Deareft dead to facrifice ;   1280
And now was iffuing out the monument,
With odors, incenfe, garlands in her hand ;
Wh'en I approacht (as one from *Cæfar* fent,)
And did her clofe thy meffage t'vnderftand.
     She turnes her backe, and with her takes me in,
Reades in thy lines thy ftrange vnlookt for tale :
And reades, and fmiles, and ftaies, and doth begin
Againe to reade, then blufht, and then vvas pale.
And hauing ended with a figh, refoldes
Thy Letter vp : and with a fixèd eye,   1290
(Which ftedfaft her imagination holds)
She muf'd a while, ftanding confufedly :
At length, Ah friend (fayd fhe) tell thy good Lord,
How deare I hold his pittying of my cafe :
That out of his fweete nature can affoord
A miferable woman fo much grace.
Tell him how much my heauy foule doth grieue
Mercileffe *Cæfar* fhould fo deale with me :
Pray him that he vvould all the counfell giue,
That might diuert him from fuch cruelty.   1300
As for my loue, fay *Antony* hath all,
Say that my heart is gone into the graue
With him, in whom it refts and euer fhall :
I haue it not my felfe, nor cannot haue.
Yet tell him, he fhall more command of me
Then any, whofoeuer liuing can.
He that fo friendly fhewes himfelfe to be
A right kind Roman, and a Gentleman.
Although his Nation (fatall vnto me,) ·

Haue had mine age a fpoyle, my youth a pray, 1310
Yet his affe&ion muft accepted be,
That fauours one diftreft in fuch decay.
  Ah, he was worthy then to haue beene lou'd,
Of *Cleopatra* whiles her glory lafted ;
Before fhe had declining fortune prou'd,
Or feene her honor wrackt, her flowre all blafted.
Now there is nothing left her but difgrace
Nothing but her affli&ion that can moue :
Tell *Dolabella*, one that's in her cafe,
(Poore foule) needs rather pity now then loue, 1320
But fhortly fhall thy Lord heare more of me.
And ending fo her fpeech, no longer ftayd,
But hafted to the tombe of *Antony* :
And this was all fhe did, and all fhe fayd.
  Dol. Ah fweet diftreffèd Lady. What hard heart
Could chufe but pity thee, and loue thee too ?
Thy worthineffe, the ftate vvherein thou art
Requireth both, and both I vow to do.
Although ambition lets not *Cæfar* fee
The vvrong he doth thy maiefty and fweetnes ; 1330
Which makes him now exa& fo much of thee,
To adde vnto his pride, to grace his greatnes,
He knowes thou canft no hurt procure vs now,
Sith all thy ftrength is feiz'd into our hands :
Nor feares he that, but rather labours how
He might fhew Rome fo great a Queene in bands :
That our great Ladies (enuying thee fo much
That ftain'd them all, and held them in fuch wonder,)
Might ioy to fee thee, and thy fortune fuch,
Thereby extolling him that brought thee vnder. 1340

  l. 1312, 'from whom all run away '¹: l. 1316, 'all' accepted from '.

But I will feeke to ftay it what I may ;
I am but one, yet one that *Cæfar* loues,
And O if now I could do more then pray,
Then fhould'ft thou know how farre affe&ion moues.
But what my powre and prayer may preuaile,
Ile ioyne them both, to hinder thy difgrace :
And euen this prefent day I will not faile
To do my beft vvith *Cæfar* in this cafe.

 Tit. And fir, euen how herfelfe hath letters fent ;
I met her meffenger as I came hither,   1350
With a difpatch as he to *Cæfar* went ;
But know not what imports her fending thither.
Yet this he told, how *Cleopatra* late
Was come from facrifice, how richly clad,
Was feru'd to dinner in moft fumptuous ftate,
With all the braueft ornaments fhe had.
How hauing din'd, fhe writes, and fends away
Him ftrait to *Cæfar*, and commanded than
All fhould depart the Tombe, and none to ftay
But her two maides, and one poore countrey man.   1360

 Dol. Why then I know, fhe fends t'haue audience
    now,
And meanes t'experience what her ftate can do :
To fee if Maieftie will make him bow
To what affli&ion could not moue him to.
And O, if now fhe could but bring a view
Of that frefh beauty fhe in youth poffeft,
(The argument wherewith fhe ouerthrew
The wit of *Iulius Cæfar*, and the reft.

---

l. 1352, 'Knowing not what meanes'⁴: l. 1355, 'with'⁴: l. 1365, 'And
now if that'⁴: l. 1366, 'rare': l. 1368, '23 adds here oddly 'condition,'
and rhymes to it below 'ambition.' It is a misplacing of lines.

Then happily *Auguſtus* might relent, 1369
Whilſt powrefull Loue, (farre ſtronger then Ambition)
Might worke in him, a minde to be content
To grant her aſking, in the beſt condition.
But being as ſhe is, yet doth ſhe merrite
To be reſpeéted, for what ſhe hath beene :
The wonder of her kinde, of rareſt ſpirit,
A glorious Lady, and a mighty Queene.
And now, but by a little weakeneſſe falling
To doe that which perhaps ſh'was forſt to doe :
Alas, an errour paſt, is paſt recalling ;
Take away weakeneſſe, and take women too, 1380
But now I goe to be thy aduocate,
Sweet *Cleopatra*, now I'le vſe mine arte.
Thy preſence will me greatly animate,
Thy face will teach my tongue, thy loue my heart.

SCEN. II.

Nuntius.

A M I ordain'd the carefull Meſſenger
    And ſad newes' bringer of the ſtrangeſt death,
Which ſelfe hand did vpon himſelfe inferre,
To free a captiue ſoule from ſeruile breath ? 1390
Muſt I the lamentable vvonder ſhew,
Which all the world muſt grieue and maruell at ?
The rareſt forme of death in earth below,
That euer pitty, glory, vvonder gat. [more
    Cho. What newes bringſt thou ? can *Egypt* yet yeeld
Of ſorrow than it hath ? vvhat can it adde

l. 1375, 'powerfull'⁴ : l. 1382, misprints 'my heart' : l. 1385, 'Scena
Secvnda'¹.

To the already ouerflowing ftore
Of fad affliction, matter yet more fad ?
Haue vve not feene the vvorft of our calamity ?
Is there behind yet fomething of diftreffe   1400
Vnfeene, vnknowne ?   Tell if that greater mifery
There be, that vve vvaile not that vvhich is leffe.
Tell vs vvhat fo it be, and tell at firft,
For forrow euer longs to heare her vvorft.

    Nun. Well then, the ftrangeft thing relate I will,
That euer eye of mortall man hath feene.

    I (as you know) euen from my youth, haue ftill
Attended on the perfon of the Queene :
And euer in all fortunes good or ill,
With her as one of chiefeft truft haue beene.   1410
And now in thefe two great extremities,
That euer could to Maieftie befall,
I did my beft in vvhat I could deuife,
And left her not, till now fhe left vs all.

    Cho. What, is fhe gone ?   Hath *Cæfar* forft her fo ?
    Nun. Yea, fhe is gone, and hath deceiu'd him to.
    Cho. What fled to *India*, to goe find her fonne?
    Nun. No, not to *India*, but to find her fonne.
    Cho. Why then there's hope fhe may her ftate recouer.
    Nun. Her ftate ? nay rather honour, and her Louer.
    Cho. Her Louer ? him fhe cannot haue againe.   1421
    Nun. Well, him fhe hath, with him fhe doth remaine.
    Cho. Why then fhe's dead.   Ift fo ? why fpeakft not
    Nun. You geffe aright, and I will tell you how. [thou ?
When fhe perceiu'd all hope was cleane bereft,
That *Cæfar* meant to fend her ftrait away,

---

l. 1415, 'her' accepted from ¹ : l. 1418, 'funne' ¹ : l. 1425, 'her' ¹.

And faw no meanes of reconcilement left,
Worke what fhe could, fhe could not worke to ftay :
She calles me to her, and fhe thus began :
O thou, whofe truft hath euer beene the fame,   1430
And one in all my fortunes, faithfull man,
Alone content t'attend difgrace and fhame.
Thou, whom the fearefull ruine of my fall,
Neuer deterr'd to leaue calamitie :
As did thofe other fmoothe ftate-pleafers all,
VVho followed but my fortune, and not me,
Tis thou muft do a feruice for thy Queene,
Wherein thy faith and fkill muft do their beft :
Thy honeft care and duty fhall be feene,
Performing this, more then in all the reft.   1440
For all what thou haft done, may die with thee,
Although tis pitty that fuch faith fhould die.
But this fhall euermore remembred be,
A rare example to pofterity.
And looke how long as *Cleopatra* fhall
In after ages liue in memory,
So long fhall thy cleare fame endure withall,
And therefore thou muft not my fute denie,
Nor contradict my will.   For what I will
I am refolu'd ; and this now muft it be :   1450
Goe finde me out with all thy art and fkill
Two Afpicks, and conuay them clofe to me.
I haue a worke to doe with them in hand ;
Enquire not what, for thou fhalt foone fee what,

l. 1427, 'her' ¹: l. 1435, '23, 'ftare-pleafers' (bad) : l. 1438, 'loyaltie
muft worke her' ⁴: ll. 1440-49 omitted in ⁴: l. 1450, 'tis thou must
doe me ¹; in ⁴ 'Thou muft feeke out with all thy induftrie': l. 1452,
'vnto' ¹.

If the heauens doe not my diſſeignes withſtand ;
But doe thy charge, and let me ſhift with that.
　　Being thus coniur'd by her t'whom I'had vow'd
My true perpetuall ſeruice, forth I went,
Deuiſing how my cloſe attempt to ſhrowde,
So that there might no art my art preuent.　　　1460
And ſo diſguiſ'd in habite as you ſee,
Hauing found out the thing for which I went,
I ſoone return'd againe, and brought with me
The Aſpickes, in a baſket cloſely pent :
Which I had filled with Figges, and leaues vpon.
And comming to the guard that kept the doore,
What haſt thou there ? ſaid they, and lookt thereon.
Seeing the figges, they deem'd of nothing more,
But ſaid, they were the faireſt they had ſeene.
Taſt ſome, ſaid I, for they are good and pleaſant. 1470
No, no, ſaid they, goe beare them to thy Queene,
Thinking me ſome poore man that brought a preſent.
Well, in I went, where brighter then the Sunne,
Glittering in all her pompeous rich aray,
Great *Cleopatra* ſate, as if ſh'had wonne
Cæſar, and all the world beſide, this day :
Euen as ſhe was when on thy criſtall ſtreames,
Cleare *Cydnos*, ſhe did ſhew what earth could ſhew ;
When *Aſia* all amaz'd in wonder, deemes
Venus from heauen was come on earth below.　　　1480
Euen as ſhe went at firſt to meete her loue,
So goes ſhe now againe to finde him.
But that firſt, did her greatnes onely proue,
This laſt her loue, that could not liue behind him.

l. 1455, 'th'' ⁴: l. 1456, 'for' ⁴: see Note before this Play for addition
here in ⁴: l. 1471, '23 'I' (bad) : l. 1475 misprinted 'their' for 'her' in all.

Yet as fhe fate, the doubt of my good fpeed,
Detraƈts mueh from the fweetnes of her looke ;
Cheere-marrer Care, did then fuch paffions breed,
That made her eye bewray the griefe fhe tooke.
But fhe no fooner fees me in the place,
But ftrait her forrow-clouded brow fhe cleares,   1490
Lightning a fmile from out a ftormy face,
Which all her tempeft-beaten fenfes cheeres.

 Looke how a ftrai'd perplexed traueller,
When chafd by thieues, and euen at point of taking,
Defcrying fuddenly fome towne not far,
Or fome vnlookt for aide to him-ward making ;
Cheeres vp his tyred fprites, thrufts forth his ftrength
To meet that good, that comes in fo good houre :
Such was her ioy, perceiuing now at length,
Her honour was t'efcape fo proude a powre.   1500
Forth from her feate fhe hafts to meete the prefent,
And as one ouer-ioy'd, fhe caught it ftrait.
And with a fmiling cheere in aƈtion pleafant,
Looking among the figs, findes the deceite.
And feeing there the vgly venemous beaft,
Nothing difmaid, fhe ftayes and viewes it well.
At length th'extreameft of her paffion ceaft,
When fhe began with words her ioy to tell.

 O rareft beaft (faith fhe) that Affrick breedes,
How dearely welcome art thou vnto me ?   1510
The faireft creature that faire *Nylus* feedes
Me thinkes I fee, in now beholding thee.
What though the euer-erring world doth deeme
That angred Nature fram'd thee but in fpight ?

l. 1509, 'all our Egypt' ⁴: l. 1510, 'now to' ⁴: ll. 1513-16 omitted
in ⁴.

Little they know what they fo light efteeme,
That neuer learn'd the wonder of thy might.
Better then Death, Deaths office thou difchargeft,
That with one gentle touch canft free our breath :
And in a pleafing fleepe our foule inlargeft,
Making our felues not priuy to our death.   1520
If Nature err'd, O then how happy error,
Thinking to make thee worft, fhe made thee beft :
Sith thou beft freeft vs from our liues worft terror,
In fweetly bringing foules to quiet reft.
When that inexorable Monfter Death
That followes Fortune, flies the poore diftreffed,
Tortures our bodies ere he takes our breath,
And loades with paines th'already weak oppreffed.
How oft haue I begg'd, pray'd, intreated him
To take my life, which he would neuer do ;   1530
And when he comes, he comes fo vgly grim,
Attended on with hideous torments to.
Therefore come thou, of wonders wonder chiefe,
That open canft with fuch an eafie key
The doore of life ; come gentle cunning thiefe
That from our felues fo fteal'ft our felues away.
Well did our Priefts difcerne fomething diuine
Shadow'd in thee, and therefore firft they did
Offrings and worfhips due to thee affigne,
In whom they found fuch myfteries were hid ;   1540
Comparing thy fwift motion to the Sunne,
That mou'ft without the inftruments that moue :

ll. 1521-32 omitted in ⁴: l. 1530, 'and yet could neuer get him?' ¹:
l. 1532, 'That who is he (if he could chufe) would let him' ¹: l. 1533,
'O welcome now' ⁴: ll. 1537-50 omitted in ⁴: l. 1540, '23 misprinted
did.'

And neuer waxing old, but alwayes one,
Dooſt ſure thy ſtrange diuinitie approue.
And therefore too, the rather vnto thee
In zeale I make the offring of my blood ;
Calamitie confirming now in me
A ſure beliefe that pietie makes good.
Which happy men negleƈt, or hold ambiguous.
And onely the affliƈted are religious.   1550
    And here I ſacrifice theſe armes to Death,
That luſt late dedicated to Delights :
Offring vp for my laſt, this laſt of breath,
The complement of my loues deareſt rites.
With that ſhe bares her arme, and offer makes
To touch her death, yet at the touch with-drawes,
And ſeeming more to ſpeake, occaſion takes,
Willing to die, and willing too to pauſe.
    Looke how a mother at her ſonnes departing
For ſome farre voyage bent to get him fame,   1560
Doth entertaine him with an ydle parting
And ſtill doth ſpeake, and ſtill ſpeakes but the ſame ;
Now bids farewell, and now recalles him backe,
Tels what was told, and bids againe farewell,
And yet againe recalles ; for ſtill doth lacke
Something that Loue would faine and cannot tell ;
Pleaf'd he ſhould goe, yet cannot let him goe.
So ſhe, although ſhe knew there was no way
But this, yet this ſhe could not handle ſo
But ſhe muſt ſhew that life deſir'd delay.   1570
Faine would ſhe entertaine the time as now,
And now would faine that Death would ſeize vpon her,

l. **1551**, 'now' **⁴**: l. **1554**, '23 misprinted 'complements': l. **1555**
misprinted 'beares' : ll. **1555-95** omitted in **⁴**.

Whilſt I might ſee preſented in her brow,
The doubtfull combate tride twixt Life and Honour.
Life bringing Legions of freſh hopes with her,
Arm'd with the proofe of time, which yeelds we ſay
Comfort and helpe, to ſuch as doe referre
All vnto him, and can admit delay.
But honour ſcorning Life, loe forth leades he
Bright Immortalitie in ſhining armour :   1580
Thorow the rayes of whoſe cleare glory, ſhe
Might ſee lifes baſeneſſe, how much it might harme her.
Beſides ſhe ſaw whole armies of Reproches,
And baſe Diſgraces, Furies fearefull ſad,
Marching with Life, and Shame that ſtill incroches
Vpon her face, in bloody colours clad.
Which repreſentments ſeeing, worſe then death
She deem'd to yeeld to Life, and therefore choſe
To render all to Honour, heart and breath ;
And that with ſpeed, leſt that her inward foes   1590
Falſe fleſh and blood, ioyning with life and hope,
Should mutinie againſt her reſolution.
And to the end ſhe would not giue them ſcope,
Shee preſently proceedes to th'execution.
And ſharpely blaming of her rebell powres,
Falſe fleſh (ſaith ſhe) and what doſt thou conſpire
With *Cæſar* too, as thou vvert none of ours,
To worke my ſhame, and hinder my deſire ?
VVilt thou retaine in cloſure of thy vaines,
That enemy, baſe Life, to let my good ?   1600
No, know there is a greater powre conſtraines
Then can be countercheckt with fearefull blood.

    l. 1596, ' What now falſe fleſh ; what? and wilt' ⁴ : l. 1598, ⁴ adds here,
' And bend thy rible parts againſt my powers.'

For to the minde that's great, nothing feemes great :/
And feeing death to be the laft of woes,
And life lafting difgrace, which I fhall get,
VVhat doe I lofe, that haue but life to lofe ? /

  This hauing faid, ftrengthned in her owne heart,
And vnion of her felfe, fenfes in one
Charging together, fhe performes that part
That hath fo great a part of glory wonne.   1610
And fo receiues the deadly poyf'ning tuch ;
That touch that tride the gold of her loue, pure,
And hath confirm'd her honour to be fuch,
As muft a wonder to all worlds endure.
Now not an yeelding fhrinke or touch of feare,
Confented to bewray leaft fenfe of paine :
But ftill in one fame fweete vnaltred cheare,
Her honour did her dying thoughts retaine.

  Well, now this worke is done (faith fhe) here ends
This act of Life, that part the Fates affign'd ;   1620
VVhat glory or difgrace here this world lends,
Both haue I had, and both I leaue behind.
And now O earth, the Theater where I
Haue acted this, witneffe I die vnforft ;   /
Witneffe my foule parts free to *Antony*,   /
And now prowde tyrant *Cæfar* doe thy worft.

  This faid, fhe ftaies, and makes a fudden paufe,
As twere to feele whether the poyfon vvrought :
Or rather elfe the vvorking might be caufe
That made her ftay, and intertain'd her thought. 1630

l. 1599, 'Wouldft' [4]: l. 1603, 'a' [4]: ll. 1607-14 omitted in [4]: ll. 1615-18
in [4] are fpoken by *Eras* : l. 1615, 'See not a' [4] : l. 1616, 'Confents now' :
l. 1618, 'fpirits' [4] : l. 1619, "of mine is done [4] : l. 1620, 'me' [1] : l. 1621,
'could lend' [4]: l. 1622, 'mee' [1] : l. 1623, 'And Egypt now' [4] : l. 1626, see
Note before this Play for new paffage here : l. 1630, ' as likewife may be.'

For in that inftant I might vvell perceiue
The drowfie humour in her falling brow :
And how each powre, each part oppreft did leaue
Their former office, and did fenfeleffe grow.
Looke how a new pluckt branch againft the Sun,
Declines his fading leaues in feeble fort ;
So here difioyned ioyntures as vndone,
Let fall her weake diffolued limbes fupport.
Yet loe that face the vvonder of her life,
Retaines in death, a grace that graceth death,   1640
Colour fo liuely, cheere fo louely rife,
That none would thinke fuch beauty could want breath.
And in that cheere th'impreffion of a fmile,
Did feeme to fhew fhe fcorn'd death and *Cæfar*,
As glorying that fhe could them both beguile,
And telling Death how much her death did pleafe her.
Wonder it vvas to fee how foone fhe vvent !
She went with fuch a will, and did fo hafte it,
That fure I thinke fhe did her paine preuent,
Fore-going paine, or ftaying not to tafte it.   1650
And fenceleffe, in her finking downe fhe wryes
The Diademe vvhich on her head fhe vvore :
Which *Charmion* (poore weake feeble maid) efpies,
And haftes to right it as it vvas before.
For *Eras* now was dead, and *Charmion* too
Euen at the point, for both vvould immitate
Their Miftreffe glory, ftriuing like to doo.
But *Charmion* vvould in this exceed her mate,

l. 1639, 'O fee this'⁴: l. 1640, 'graces'⁴: l. 1643, 'this'⁴: l. 1644,
'fkorns both'⁴: l. 1645, 'And glories'⁴: l. 1646, 'And here tells . . .
well . . . death'⁴: ll. 1647-59 omitted, except in lines worked in : l. 1651,
'23 'wrines' (bad).

For fhe vvould haue this honour to be laft,
That fhould adorne that head that muft be feene   1660
To weare a Crowne in death, that life held faft,
That all the world may know fhe dide a Queene.
And as fhe ftood, fetting it fitly on,
Loe, in rufh *Cæfars* meffengers in haft,
Thinking to haue preuented vvhat vvas done
But yet they came too late, for all vvas paft.
For there they found ftretcht on a bed of gold,
Dead *Cleopatra* ; and that proudly dead,
In all the rich attire procure fhe could ;
And dying *Charmion* trimming of her head,   1670
And *Eras* at her feete, dead in like cafe.
Charmion, is this well done ? fayd one of them.
Yea, well fayd fhe, and her that from the race
Of fo great Kings defcends, doth beft become.
And with that word, yeelds to her faithfull breath,
To paffe th'affurance of her loue with death.
    Cho. But how knew *Cæfar* of her clofe intent ?
    Nun. By Letters which before to him fhe fent.
For when fhe had procur'd this meanes to die,
She writes, and earneftly intreates, fhe might   1680
Be buried in one Tombe with *Antony*.
Whereby then *Cæfar* gef'd all went not right.
And forthwith fends ; yet ere the meffage came
She was difpatcht, he croft in his intent ;
Her prouidence had ordred fo the fame,
That fhe was fure none fhould her plot preuent.

CHORVS.

T Hen thus we haue beheld
    Th'accomplifhment of woes

The full of ruine, and				1690
The worft of worft of ills :
And feene all hope expeld,
That euer fweete repofe
Shall repoffeffe the Land,
That Defolation fills.
And where Ambition fpills
With vncontrouled hand,
All th'iffue of all thofe
That fo long rule haue held :
To make vs no more vs,				1700
But cleane confound vs thus.

And canft O Nylus thou,
Father of flouds indure,
That yellow Tyber fhould
With fandy ftreames rule thee ?
Wilt thou be pleaf'd to bow
To him thofe feete fo pure,
Whofe vnknowne head we hold
A powre diuine to be ?
Thou that didft euer fee				1710
Thy free bankes vncontrould,
Liue vnder thine owne cure ?
Ah wilt thou beare it now ?
And now wilt yeeld thy ftreames
A prey to other Reames ?

Draw backe thy waters floe
To thy concealèd head :
Rockes ftrangle vp thy waues,
Stop Cataractes *thy fall.*
And turne thy courfes fo,				1720

That sandy Desarts dead,
(The world of dust that craues
To swallow thee vp all,)
May drinke so much as shall
Reuiue from vasty graues
A liuing greene, which spred
Far florishing, may grow
On that wide face of Death,
Where nothing now drawes breath.

Fatten some people there,   1730
Euen as thou vs hast done,
With plenties wanton store,
And feeble luxury :
And them as vs prepare
Fit for the day of mone
Respected not before.
Leaue leuell'd Egypt drie,
A barren prey to lie,
Wasted for euer-more.
Of plenties yeelding none   1740
To recompence the care
Of Victors greedy lust,
And bring forth nought but dust.

And so O leaue to be,
Sith thou art what thou art :
Let not our race possesse
Th'inheritance of shame,
The fee of sin, that we
Haue left them for their part :

l. 1736, '23 misprinted ' respect ' ; in ' -ed— accepted.

The yoake of whofe diftreffe   1750
Muft ftill vpbraid our blame,
Telling from whom it came.
Our weight of wantonneffe
Lies heauy on their heart,
Who neuer-more fhall fee
The glory of that worth
They left, who brought vs forth.

O then all-feeing light,
High Prefident of Heauen,
You Magiftrates, the Starres   1760
Of that eternall Court
Of Prouidence and Right,
Are thefe the bounds y'haue giuen
Th'vntranfpaffable barres,
That limit Pride fo fhort?
Is greatneffe of this fort,
That greatneffe greatneffe marres,
And wrackes it felfe, felfe-driuen
On Rockes of her owne might?
Doth Order order fo   1770
Diforders ouerthrow?

FINIS.

In ¹ on verso of last leaf :—

AT LONDON
 Printed by *Iames Roberts,* and
Edward Allde, for Simon Waterfon.   1594.

II.

PHILOTAS.

1607.

The first edition of 'Philotas' was published in 1605 in the 'Certaine Small Workes' (as before). It was succeeded by two editions in 1607— the one in the 1607 'Certaine Small Workes,' and the other in a charming little volume (18mo), worthy to rank with the 1594 'Delia.' Its title-page, within a two-banded bordering, is as follows :—

THE

T R A G E D I E

of

PHILOTAS.

By

SAM. DANIEL.

LONDON
Printed by *Melch. Bradwood*
for *Edw. Blount.*
1607.

It was reprinted in the 'Certaine Small Workes' of 1609 and 1611. A collation of these shows only very trivial changes beyond orthography; but a recurrence to [1] has enabled various misprints of '23 and others to be corrected. This '1607' volume contains the following other pieces by Daniel:—" Panegyrike . . . . alfo certaine Epiftles, with a Defence of Ryme heretofore written, and now publifhed by the Author"—the 'Defence' having a separate title-page. These three tiny volumes are met with separately. My signs are—

1605 = [1].
1607 = [2] (the 18mo edition).

All the others yield only slight orthographical changes.   G.

THE
TRAGEDY
OF
PHILOTAS.

By SAM. DANIEL.

LONDON,
Printed by NICHOLAS OKES for
SIMON WATERSON.
1623.

To the Prince.

O you moſt hopefull Prince, not as you are,
But as you may be, doe I giue theſe lines:
That when your iudgement ſhall arriue
  ſo farre,
As t'ouer-looke th'intricate deſignes
Of vncontented man : you may beholde
With what encounters greateſt fortunes
  cloſe,
What dangers, what attempts, what manifolde
Incumbrances ambition vndergoes :
How hardly men digeſt felicitie ;   I O
How to th'intemprate, to the prodigall,
To wantonneſſe, and vnto luxurie,
Many things want, but to ambition all.
And you ſhall finde the greateſt enemie
That man can haue, is his proſperitie.
 Here ſhall you ſee how men diſguiſe their ends,
And plant bad courſes vnder pleaſing ſhewes ;
How well preſumptions broken wayes defends,
Which cleere-eyed Iudgement grauely doth diſcloſe,

Here fhall you fee how th'eafie multitude   20
Tranfported, take the partie of diftreffe ;
And onely out of paffions doe conclude,
Not out of iudgement, of mens practifes ;
How pow'rs are thought to wrong, that wrongs debar,
And Kings not held in danger, though they are.
Thefe ancient reprefentments of times paft
Tell vs that men haue, doe, and alwayes runne
The felfe fame line of action, and doe caft
Their courfe alike, and nothing can be done,
Whilft they, their ends, and nature are the fame: 30
But will be wrought vpon the felfe fame frame.
    This benefit, moft noble prince, doth yeeld
The fure records of Bookes, in which we finde
The tenure of our State, how it was held
By all our Anceftors, and in what kinde
We holde the fame, and likewife how in the end
This fraile poffeffion of felicitie,
Shall to our late pofteritie defcend
By the fame Patent of like deftinie.
In them we find that nothing can accrew   40
To man, and his condition that is new.
Which images here figured in this wife
I leaue vnto your more mature furuay,
Amongft the vowes that others facrifice
Vnto the hope of you, that you one day
Will giue grace to this kinde of Harmonie.
For know, great Prince, when you fhall come to know
How that it is the faireft Ornament
Of worthy times, to haue thofe which may fhew

ll. 42—53 not in ¹, ² : ll. 44-6 repeated at ll. 61-3.

The deedes of power, and liuely reprefent 50
The actions of a glorious Gouernement.
　And is no leffer honor to a Crowne
T'haue Writers then haue Actors of renowne.
　And though you haue a Swannet of your owne,
Within the bankes of Douen *meditates*
Sweet notes to you, and vnto your renowne
The glory of his Muficke dedicates,
And in a lofty tune is fet to found
The deepe reports of fullen Tragedies :
Yet may this laft of me be likewife found 60
Amongft the vowes that others facrifice
Vnto the hope of you, that you one day
May grace this now neglected Harmonie,
Which fet vnto your glorious actions, may
Record the fame to all pofteritie.
　Though I the remnant of another time
Am neuer like to fee that happineffe,
Yet for the zeale that I haue borne to rime
And to the Mufes, wifh that good fucceffe
To others trauell, that in better place, 70
And better comfort, they may be incheerd
Who fhall deferue, and who fhall haue the grace
To haue a Mufe held worthy to be heard.
And know, fweet Prince, when you fhall come to know,
That tis not in the pow'r of Kings to raife
A fpirit for Verfe that is not borne thereto,
Nor are they borne in euery Princes dayes :
For late Eliza's *raigne gaue birth to more*
Then all the Kings of England *did before.*

　L 53 : the '1607' text here ends in British Museum exemplar (probably
imperfect). So, too, 1611 in 'Certaine Small Workes.'

And it may be, the Genius of that time
Would leaue to her the glory in that kind,
And that the vtmoſt powers of Engliſh Rime
Should be within her peacefull raigne confin'd ;
For ſince that time our Songs could neuer thriue,
But laine as if forlorne ; though in the prime
Of this new raiſing ſeaſon, we did ſtriue
To bring the beſt we could vnto the time.

And I although among the latter traine,
And leaſt of thoſe that ſung vnto this land,
Haue borne my part, though in an humble ſtraine,   90
And pleaſd the gentler that did vnderſtand :
And neuer had my harmeleſſe pen at all
Diſtain'd with any looſe immodeſtie,
Nor euer noted to be toucht with gall,
To aggrauate the worſt mans infamie.
But ſtill haue done the faireſt offices
To vertue and the time, yet naught preuailes,
And all our labours are without ſucceſſe,
For either fauour or our vertue failes.
And therefore ſince I haue out-liu'd the date   100
Of former grace, acceptance and delight,
I would my lines late-borne beyond the fate
Of her ſpent line, had neuer come to light.
So had I not beene tax'd for wiſhing well,
Nor now miſtaken by the cenſuring Stage,
Nor, in my fame and reputation fell,
Which I eſteeme more then what all the age
Or th'earth can giue.   But yeeres hath done this wrong,
To make me write too much, and liue too long.

And yet I grieue for that vnfiniſht frame,   110
Which thou deare Muſe didſt vow to ſacrifice,

of Peace, and in the fame
our happineffe to memorize,
Muft, as it is, remaine : though as it is,
It fhall to after-times relate my zeale
To Kings, and vnto right, to quietneffe,
And to the vnion of the Common-weale.
But this may now feeme a fuperfluous vow,
We haue this peace ; and thou haft fung enow,
   And more then will be heard, and then as good   120
   As not to write, as not be vnderftood.

SAM. DAN.

THE ARGVMENT.

*Hilotas* the Sonne of *Parmenio,* was a man of great eſtimation, among the *Macedonians,* and next vnto *Alexander,* held to be the moſt-valiant of the *Greekes* (*Plutarch* in the life of *Alex.*) : patient of trauell, exceeding bountifull, and one that loued his men and friends better then any Noble-man of the Campe : but otherwiſe ; noted of vaine-glory and prodigalitie, inſomuch, as his 10 father (hauing notice of his carriage) warned him to make himſelfe leſſe then he was, to auoide the enuie of the Campe, and the diſlike of the King, who grew ſuſpicious of him, in reſpeƈt of the greatneſſe of his father, and his owne popularitie, and by hauing intelligence of certaine vaunts of his, vſed to *Antigona,* a faire Curtizan, borne in the City of *Pidna* ; with whom being in loue, hee let fall many braue words and boaſts of a Souldier, to aduance his owne aƈtions and his fathers, terming *Alexander* at euery word, The 20 yong man. Which ſpeeches *Antigona* reuealing to a Companion of hers, were at length brought to *Craterus*

who with the woman, carried them to *Alexander* (*Q,*
Curtius lib. 6.) ; whereby *Philotas* lay open to all the
aduantages that might worke his ouerthrow : and in
the end, concealing a confpiracie (which was reuealed
vnto him) intended againft the King, was thereby
fufpected to haue beene a party in the plot : but
brought before *Alexander*, he fo defended himfelfe, 30
that hee obtained his pardon for that 'time, fupped
with the King that night, and yet the next day, not-
withftanding, was arraigned for the fame fact ; which
hee ftoutly denying, was afterward put to torture, and
then confeft his treafon.   And indeede, *Alexanders*
drawing a Pedegree from Heauen, with affuming the
Perfian magnificence, was the caufe that withdrew
many [of] the hearts of the Nobilitie and people from
him, and by the confeffion of *Philotas* was that, which
gaue a purpofe to him and his father to haue fubuerted 40
the King as foone as hee had eftablifhed *Afia*, and
freed them from other feares ; which being by *Epheftion*
and *Craterus*, two the moft efpeciall Councellers of
Alexander, grauely and prouidently difcerned, was pro-
fecuted in that manner as became their neereneffe and
deereneffe with their Lord and Mafter, and fitting to
the fafety of the State, in the cafe of fo great an
Afpirer ; who, no doubt, had he not beene preuented
(howfoeuer popularly in the Army it might be other-
wife deemed) hee had turned the courfe of gouernement 50
vpon his father himfelfe, or els by his imbroilements
made it a ⸳monfter of many heads, as it afterward
proued vpon the death of *Alexander*.   The *Chorus*
confifting of three *Græcians* (as of three eftates of a
Kingdome) and one *Perfian*, reprefenting the multi-

tude and body of a People, who vulgarly (according
to their affections, carried rather with compaffion
on Great-mens misfortunes, then with the
confideration of the caufe) frame their
imaginations by that fquare, and   60
cenfure what is done.

The Names of the Actors.

Philotas.
Chaliſthenes.
Alexander.
Epheſtion.
Craterus.
Thais a Curtezan.
Antigona, fometimes one
  of the Concubines of
  Darius.
Attarras.

Soſtratus.
Chorus.
Cebalinus.
Polidamas.
Nichomachus.
Metron.
Clitus.
Perdiceas.
Three *Græcians* and a
  Perſian.

THE TRAGEDY OF
Philotas.

A C T V S I. *Philotas. Chaliſthenes.*

Philotas reading his fathers Letter.

"Ake thy felfe leſſe *Philotas* then
  thou art."
What meanes my father thus to
  write to me?
Leſſe than I am? In what? How
  can that be?
Muſt I be then fet vnderneath my
  hart?
Shall I let goe the hold I haue of grace,
Gain'd with ſo hard aduenture of my blood,
And ſuffer others mount into my place,
And from below, looke vp to where I ſtood?   10
Shall I degrade th'opinion of my worth?
By putting off imployment; as vndone

In fpirit or grace : whilft other men fet forth
To get that ftart of aftion I haue wonne?
As if fuch men as I, had any place,
To ftay betwixt their ruine and their grace.
Can any goe beyond me, but they will
Goe ouer me, and trample on my ftate,
And make their fortunes good vpon my ill,   19
Whilft feare hath powre to wound me worfe then hate?
    Chal. Philotas, you deceiue your felfe in this,
Your father meanes not you fhould yeeld in place,
But in your popular dependences,
Your entertainements, gifts and publike grace ;
That doth in iealous Kings, diftafte the Peeres,
And makes you not the greater but in feares.
    Phi. Alas, what popular dependences
Doe I retaine? Can I fhake off the zeale
Of fuch as doe out of their kindneffes,
Follow my fortunes in the Common-weale?   30
    Cha. Indeed *Philotas* therein you fay true :
They follow doe your fortunes, and not you.
    Phi. Yea, but I find their loue to me fincere.
    Cha. Euen fuch as to the Woolfe the Fox doth
        beare,
That vifits him but to partake his pray,
And feeing his hopes deceiu'd, turnes to betray.
    Phi. I know they would, if I in danger ftood,
Runne vnto me with hazzard of their blood.
    Cha. Yes, like as men to burning houfes run,
Not to lend aide, but to be lookers on   40
    Phi. But I with bountie and with gifts haue tide
Their hearts fo fure, I know they will not flide.

l. 20, 'than'² : l. 29, 'kindneffes' accepted from ¹, ², for 'kindneffe' of '23.

Cha. Bountie and gifts lofe more than they doe
    finde,
Where many looke for good, few haue their minde ;
'Each thinkes he merits more then that he hath ;
And fo gifts laide for loue, doe catch men wrath.
    Phi. But many meerely out of loue attend.
    Cha. Yea, thofe that loue and haue no other end !
Thinke you that men can loue you when they know
You haue them not for friendfhip, but for fhow ?   50
And as you are ingag'd in your affaires,
And haue your ends, thinke likewife they haue theirs.
    Phi. But I doe truly from my heart affeƈt
Vertue and worth where I doe find it fet :
Befides, my foes doe force me in effeƈt
To make my party of opinion great,
And I muft arme me thus againft their fcornes :
Men muft be fhod that goe amongft the thornes.
    Cha. Ah, good *Philotas*, you your felfe beguile,
Tis not the way to quench the fire with Oile :   60
The meeke and humble Lambe with fmall adoo
Suckes his own damme, we fee, and others too.
In Courts men longeft liue, and keepe their rankes,
By taking iniuries, and giuing thankes.
    Phi. And is it fo ?   Then neuer are thefe haires
Like to attaine that fober hew of gray;
I cannot plafter and difguife m'affaires
In other colours then my heart doth lay.
Nor can I patiently endure this fond
And ftrange proceeding of authoritie,   70
That hath ingroft vp all into their hand
By idol-liuing feeble Maieftie,

l. 72—qy. 'idle-'?

And impioufly doe labour all they can
To make the King forget he is a man ;
Whilft they diuide the fpoyles, and pray for powre,
And none at all refpect the publike good :
Thofe hands that guard and get vs what is our,
The Sold[i]erie ingag'd to vent their blood,
In worfe cafe feeme then *Pallas* old-grow'n Moile
Th'*Athenians* foftred at their publike coft ;   80
For thefe poore foules confum'd with tedious toile,
Remaine neglected, hauing done their moft,
And nothing fhall bring home of all thefe warres,
But empty age, and bodies charg'd with fcarres.
    Cha. Philotas, all this publike care, I feare,
Is but fome priuate touch of your diflike,
Who feeing your owne defignes not ftand to
        fquare
With your defires, no others courfes like.
The griefe you take things are not ordered well,
Is, that you feele your felfe, I feare, not well ;   . 90
But when your fortunes fhall ftand paralell
With thofe you enuie now, all will be well :
For you Great-men, I fee, are neuer more,
Your end attain'd, the fame you were before.
You with a finger can point out the ftaines
Of others errours now, and now condem
The traine of ftate, whil'ft your defire remaines
Without.   But once got in, you iumpe with them,
And interleague yee with iniquitie,
And with a like neglect doe temporize   100
And onely ferue your owne commoditie :
Your fortune then viewes things with other eyes.   .

                l. 75, 'of' ¹,².

For either greatneſſe doth transforme the hart ·
In t'other ſhapes of thoughts, or certainely
This vulgar honeſtie doth dwell apart·
From pow'r, and is ſome priuate quality.
Or rather thoſe faire parts which we eſteeme
In ſuch as you, are not the ſame they ſeeme :
You double with your ſelues or els with vs.
And therefore now, *Philotas*, euen as good   110
T'imbrace the times, as ſwell and doe no good.
   Phi. Alas, *Chaliſthenes*, you haue not laid
True leuell to my nature, but are wide
From what I am within : all you haue ſaid
Shall neuer make me of another ſide
Then that I am, and I doe ſcorne to clime
By ſhaking hands with this vnworthy time.
  · *Cha*. The time, *Philotas*, then will breake thy necke.
   Phi. They dare not, friend, my father will keepe my
       necke :
My ſeruice to the State hath cauſioned
So ſurely for mine honor, as it ſhall
Make good the place my deedes haue purchaſed,
With danger, in the loue and hearts of all.
   Cha. Thoſe ſeruices will ſerue as weights to charge
And preſſe you vnto death, if your foot faile
Neuer ſo little vnderneath your charge,
And will be deem'd, done for your owne auaile.
And who haue ſpirits to doe the greateſt good,
May doe moſt hurt, if they remaine not good.
   Phi. Tuſh, they cannot want my ſeruice in the
      State.   130
   Cha. Theſe times want not men to ſupply the State.

       l. 112, ² oddly misprints 'yaue.'

Phi. I feare not whilſt *Parmenios* forces ſtand.

Cha. Water farre off quenches not fire neere hand.
You may be faire diſpatcht, ere he can heare,
Or if he heard, before he·could be here.
And therefore doe not build vpon ſuch ſand,
It will deceiue your hopes when all is done ;
For though you were the Minion of the Land,
If you breake out, be ſure you are vndone.
When running with the current of the State,   140
Were you the weakeſt man of men aliue,
And in Conuentions and in Counſell ſate,
And did but ſleepe or nod, yet ſhall you thriue ;
Theſe motiue ſpirits are neuer fit to riſe,
And tis a danger to be held ſo wiſe.

Phi. What call you running with the State ? Shall I
Combine with thoſe that doe abuſe the State ?
Whoſe want of iudgement, wit and honeſty,
I am aſham'd to ſee, and ſeeing hate.

Cha. Tuſh, tuſh, my Lord, thinke not of what were
        fit :   • 150
The world is gouern'd more by forme, then wit.
He that will fret at Lords, and at the raine,
Is but a foole, and grieues himſelfe in vaine.
Cannot you Great-men ſuffer others to
Haue part in rule, but muſt haue all to do ?
Now good my Lord confǒrme you to the reſt,
Let not your wings be greater then your neſt.

Phi. ſolus. See how theſe vaine diſcourſiue Book-men
Out of thoſe ſhadowes of their ayrie powers,   [talke,
And doe not ſee how much they muſt defalke   160
Of their accounts, to make them gree with ours.

l. 151, 'than' ².

They little know to what neceffities
Our courfes ftand allied, or how we are
Ingag'd in reputation otherwife,
To be our felues in our particular.
They thinke we can command our harts to lie
Out of their place ; and ftill they preach to vs
Pack-bearing Patience ; that bafe propertie,
And filly gift of th'all enduring Affe.
But let them talke their fill, it is but winde,   170
I muft fayle by the Compaffe of my minde.

Enters a Meffenger.

My Lord, the King call's for you, come my Lord away.
Phi. Well then I know ther's fome new ftratagem
In hand, to be confulted on to day,
That I am fent for, with fuch fpeede, to him,
Whofe youth and fortune cannot brooke delay.
But here's a futer ftands t'impeach my hafte :
I would I had gone vp the priuie way,
Whereby we efcape th'attending multitude ;   180
Though, I confeffe, that in humanity
Tis better to denie, then to delude.

Enters Cebalinus.

My Lord *Philotas*, I am come with newes
Of great importance, that concernes vs all ;
And well hath my good fortune met with you,
Who beft can heare, and beft difcharge my care.
Phi. Say what it is, and pray-thee friend be briefe.
Ceb. The cafe requires your patience, good my Lord
And therefore I muft craue your eare a while.   190
III.   8

Phi. I cannot now be long from *Alexander*.

Ceb. Nor *Alexander* will be long with vs,
Vnleffe you heare : and therefore know, the newes
I bring, concernes his life ; and this it is :
There is one *Dymnus* here within the Campe,
Whofe low eftate, and high affections,
Seeme to haue thruft him int'outragious wayes.
This man, affecting one *Nichomachus*,
A youth, my brother : whom one day h'allures
Int'a Temple ; where being both alone,   200
He breakes out in this fort : *Nichomacus*,
Sweet louely youth ; ah, fhould I not impart
To thee the deepeft fecrets of my heart !
My heart that hath no locke fhut againft thee,
Would let it out fometimes vnwares of me ;
But as it iffues from my faithfull loue,
So clofe it vp in thine, and keepe it faft.
Sweare to be fecret, deare *Nichomacus*,
Sweare by the facred God-head of this place,
To keepe my counfell, and I will reueale   210
A matter of the greateft confequence
That euer man imparted to his friend.
Youth and defire, drawne with a loue to know,
Swore to be fecret, and to keepe it clofe.
Then *Dymnus* tels him, That within three dayes
There fhould b'effected a confpiracy
On *Alexanders* perfon, by his meanes
And diuers more of the Nobility,
To free their labours, and redeeme them home.
Which when *Nichomacus* my brother heard :   220
Is this your tale ? fayth he, O God forbid
Mine oath fhould tie my tongue to keepe in this !

This ougly finne of treafon, which to tell
Mine oath compels me ; faith againft my faith
Muft not be kept.   My falfhood here is truth,
And I muft tell.   Friend or friend not, I'l tell.
Dymnus amaz'd, hearing beyond conceit
The felfe-will'd youth vow to reueale their plot,
Stands ftaring on him, drawing backe his breath,
Or els his breath confounded with his thoughts   230
Bufied with death and horror, could not worke :
Not hauing leafure now to thinke what was,
But what would be, his feares were runne before,
And at miffortune ere fhe came to him.
At length yet, when his reafon had reduc'd
His flying thoughts backe to fome certaine ftand,
Perceiuing yet fome diftance was betwixt
Death and his feares, which gaue him time to worke,
With his returning fpirits he drew his fword,
Puts it t'his owne then to my brothers throat,   240
Then laies it downe, then wrings his hands, then kneeles,
Then ftedfaft lookes, then takes him in his armes,
Weeps on his necke, no word, but, O wilt thou ?
VVilt thou, be the deftruction of vs all ?
And finding no relenting in the youth,
His miferies grew furious, and againe
He takes his fword, and fweares to facrifice
To filence and their caufe, his deareft bloud
The boy amaz'd, feeing no other way,
VVas faine to vow, and promife fecrecy ;
And as if woon t'allow and take that part,
Prayes him tell, who were his complices.
Which, though perplext with griefe for what was done,
Yet thinking now t'haue gain'd him to his fide,

Dymnus replies : No worſe than *Loceus*,
Demetrius of the priuy Chamber, and
Nicanor, *Amyntas*, and *Archelopis*,
Drocenus, *Aphebetus*, *Leuculaus*,
Shall be th'aſſociats of *Nichomacus*.
This when my brother once had vnderſtood,   260
And after much adoe had got away,
He comes, and tells me all the whole diſcourſe,
Which here I haue related vnto you ;
And here will I attend t'auouch the ſame,
Or bring my brother to confirme as much,
Whom now I left behinde, left the conſpirators
Seeing him here vnuſing to this place,
Suſpecting t'b'appeach'd, might ſhift away.
    Phil. Well fellow, I haue heard thy ſtrange report,
And will find time t'acquaint the King therewith. 270

SCENA SECVNDA.

Antigona, and *Thais*.

VV Hat can a free eſtate affoord me more
         Than my incaptiu'd fortune doth allow ?
Was I belou'd, inrich'd, and grac'd before?
Am I not lou'd, inrich'd, and gracèd now ?
    Tha. Yea, but before thou wert a Kings delight.
    Ant. I might be his, although he was not mine.
    Tha. His greatnes made thee greater in mens ſight.
    Ant. More great perhaps without, but not within :
My loue was then aboue me: I am now   281
Aboue my loue. *Darius* then had thouſands more :
Philotas hath but me as I do know,
Nor none els will he haue, and ſo he ſwore.

Tha. Nay, then you may beleeue him, if he fwore.
[*Afide*] Alas, poore foule, fhe neuer came to know
Nor liberty, nor louers periuries.

    Ant. Stand I not better with a meaner loue,
That is alone to me, than with thefe powres,
Who out of all proportion muft b'aboue   290
And haue vs theirs, but they will not be ours.
And *Thais*, although thou be a Grecian,
And I a Perfian, do not enuy me,
That I embrace the onely gallant man
Perfia, or *Greece*, or all the world can fee.
Thou, who art entertein'd and grac'd by all
The flowre of honour els, do not defpife,
That vnto me, poore captiue, fhould befall
So great a grace in fuch a worthies eyes.

    Tha. Antigona, I enuy not thy loue,   300
But thinke thee bleft t'enioy him in that fort.
But tell me truly, Didft thou euer proue
Whether he lou'd in earneft or in fport?

    Ant. Thais, let m'a little glory in my grace,
Out of the paffion of the ioy I feele,
And tell the'a fecret; but in any cafe,
As y'are a woman, do not it reueale.
One day, as I was fitting all alone,
·In comes *Philotas* from a victory,
All blood and duft, yet iolly, hauing wonne   310
The glory of the day moft gallantly:
And warm'd with honour of his good fucceffe,
Relates to me the dangers he was in:
Whereat I wondring, blam'd his forwardneffe.
Faith wench, fayes he, thus muft we fight, toyle, win,

l. 287, ' Her liberty ' [1], [2].

To make that yong-man proud : thus is he borne
Vpon the wings of our deferts ; our blood
Sets him aboue himfelfe, and makes him fcorne
His owne, his country, and the authors of his good.
My father was the firft that out from *Greece*   320
Shew'd him the way of *Afia*, fet him on,
And by his proiect raif'd the greateft peece
Of this proud worke which now he treads vpon.
Parmenio without *Alexander* much hath wrought,
Without *Parmenio, Alexander* hath done nought.
But let him vfe his fortune whilft he may,
Times haue their change, we muft not ftill be led.
And fweet *Antigona* thou mayft one day
Yet, bleffe the houre t'haue knowne *Philotas* bed ;
Wherewith he fweetly kift me.   And now deeme, 330
If that fo great, fo wife, fo rare a man
Would, if he held me not in deare efteeme,
Haue vttred this t'a captiue Perfian.
But *Thais* I may no longer ftay, for feare
My Lord returne, and find me not within ;
Whofe eyes yet neuer faw me any where
But in his chamber, where I fhould haue been :
And therefore *Thais* farewell.
     Tha. Farewell *Antigona.*
Now haue I that, which I defirèd long,   340
Layd in my lap by this fond woman heere,
And meanes t'auenge me of a fecret wrong
That doth concerne my reputation neere.
This gallant man, whom this foole in this wife
Vants to be hers, I muft confeffe t'haue lou'd,
And vi'd all th'engins of thefe conquering eyes,
Affections in his hie-built heart t'haue mou'd,

Yet neuer could : for what my labour feekes
I fee is loft vpon vaine ignorance,
Whil'ft he that is the glory of the Greekes,   350
Virtues vpholder, honours countenance,
Out of this garnifh of his worthy parts
Is fall'n vpon this foolifh Perfian,.
To whom his fecrets grauely he imparts ;
Which fhe as wifely keepe and gouerne can.
Tis ftrange to fee the humour of thefe men,
Thefe great afpiring fpirits, that fhould be wife ;
We women fhall know all : for now and then,
Out of the humour of their iollities,
The fmoake of their ambition muft haue vent,   360
And out it comes what racks fhould not reueale :
For this her humour hath fo much of windе,
That it will burft it felfe if too clofe pent ;
And none more fit than vs their wifdomes finde,
Who will for loue or want of wit conceale.
For being the nature of great fpirits, to loue
To be where they may be moft eminent ;
And rating of themfelues fo farre aboue
Vs in conceit, with whom they do frequent,
Imagine how we wonder and efteeme   370
All that they do or fay ; which makes them ftriue
To make our admiration more extreme :
Which they fuppofe they cannot, 'leffe they giue
Notice of their extreme and higheft thoughts :
And then the opinion, that we loue them too,
Begets a confidence of fecrecy ;

l. 358, ' now ' from ¹, ², accepted for '23 ' how ' : l. 359, *Ibid.* ' their ' for ' thefe.'

Whereby what euer they intend to doo,
We fhall be fure to know it prefently.
　　But faith, I fcorne that fuch a one as fhe,
A filly wittied wench, fhould haue this grace　　380
To be preferr'd and honor'd before me,
Hauing but only beauty, and a face.
I that was euer courted by the great
And gallant'ft Peeres and Princes of the Eaft,
Whom *Alexander* in the greateft ftate
The earth did euer fee him, made his gueft.
‧There where this tongue obtainèd for her merit
Eternity of Fame : there where thefe hands
Did write in fire the glory of my fpirit,
And fet a trophey that for euer ftands :　　390
Thais aftion with the Grecian afts fhall be
Inregiftred alike.　　*Thais*, fhe that fir'd
The ftatelieft palace th'earth did euer fee ;
Darius houfe, that to the clouds afpir'd :
She is put backe behinde *Antigona*.
　　But foone *Philotas* fhall his error fee,
Who thinkes that beauty beft, mens paffions fits
For that they vfe our bodies, not our wits :
And vnto *Craterus* will I prefently,
And him acquaint with all this whole difcourfe,　　400
Who, I am fure, will take it well of vs :
For thefe great Minions, who with enuious eie
Looke on each others greatneffe, will be glad,
In fuch a cafe of this importancy,
To haue th'aduantage that may here be had.

CHORVS.

*W*E *as the Chorus of the vulgar, ftand*
  Spectators heere, to fee thefe great men play
Their parts both of obedience and command,
And cenfure all they do, and all they fay. 410
For though we be efteem'd but ignorant,
Yet are we capable of truth, and know
Where they do well, and where their actions want
The grace that makes them proue the beft in fhow.
And though we know not what they do within,
Where they attire, their myfteries of State,
Yet know we by th'euents, what plots haue beene,
And how they all without do perfonate,
  We fee who well a meaner part became,
  Faile in a greater, and difgrace the fame. 420
We fee fome worthy of aduancement deem'd,
Saue when they haue it: fome againe haue got
Good reputation, and beene well efteem'd
In place of greatneffe, which before were not.
  We fee affliction act a better fcæne
  Than profperous fortune which hath marr'd it cleane.
We fee that all which we haue praifd in fome,
Haue only beene their fortune, not defart:
Some warre haue grac'd, whom peace doth ill become,
And luftfull eafe hath blemifht all their part. 430
We fee Philotas *acts his goodneffe ill,*
And makes his paffions to report of him
Worfe than he is: and we do feare he will
Bring his free nature to b'intrapt by them.
For fure there is fome engin clofely laid
Againft his grace and greatneffe with the King:

And that vnleſſe his humors proue more ſtaid,
We ſoone ſhall ſee his vtter ruining.
  And his affliction our compaſſion drawes,
  Which ſtill lookes on mens fortunes, not the cauſe. 440

ACTVS II. SCENA I.

Alexander, Epheſtion, Craterus.

Alexander.

E *Pheſtion,* thou doeſt *Alexander* loue,
  Craterus, thou the King : yet both you meet
In one ſelfe point of loyalty and loue,
And both I find like carefull, like diſcreet ;
Therefore my faithfull'ſt Counſellers, to you
I muſt a weighty accident impart,
Which lies ſo heauy, as I tell you true   450
I finde the burthen much t'oppreſſe my hart.
  Ingratitude and ſtubburne carriage,
In one of whom my loue deſeru'd reſpect,
Is that which moues my paſſion into rage,
And is a thing I ought not to neglect.
  You ſee how I *Philotas* raiſèd haue
Aboue his ranke, his Peeres, beyond his terme ;
You ſee the place, the offices I gaue,
As th'earneſt of my loue to binde his firme :
But all, he deeming rather his deſarts,   · 460
Than the effects of my grace any way,
Beginnes to play moſt peremptory parts,
As fitter to controule than to obay.
And I haue beene inform'd, he foſters too
The faction of that home-bent cowardize,

I. 446, 'one' from ¹, ², accepted for 'on' of '23.

That would run backe from glory, and vndoo
All the whole wonder of our enterprize ;
And one day to our felfe prefumes to write,
(Seeming our ftile and title to abraid,
Which th'oracles themfelues held requifite,   470
And which not I, but men on me haue laid)
And fayd he pitied thofe who vnder him fhould liue,
Who held himfelfe the fonne of *Iupiter.*
Alas good man, as though what breath could giue
Could make mine owne thoughts other than they are !
I that am Arbitrer betwixt my heart
And their opinion, know how it ftands within,
And finde that my infirmities take part
Of that fame frailty other men liue in.
And yet, what if I were difpof'd to winke   480
At th'entertain'd opinion fpred fo farre,
And rather was content the world fhould thinke
Vs other than we are, than what we are ?
In doing which, I know I am not gone
Beyond example, feeing that maiefty
Needs all the props of admiration
That may be got, to beare it vp on hie ;
And much more mine, which but eu'n now begun
By miracles of fortune, and our worth,
Needs all the complements to reft vpon
That reu'rence and opinion can bring forth ;   490
Which this wife man conceiues not, and yet takes
Vpon him to inftruct vs what to do.
But thefe are but the flourifhes he makes
Of greater malice he is bent vnto :

l. 469, 'obrayd' ¹, 'obraid' ² : l. 483, 'than' of ² corrects 'that' of '23;
'then' ¹.

For fure, me thinkes, I view within his face
The map of change and innouation :
I fee his pride contented with no place,
Vnleffe it be the throne I fit vpon.
   Epheft. Had I not heard this from your facred
        tongue,
Deare Souereigne, I would neuer haue beleeued   501
Philotas folly would haue done that wrong
To his owne worth and th'honours he receiued :
And yet me thought, of late, his carriage
In fuch exceeding pompe and gallantry,
And fuch a world of followers, did prefage
That he affected popularity,
Efpecially, fince for his feruice done
He was adiudg'd to haue the fecond place
In honour with *Antigonus*: which wonne   510
To fome th'opinion to be high in grace ;
Then his laft action, leading the right wing,
And th'ouerthrow he gaue, might hap inlarge   .
Th'opinion of himfelfe, confidering
Th'efpeciall grace and honour of his charge ;
Whereby perhaps in rating his owne worth,
His pride might vnder-value that great grace
From whence it grew, and that which put him forth,
And made his fortune futing to the place.
But yet I thinke he is not fo vnwife   520
Although his fortune, youth, and iollity
Makes him thus mad, as he will enterprife
Ought againft courfe, his faith, and loyalty :
And therefore, if your Grace did but withdraw
Thofe beames of fauour, which do daze his wits,

l. 497, 'inouacion' of¹ and 'innouation' of² corrects '23 'invocation.'

He would be foone reduc'd t'his ranke of aw,
And know himfelfe, and beare him as befits.

 Alex. Withdraw our grace? and how can that be done,
Without fome fulliuation to enfue!
Can he be fafe brought in, being so farre gone? 530
I hold it not. Say *Craterus,* What thinke you?

 Cra. Souereigne, I know the man: I finde his fpirit;
And malice fhall not make me (I proteft)
Speake other than I know his pride doth merit:
And what I fpeake, is for your intereft,
Which long ere this I would haue vttered,
But that I fear'd your Maiefty would take,
·That from fome priuate grudge it rather bred,
Than out of care, for your deare fifters fake;
Or rather, that I fought to croffe your Grace, 540
Or, to confine your fauour within bounds:
And finding him to hold fo high a place
In that diuine conceit which ours confounds;
I thought the fafeft way to let it reft,
In hope, that time fome paffage open would,
To let in thofe cleere lookes into that breft
That doth but malice and confufion hold.
And now I fee you haue difcern'd the man
Whom (I proteft) I hold moft dangerous.
And that you ought, with all the fpeede you can, 550
Worke to repreffe a fpirit fo mutinous:
For eu'n already he is fwoll'n fo hie,
That his affe&ctions ouerflow the brim
Of his owne pow'rs, not able to deny
Paffage vnto the thoughts that gouerne him:
For but eu'n now I heard a ftrange report,
Of fpeeches he fhould vfe t'his Curtizan;

Vanting what he had done, and in what fort
He labour'd to aduance that proud yong man.
(So terming of your facred Maiefty)   560
With other fuch extrauagant difcourfe,
Whereof we fhall attaine more certeinty
(I doubt not) fhortly, and difcry his courfe.
Meane while, about your perfon (I aduife)
Your Grace fhould call a more fufficient guard,
And on his actions fet fuch wary eyes,
As may thereof take fpeciall good regard ;
And note what perfons chiefly he frequents,
And who to him haue the moft free acceffe ;
How he beftowes his time ; where he prefents   570.
The large reuenue of his bounteoufneffe.
And for his wench that lies betwixt his armes,
And knowes his heart, I will about with her ;
She fhalbe wrought t'apply her vfuall charmes,
And I will make her my difcouerer.

   Alex. This counfell (*Craterus*) we do well allow,
And giue thee many thankes for thy great care : ·
But yet we muft beare faire, left he fhould know
That we fufpect what his affections are :
For that you fee he holds a fide of pow'r,   580
Which might perhaps call vp fome mutiny:
His father, old *Parmenio*, at this howre
Rules *Medeæ* with no leffer pow'rs than I ;
Himfelfe, you fee, gallantly followed,
Holds next to vs a fpeciall gouernment;
Cænus, that with his fifter married,
Hath vnder him againe commandement ;
Amintas and *Symanus*, his deare friends,
With both their honourable offices ;

And then the priuate traine that on them tends,   590
With all particular dependences,
Are motiues to aduife vs how to deale.
    Crat. Your Grace faies true, but yet thefe clouds of
        fmoke
Vanifh before the fun of that refpeſt
Whereon mens long-inur'd affeſtions looke
With fuch a natiue zeale, and fo affeſt,
As that the vaine and fhallow praſtifes
Of no fuch giddy traytour (if the thing
Be tooke in time with due aduifedneffe)
Shal the leaft fhew of any fearing bring.   600
    Alex. Well, then to thee (deare *Craterus*) I refer
Th'efpeciall care of this great bufineffe.

S c e n a S e c v n d a.   *Philotas, Ceballinus, Seruus.*

          Ceballinus.

M Y Lord, I here haue long attendance made,
    Expeſting to be call'd t'auouch my newes,
    Phi. In troth (my friend) I haue not found the King
At any leafure yet to heare the fame.
    Ceb. No, not at leafure to preuent his death?
And is the matter of no more import?   610
I'l try another.   Yet me thinkes fuch men
As are the eyes and eares of Princes, fhould
Not weigh fo light fuch an intelligence.
    Ser. My Lord, the fumme you willèd me to giue
The captaine that did vifit you to day;
To tell you plaine, your coffers yeeld it not.
    Phi. How if they yeeld it not? Haue I not then

Apparell, plate, iewels? Why fell them,
And go your way, difpatch, and giue it him.

Philotas alone.   620

Me thinkes I find the King much chang'd of late,
And vnto me his graces not fo great :
Although they feeme in fhew all of one rate,
Yet by the touch, I find them counterfet :
For when I fpeake, although I haue his eare,
Yet do I fee his mind is other where :
And when he fpeakes to me, I fee he ftriues
To giue a colour vnto what is not :
For he muft think, that we, whofe ftates, whofe liues
Depend vpon his Grace, learne not by rote   630
T'obferue his actions, and to know his trym.
And though indeed Princes be manifold,
Yet haue they ftill fuch eyes to wait on them,
As are too piercing, that they can behold
And penetrate the inwards of the heart,
That no deuice can fet fo clofe a doore   .
Betwixt their fhew and thoughts, but that their art
Of fhadowing it, makes it appeare the more.
But many, malicing my ftate of grace,
I know no worke, with all the power they haue   640
Vpon that eafie nature, to difplace
My fortunes, and my actions to depraue.
And though I know they feeke t'inclofe him in,
And faine would locke him vp and chamber him,
Yet will I neuer ftoppe, and feeke to win
My way by them, that came not in by them ;

l. 619, ' *Plutarch* in the life of *Alexander* ' (in margin) : l. 629, ' whofe '
of ¹, ², corrects '23 ' who' : l. 637, ' fhewes ' ¹, ².

And fcorne to ftand on any other feet
Than thefe of mine owne worth ; and what my plaine
And open actions cannot fairely get,
Bafeneffe and fmoothing them, fhall neuer gaine.   650
And yet, I know, my prefence and acceffe
Cleeres all thefe mifts which they haue raif'd before,
Though, with my backe, ftraight turnes that happineffe,
And they againe blow vp as much or more.
　　Thus do we roule the ftone of our owne toyle,
　　And men fuppofe our hell, a heauen the while.

　　S c e n a I I I.   *Craterus, Antigona.*

　　　　　Craterus.

A*Ntigona*, there is no remedy,
　　You needs muft iuftifie the fpeech you held 660
With *Thais*, who will your confrence verifie,
And therefore now it can not be conceal'd.
　　Ant. O, my good Lord, I pray you vrge me not :
Thais only of a cunning enuious wit,
Scorning a ftranger fhould haue fuch a lot,
Hath out of her inuention forgèd it.
　　Crat. Why then, fhall racks and tortures force thee
　　　　fhow
Both this and other matters which we know ?
Thinke therefore, if't were not a wifer part
T'accept of reft, rewards, preferment, grace,   670
And being perhaps, fo beautious as thou art,
Of faire election for a neerer place ;
To tell the truth, than to be obftinate,
And fall with the misfortune of a man,

III.　　　　　　　　　　　　　　　　　9

Who, in his dangerous and concuffed ftate,
No goode to thee, but ruine render can.
Refolue thee of this choice, and let me know
Thy minde at full, at my returning backe.
 Ant. What fhall I do, fhall I betray my Loue,
Or die difgrac'd ? What, do I make a doubt ! 680
Betray my Loue ? O heauenly pow'rs aboue
Forbid that fuch a thought fhould iffue out
Of this confufèd breft : Nay rather firft
Let tortures, death and horror do their worft.
But out alas, this inconfiderate tongue,
Without my hearts confent and priuity,
Hath done already this vnwilling wrong,
And now it is no wifdome to deny.
No wifdome to deny ? Yes, yes, that tongue
That thus hath beene the traytour to my heart, 690
Shall either pow'rfully redeeme that wrong,
Or neuer more fhall words of breath impart.
Yet, what can my deniall profit him,
Whom they perhaps, whether I tell or not,
Are purpof'd, vpon matters knowne to them,
To ruinate on fome difcouered plot ?
Let them do what they will. Let not thy heart
Seeme to be acceffary in a thought,
To giue the leaft aduantage of thy part,
To haue a part of fhame in what is wrought. 700
O this were well, if that my dangers could
Redeeme his perill, and his grace reftore ;
For which, I vow, my life I render would,
If this poore life could fatisfie therefore.
But tis not for thy honour to forfake
Thy Loue for death, that lou'd thee in this fort.

Alas, what notice will the world take
Of fuch refpects in women of my fort ?
This act may yet put on fo faire [a] coate
Vpon my foule profeffion, as it may   710
Not blufh t'appeare with thofe of cleaneft note,
And haue as hie a place with fame as they.
What do I talke of fame ? Do I not fee
This faction of my flefh, my feares, my youth
Already entred ; and haue bent at me,
The ioyes of life, to batter downe my truth ?
O my fubdued thoughts ! what haue you done ?
To let in feare, falfhood to my heart.
Whom though they haue furpriz'd, they haue not won ;
For ftill my loue fhall hold the deareft part.   720
   Crat. Antigona, What, are you yet refolu'd ?
   Ant. Refolu'd, my Lord, t'endure all mifery ?
   Crat. And fo be fure you fhall, if that b'your choice.
   Ant. What will you haue me do, my Lord, I am
Content to fay what you will haue me fay.
   Crat. Then come, go with me to *Alexander.*

CHORVS.

H Ow doft thou weare, and weary out thy dayes,
    Reftleffe ambition, neuer at an end !
Whofe trauels no Herculean pillar ftayes,   730
But ftill beyond thy reft thy labours tend :
Aboue good fortune thou thy hopes doft raife,
Still climing, and yet neuer canft afcend :
   For when thou haft attaind vnto the top
   Of thy defires, thou haft not yet got vp.

That height of fortune either is controld
By ſome more pow'rfull ouerlooking eye,
(That doth the fulneſſe of thy grace withhold)
Or counter-checkt with ſome concurrency,
That it doth coſt farre more ado to hold   740
The height attain'd, than was to get ſo hie ;
   Where ſtand thou canſt not, but with carefull toile,
   Nor looſe thy hold without thy vtter ſpoile.
There doſt thou ſtruggle with thine owne diſtruſt,
And others iealouſies, their counterplot,
Againſt ſome vnder-working pride, that muſt
Supplanted be, or els thou ſtandeſt not.
There wrong is playd with wrong, and he that thruſt
Downe others, comes himſelfe to haue that lot.
   The ſame concurſſion doth afflict his breſt   750
   That others ſhooke: oppreſſion is oppreſt,
That either happineſſe dwells not ſo hie,
Or els aboue, whereto pride cannot riſe :
And that the highſt of mans felicity,
But in the region of affliction lies :
And that we climbe but vp to miſery :
High fortunes are but high calamities.
   It is not in that Sphere, where peace doth moue;
   Reſt dwell's below it, happineſſe aboue.
For in this height of fortune are imbred   760
Thoſe thundring fragors that affright the earth:
From thence haue all diſtemp'ratures their head,
That brings forth deſolation, famine, dearth:
There certaine order is diſordered :
And there it is confuſion hath her birth.
   It is that height of fortune doth vndoo
   Both her owne quietneſſe and others too.

ACTVS TERTIVS.

*Alexander, Metron, Ceballinus, Craterus, Perdiceas,
Epheſtion.*

Alexander. 770

COme, *Metron* ſay, of whom haſt thou receiued
   Th'intelligence of this conſpiracy,
Contriu'd againſt our perſon, as thou ſayſt,
By *Dymnus* and ſome other of the Campe ?
Is't not ſome vaine report borne without cauſe,
That enuy or imagination drawes
From priuate ends, to breed a publike feare,
T'amuze the world with things that neuer were ?
   Met. Here, may it pleaſe your Highneſſe is the man,
One *Ceballinus,* that brought me the newes.   780
   Ceb. O, *Alexander !* I haue ſau'd thy life ;
I am the man that haue reueal'd their plot.
   Alex. And how cam'ſt thou to be inform'd thereof ?
   Ceb. By mine owne brother, one *Nichomacus,*
Whom *Dymnus,* chiefe of the conſpiratours,
Acquainted with the whole of their intents.
   Alex. How long ſince is it, this was told to thee ?
   Ceb. About ſome three dayes, my ſouereigne Lord.
   Alex. What, three dayes ſince ! and haſt thou ſo long
      kept   790
The thing conceal'd from vs, being of that weight ?
Guard, Take and lay him preſently in hold.
   Ceb. O, may it pleaſe your Grace, I did not keep
The thing conceal'd one houre, but preſently
Ran to acquaint *Philotas* therewithall,
Suppoſing him a man, ſo neere in place,

Would beſt reſpect a caſe that toucht ſo neere;
And on him haue I waited theſe two dayes,
Expecting t'haue beene brought vnto your Grace;
And ſeeing him weigh it light, pretending that
Your Graces leaſure ſeru'd not fit to heare,   800
I to the Maſter of your armoury
Addreſt my ſelfe forthwith, to *Metron* here;
Who, without making any more delay,
Preſt in vnto your Grace, being in your bath;
Locking me vp the while in th'armoury:
And all what I could ſhew reuealèd hath.
    Alex. If this be ſo, then, fellow, I confeſſe,
Thy loyall care of vs was more than theirs,
Who had more reaſon theirs ſhould haue bin more.
Cauſe *Dymnus* to be preſently brought forth,   810
And call *Philotas* ſtreight; who, now I ſee,
Hath not deceiu'd me, in deceiuing me.
Who would haue thought one, whom I held ſo neere,
Would from my ſafety haue beene ſo farre off,
When moſt it ſhould and ought import his care,   •
And wherein his allegeance might make proofe
Of thoſe effects my fauours had deſeru'd,
And ought t'haue claim'd more duty at his hands
Than any of the reſt?   But thus w'are ſeru'd,
When priuate grace out of proportion ſtands,   820
And that we call vp men from of[f] below,
From th'element of baſer property;
And ſet them where they may behold and know
The way of might, and worke of maieſty;
VVhere ſee'ng thoſe rayes, which being ſent far off,
Reflect a heate of wonder and reſpect,
To faile neere hand, and not to ſhew that proofe,

(The obiect only working that effect)
Thinke (feeing themfelues, though by our fauour, fet
VVithin the felfe fame orbe of rule with vs)   830
Their light would fhine alone, if ours were fet ;
And fo prefume t'obfcure or fhadow vs.
But he fhall know, although his neerenefle hath
Not felt our heat, that we can burne him too ;
And grace that fhines, can kindle vnto wrath ;
And *Alexander* and the King are two.
But here they bring vs *Dymnus*, in whofe face
I fee is guilt, defpaire, horror, and death.
     Guar. Yea, death indeed, for ere he could b'attach'd
He ftabb'd himfelfe fo deadly to the heart,   840
As tis impoffible that he fhould liue.
     Alex. Say *Dymnus*, what haue I deferud of thee,
That thou fhouldft thinke worthier to be thy King,
Philotas, than our felfe ? hold, hold, he finks ;
Guard keepe him vp, get him to anfwer vs.
     Guar. He hath fpoke his laft, h'wil neuer anfwer more.
     Alex. Sorry I am for that, for now hath Death
Shut vs cleane out from knowing him within,
And lockt vp in his breft all the others hearts.
But yet this deed argues the truth in groffe,   850
Though we be barr'd it in particular.
Philotas, are you come ? Looke here, this man,
This *Ceballinus* fhould haue fuffred death,
Could it but haue beene prou'd he had conceal'd
Th'intended treafon from vs thefe two dayes ;
Wherewith (he fayes) he ftreight acquainted thee.
Thinke, the more neere thou art about our felfe,
The greater is the fhame of thine offence :
And which had beene leffe foule in him than thee.

Phil. Renowmed Prince, for that my heart is cleere,
Amazement cannot ouer caſt my face,　　　　　861
And I muſt boldly with th'aſſurèd cheere
Of my vnguilty confcience, tell your Grace,
That this offence (thus hapning) was not made
By any the leaſt thought of ill in me ;
And that the keeping of it vnbewrai'd,
Was, that I held the rumour vaine to be,
Confidering fome, who were accuf'd, were knowne
Your ancient and moſt loyall feruitours,
And fuch, as rather would let out their owne　　　870
Heart blood, I know, than once indanger yours.
And for me then, vpon no certaine note,
But on the brabble of two wanton youthes,
T'haue tolde an idle tale, that would haue wrought
In you diſtruſt, and wrong to others truths,
And to no end, but only to haue made
My felfe a fcorne, and odious vnto all.
(For which I rather tooke the bait was layd,
Than els for any treachery at all.)
I muſt confeſſe, I thought the fafeſt way　　　880
To fmoother it a while, to th'end I might,
If fuch a thing could be, fome proofes bewray,
That might yeeld probability of right ;
Proteſting that mine owne vnfpotted thought
A like beleefe of others truth did breed,
Iudging no impious wretch could haue bin wrought
T'imagine fuch a deteſtable deed.
And therefore, O dread Souereigne, do not way
Philotas faith by this his ouerfight,
But by his actions paſt, and only lay　　　890
Error t'his charge, not malice or defpight.

Alex. Well, loe, thou haſt a fauourable Iudge,
When, though thou haſt not pow'r to cleere thy blame,
Yet hath he pow'r to pardon thee the fame ;
Which take not as thy right, but as his grace,
Since here the perſon alters not the caſe.
And here, *Philotas*, I forgiue the offence,
And to confirme the fame, loe here's my hand.

   Phi. O ſacred hand, the witneſſe of my life !
By thee I hold my ſafety as ſecure   900
As is my conſcience free from treachery.

   Alex. Well, go t'your charge, and looke to our affaires,
For we to morrow purpoſe to remoue.   *Exit.*

   Alex. In troth I know not what to iudge herein,
Me thinkes that man ſeemes ſurely cleere in this,
How euer otherwiſe his hopes haue beene
Tranſported by his vnaduiſedneſſe :
It cannot be, a guilty conſcience ſhould
Put on ſo ſure a brow ; or els by art
His lookes ſtand newtrall, ſeeming not to hold   910
Reſpondency of int'reſt with his heart.
Sure, for my part, he hath diſſolu'd the knot
Of my ſuſpition, with ſo cleere a hand,
As that I thinke in this (what euer plot
Of miſchiefe it may be) he hath no hand.

   Crat. My Lord, the greater confidence he ſhewes,
Who is ſuſpected, ſhould be fear'd the more :
For danger from weake natures neuer growes ;
Who muſt diſturbe the world, are built therefore.
   He more is to be fear'd, that nothing feares,   920
   And malice moſt effects, that leaſt appeares.
Preſumption of mens pow'rs as well may breed
Aſſuredneſſe, as innocency may ;

d mifchiefe feldome but by truft doth fpeed;
10 Kings betray, firft their beleefe betray.
'ould your Grace had firft conferr'd with vs,
ce you would needs fuch clemency haue fhown,
at we might yet haue aduif'd you thus,
at he his danger neuer might haue know'n.
In faults wherein an after-fhame will liue,   930
Tis better to conceale, than to forgiue :
r who are brought vnto the blocke of death,
inke rather on the perill they haue paft,
an on the grace which hath preferu'd their breath ;
id more their fuffrings than their mercy taft :
: now to plot your danger ftill may liue,
t you his guilt not alwayes to forgiue.
Know, that a man fo fwoll'n with difcontent,
) grace can cure, nor pardon can reftore ;
: knowes how thofe who once hath mercy fpent, 940
n neuer hope to haue it any more.
But fay, that through remorfe he calmer proue,
ill great *Parmenio* fo attended on   •
ith that braue army, foftred in his loue,
 thankfull for this grace you do his fonne ?
me benefits are odious, fo is this,
iere men are ftill afhamèd to confeffe
 haue fo done, as to deferue to die ;
d euer do defire, that men fhould geffe
ey rather had receiu'd an iniury   950
an life ; fince life they know in fuch a cafe
iy be reftor'd to all, but not to grace.
Perd. And for my part, my liege, I hold this minde,
at fure,. he would not haue fo much fuppreft
e notice of a treafon in that kinde,

Vnleſſe he were a party with the reſt.
Can it be thought that great *Parmenios* ſonne,
The generall commander of the horſe,
The minion of the campe, the only one
Of ſecret counſell, and of free recourſe,   960
Should not in three dayes ſpace haue found the King
At leaſure t'heare three words of that import ;
Whil'ſt he himſelfe in idle lauiſhing
Did thouſands ſpend t'aduance his owne report ?
    Crat. And if he gaue no credit to the youth,
Why did he two dayes ſpace delay him then ?
As if he had beleeu'd it for a truth,
To hinder his addreſſe to other men.
If he had held it but a vaine conceit,
I pray why had he not diſmiſt him ſtreight ?   970
Men in their priuate dangers may be ſtout,
But in th'occaſions and the feares of Kings
We ought not to be credulous, but doubt
The intimation of the vaineſt things.
    Alex. Well, howſoeuer, we will yet this night
Diſport and banquet in vnuſuall wiſe,
That it may ſeeme, we weigh this practiſe light,
How euer heavy, here, within it lies.
Kings may not know diſtruſt, and though they feare,
They muſt not take acquaintance of their feare.   980

Scena II.

Antigona, Thais.

OY'are a ſecret counſell-keeper, *Thais :*
    In troth I little thought you ſuch a one.
    Tha. And why, *Antigona*, what haue I done ?

Ant. You know ful-well, your confcience you
        bewraies.
Tha. Alas, good foule, would you haue me conceale
That, which your felfe could not but needs reueale?
Thinke you, another can be more to you,
In what concernes them not, than you can be   990
Whom it imports? Will others hold them true,
When you proue falfe to your o[w]ne fecrecy?
But yet this is no wonder: for we fee
Wifer than we do lay their heads to gage
For riotous expences of their tongues,
Although it be a property belongs
Efpecially to vs, and euery age
Can fhew ftrange prefidents what we haue been
In cafes of the greateft plots of men;
And t'is the Scene on this worlds ftage we play,   1000
Whofe reuolution we with men conuert,
And are to act our part as well as they,
Though commonly the weakeft, yet a-part.
    For this great motion of a State we fee
Doth turne on many wheeles, and fome (thogh fmal)
Do yet the greater moue, who in degree
Stirre thofe who likewife turne the great'ft of all.
For though we are not wife, we fee the wife
By vs are made, or make vs parties ftill
In actions of the greateft qualities   1010
That they can manage, be they good or ill.
    Ant. I cannot tell: but you haue made me doo
That which muft euermore afflict my heart.
And if this be my wofull part, t'vndoo
My deareft Loue, would I had had no part!
How haue I filly woman fifted been,

Examin'd, tri'd, flatt'red, terrifi'd,
By *Craterus*, the cunningeſt of men ;
That neuer left me till I had deſcri'd
What euer of *Philotas* I had know'n !　　　　　1020
　　Tha. What, is that all ? Perhaps I haue thereby
Done the[e] more good than thou canſt apprehend.
　　Ant. Such good I rather you ſhould get than I,
If that can be a good t'accuſe my friend.
　　Tha. Alas, thy accuſation did but quote
The margin of ſome text of greater note.
　　Ant. But that is more then thou or I can tell.
　　Tha. Yes, yes, *Antigona*, I know it well.
For be thou ſure, that alwayes thoſe who ſeeke
T'attacke the Lyon, ſo prouide, that ſtill　　　　1030
Their toyles be ſuch, as that he ſhall not ſcape
To turne his rage on thoſe that wrought his ill.
Philotas neither was ſo ſtrong nor hie,
But malice ouerlookt him, and diſcride
Where he lay weake, where was his vanity,
And built her countermounts vpon that ſide,
In ſuch ſort, as they would be ſure to race
His fortunes with the engins of diſgrace.
And now mayſt thou, perhaps, come great hereby,
And gracious with his greateſt enemy :　　　　1040
For ſuch men thinke, they haue no full ſucces,
Vnleſſe they likewiſe gaine the miſtreſſes
Of thoſe they maſter, and ſucceed the place
And fortunes of their loues with equall grace.
　　Ant. Loues ! Out alas ! Loue ſuch a one as he,
That ſeekes t'vndoo my Loue, and in him me ?
　　Tha. Tuſh, loue his fortunes, loue his ſtate, his place,
What euer greatneſſe doth, it muſt haue grace.

Ant. I weigh not greatneſſe, I muſt pleaſe mine eye.
Tha. Th'eye nothing fairer ſees than dignity.   1050
Ant. But what is dignity without our loue?
Tha. If we haue that, we cannot want our loue.
Ant. Why, that giues but the out-ſide of delight:
The day time ioy, what comfort hath the night?
Tha. If pow'r procure not that, what can it do?
Ant. I know not how that can b'attain'd vnto.
Tha. Nor will I teach thee, if thou know'ſt it not:
Tis vaine, I ſee, to learne an Aſian wit.   *Exit.*

Ant. If this be that great wit, that learnèd ſkill,
You Greeks profeſſe, let me be fooliſh ſtill,   1060
So I be faithfull.   And now, being here alone,
Let me record the heauy notes of mone.

Scena III.

Craterus, Epheſtion, Clitus, &c.

Craterus.

MY Lords, you ſee the flexible conceit
        Of our indangered ſouereigne: and you know
How much his perill, and *Philotas* pride,
Imports the State and vs; and therefore now
We either muſt oppoſe againſt deceit,   1070
Or be vndone: for now hath time diſcride
An open paſſage to his fartheſt ends;
From whence, if negligence now put vs backe,
Returne we neuer can without our wracke.

And, good my Lords, ſince you conceiue as much,
And that we ſtand alike, make not me proſecute
The cauſe alone, as if it did but touch
Only my ſelfe; and that I did both breed

And vrge thefe doubts out of a priuate griefe.
Indeed, I know, I might with much more eafe   1080
Sit ftill like others ; and if dangers come,
Might thinke to fhift for one, as well as they :
But yet the faith, the duty, and refpect
We owe both to our fouereigne and the State,
My Lords, I hold, requires another care.

   Eph. My Lord, affure you we will take a time
To vrge a ftricter count of *Dymnus* death.   :

   Crat. My Lords, I fay, vnleffe this be the time,
You will apply your phyficke after death.
You fee the King inuited hath this night   1090
Philotas with the reft, and entertaines
Him with as kinde an vfage (to our fight)
As euer : and you fee the cunning ftraines
Of fweet infinuation, that are vf'd
T'affure the eare of grace with falfe reports :
So that all this will come to be excuf'd
With one remoue ; one action quite tranfports
The Kings affections ouer to his hopes,
And fets him fo beyond the due regard
Of his owne fafety, as one enterprize   1100
May ferue their turne, and may vs all furprize.

   Clit. But now, fince things thus of themfelues breake
We haue aduantage to preuent the worft,   [out,
And eu'ry day will yeeld vs more, no doubt ;
For they are fau'd, that thus are warnèd firft.

   Crat. So, my Lord *Clitus*, are they likewife warn'd
T'accelerate their plot, being thus bewrai'd.

   Cli. But that they cannot now, it is too late :
For treafon taken ere the birth, doth come
Abortiue, and her wombe is made her tombe.   1110

Crat. You do not know how farre it hath put forth
The force of malice, nor how farre is fpred
Already the contagion of this ill.

Clit. Why then there may fome one be tortured
Of thofe whom *Ceballinus* hath reueal'd,
Whereby the reft may be difcouered.

Crat. That one muft be *Philotas*, from whofe head
All this corruption flowes ; take him, take all.

Clit. Philotas is not nam'd, and therefore may
Perhaps not be acquainted with this plot.   1120

Crat. That, his concealing of the plot bewraies :
And if we do not caft to find him firft,
His wit (be fure) hath layd fo good a ground,
As he will be the laft that will be found.

Clit. But if he be not found, then in this cafe
We do him more, by iniuring his grace.

Crat. If that he be not found t'haue dealt in this,
Yet this will force out fome fuch thoughts of his,
As will vndoo him : for you feldome fee
Such men arraign'd, that euer quitted be.   1130

Eph. Well, my Lord *Craterus*, we will moue his
          Grace
(Though it be late) before he take his reft,
That fome courfe may be taken in this cafe :
And God ordaine, it may be for the beft.   *Exeunt.*

CHORVS.

*SE how thefe great men cloath their priuate hate
    In thofe faire colours of the publike good ;
And to effect their ends, pretend the State,
As if the State by their affections ftood :*

And arm'd with pow'r and Princes iealousies,　　1140
Will put the least conceit of discontent
Into the greatest ranke of treacheries,
That no one action shall seeme innocent:
Yea, valour, honour, bounty, shall be made
As accessaries vnto ends vniust :
And euen the seruice of the State must lade
The needfull'st vndertakings with distrust.
　　So that base vilenesse, idle luxury
　　Seeme safer farre, than to do worthily.
Suspition full of eyes, and full of eares,　　1150
Doth thorow the tincture of her owne conceit
See all things in the colours of her feares,
And truth it selfe must looke like to deceit ;
That what way s'euer the suspected take,
Still enuy will most cunningly forelay
The ambush of their ruine, or will make
Their humors of themselues to take that way.
　　But this is still the fate of those that are
　　By nature or their fortunes eminent,
Who either carried in conceit too farre,　　1160
Do worke their owne or others discontent,
Or els are deemèd fit to be supprest,
Not for they are, but that they may be ill ;
Since States haue euer had far more vnrest
By spirits of worth, then men of meaner skill ;
　　And find, that those do alwayes better proue,
　　Wh' are equall to imployment, not aboue.
For selfe-opinion would be seene more wise,
Than present counsels, custtomes, orders, lawes :
And to the end to haue them otherwise,　　1170
The Common-wealth into combustion drawes,

III.　　　　　　　　　　　　　　　　　　10

As if ordaind t'imbroile the world with wit,
As well as grofneffe, to difhonour it.

ACTVS IIII. SCENA I. *Attaras, Softratus.*

Softratus.

CAn there be fuch a fudden change in Court
    As you report ? Is it to be beleeu'd,
That great *Philotas*, whom we all beheld
In grace laft night, fhould be arraign'd to day ?
    Att. It can be : and it is as I report :   1180
For ftates of grace are no fure holds in Court.
    Soft. But yet tis ftrange they fhould be ouerthrow'n
Before their certeine forfeitures were know'n.
    Att. Tufh, it was breeding long, though fuddenly
This thunder-cracke comes but to breake out now.
    Soft. The time I waited, and I waited long,
Vntill *Philotas*, with fome other Lords,
Depart the Prefence, and as I conceiu'd,
I neuer faw the King in better mood,   •
Nor yet *Philotas* euer in more grace :   1190
Can fuch ftormes grow, and yet no clouds appeare ?
    Att. Yea, court ftormes grow, when fkies there feeme
It was about the deepeft of the night,   [moft cleare.
The blackeft houre of darkneffe and of fleepe,
When, with fome other Lords, comes *Craterus*,
Falles downe before the King, intreates, implores,
Coniures his Grace, as euer he would looke
To faue his perfon and the State from fpoile,
Now to preuent *Philotas* pra&tifes ;
Whom they had plainly found to be the man   1200.
Had plotted the deftru&tion of them all.

.The King would faine haue put them off to time
And farther day, till better proofes were knowne :
Which they perceiuing, preſt him ſtill the more,
And reinforc'd his dangers and their owne ;
And neuer left him till they had obtain'd
Commiſſion t'apprehend *Philotas* ſtreight.
 Now, to make feare looke with more hideous face,
Or els, but to beget it out of forme,
And carefull preparations of diſtruſt ;   1210
About the Palace men in armour watch,
In armour men about the King attend ;
All paſſages and iſſues were forelayd
With horſe, t'interrupt what euer newes
Should hence breake out into *Parmenios* campe.
I, with three hundred men in armour charg'd,
Had warrant to attach and to commit
The perſon of *Philotas* preſently :
And comming to his lodging where he lay,
Found him imburied in the ſoundeſt ſleepe   1220
That euer man could be ; where neither noyſe
Of clattering weapons, or our ruſhing in
With rude and trampling rumour, could diſſolue
The heauy humours of that drowſie brow ;
Which held perhaps his fences now more faſt,
As loth to leaue, becauſe it was the laſt.
 Soſt. Attaras, what can treaſon ſleepe ſo found ?
Will that lowd hand of Horror that ſtill beats
Vpon the guilty conſcience of diſtruſt
Permit it t'haue ſo reſolute a reſt ?   1230
 Att. I cannot tell : but thus we found him there,
Nor could we (I aſſure you) waken him,
Till thrice I call'd him by his name, and thrice

Had fhooke him hard ; and then at length he wakes :
And looking on me with a fetled cheere,
Deare friend *Attaras*, what's the newes ? (fayd he)
What vp fo foone, to haften the remoue,
Or raif'd by fome alarme or fome diftruft ?
I told him, that the King had fome diftruft :
VVhy, what will *Nabarzanes* play (fayth he)   1240
The villaine with the King, as he hath done
Already with his miferable Lord ?
I feeing he would not or did not vnderftand
His owne diftreffe, told him the charge I had :
Wherewith he rofe, and rifing vf'd thefe words ;
O *Alexander* ! now I fee my foes
Haue got aboue thy goodneffe, and preuail'd
Againft my innocency and thy word.
And as we then inchain'd and fettred him,
Looking on that bafe furniture of fhame ;   1250
Poore body (fayd he) hath fo many alarme
Raif'd thee to blood and danger from thy reft,
T'inueft thee with this armour now at laft ?
Is this the feruice I am call'd to now ?
    But we, that were not to attend his plaints,
Couering his head with a difgracefull weed,
Tooke and conuai'd him fuddenly to ward ;
From whence he fhalbe inftantly brought forth,
Here to b'arraign'd before the King ; who fits
(According to the Macedonian vfe)   1260
In cafes capitall, himfelfe as Iudge.
    Soft. Well, then I fee, who are fo high aboue,
Are neere to lightning, that are neere to *Ioue.*

l. 1257, 'to warde' of [1] and 'to ward' of [2] correct ‑ 'toward' of '23.

Scena Secvnda.

Alexander, with all his Councell, the dead body of Dymnus, the Reuealers of the confpiracy, Philotas.

THe hainous treafon of fome few had like
    T'haue rent me from you, worthy fouldiers ;
But by the mercy of th'immortall Gods
I liue, and ioy your fight, your reuerend fight ;   1270
Which makes me more t'abhor thofe paricides,
Not for mine owne refpect, but for the wrong
You had receiued, if their defigne had ftood ;
Since I defire but life to do you good.
    But how will you be mou'd, when you fhall know
Who were the men that did attempt this fhame !
When I fhall fhow that which I grieue to fhow,
And name fuch, as would God I could not name !
But that the foulneffe of their practife now
Blots out all memory of what they were :   1280
And though I would fuppreffe them, yet I know
This fhame of theirs will neuer but appeare.
Parmenio is the man ; a man (you fee)
Bound by fo many merits both to me
And to my father, and our ancient friend ;
A man of yeeres, experience, grauity ;
Whofe wicked minifter *Philotas* is ;
Who here *Dimetrius*, *Luculaus*, and
This *Dymnus*, whofe dead body heere you fee,
With others, hath fuborn'd to flaughter me.   1290
    And here comes *Metron* with *Nichomacus*,
To whom this murdred wretch at firft reueal'd
The proiect of this whole confpiracy,
T'auere as much as was difclof'd to him.

Nichomacus, Looke heere, aduife thee well,
What, doft thou know this man that here lies dead ?
   Nic. My Souereigne Lord, I know him very well :
It is one *Dymnus*, who did three dayes fince
Bewray to me a treafon practifèd
By him and others, to haue flaine your Grace.   1300
   Alex. Where or by whom, or when did he report,
This wicked act fhould be accomplifhèd ?
   Nic. He fayd, within three daies your Maiefty
Should be within your chamber murdered
By fpeciall men of the Nobility ;
Of whom he many nam'd, and they were thefe :
Loceus, Demetrius, and *Archelopis*,
Nicanor, and *Amintas, Luculens*,
Droceas, with *Aphebœtus*, and himfelfe.
   Mac. Thus much his brother *Ceballinus* did   1310
Reueale to me from out this youths report.
   Ceb. And fo much, with the circumftance of all,
Did I vnto *Philotas* intimate.
   Alex. Then, what hath been his mind, who did
The information of fo foule a traine,   [fuppreffe
Your felues, my worthy fouldiers, well may geffe,
Which *Dymnus* death declares not to be vaine.
Poore *Ceballinus* not a moment ftayes
To redifcharge himfelfe of fuch a weight ;
Philotas careleffe, feareleffe, nothing weighes,   1320
Nor ought reueales.   His filence fhewes deceit,
And tels he was content it fhould be done :
Which, though he were no party, makes him one.
   For he that knew vpon what pow'r he ftood,
And faw his fathers greatneffe and his owne,

l. 1308, '23 mifprints ' Amentas,' as before. ' Amyntas ' in ¹, ' Amintas ' in ².

Saw nothing in the way, which now withſtood
His vaſt deſires, but only this my crowne ;
Which in reſpeᶜt that I am iſſuleſſe,
ʹHe thinkes the rather eaſie to bʹattainʹd.
But yet *Philotas* is deceiuʹd in this ;   1330
I haue who ſhall inherit all I gainʹd.
In you I haue both children, kindred, friends ;
You are the heires of all my purchaſes,
And whilʹſt you liue I am not iſſuleſſe.

    And that theſe are not ſhadowes of my feares
(For I feare nought but want of enemies)
See what this intercepted letter beares,
And how *Parmenio* doth his ſonnes aduiſe.
This ſhewes their ends. Hold, reade it *Craterus.*
Crat. reads it. My ſonnes, firſt haue a ſpeciall care vnto
                    your ſelues,   1340
Then vnto thoſe which do depend on you :
So ſhall you do what you intend to do.

    Alex. See but how cloſe he writes, that if theſe lines
Should come vnto his ſonnes, as they are ſent,
They might incourage them in their deſignes ;
If enterprizʹd, might mocke the ignorant.
But now you ſee what was the thing was meant,
ʹYou ſee the fathers care, the ſonnes intent.

    And what if he, as a conſpirator,
Was not by *Dymnus* namʹd among the reſt ?   ·1350
That ſhewes not his innocency, but his powʹr,
Whom they account too great to be ſuppreſt,
And rather will accuſe themſelues than him :
For that whilʹſt he ſhall liue, thereʹs hope for them.
And how hʹhath borne himſelfe in priuate ſort,
I will not ſtand to vrge, itʹs too well knowne ;

Nor what hath beene, his arrogant report,
T'imbafe my actions, and to brag his owne ;
Nor how he mockt my letter which I wrote :
To fhew him of the ftile beftow'd on me,   1360
By th'Oracle of *Ioue.*   Thefe things I thought
But weakneffes, and words of vanity,
(Yet words that read the vlcers of his heart)
Which I fuppreft ; and neuer ceaft to yeeld
The chiefe rewards of worth, and ftill compart
The beft degrees and honors of the field,
In hope to win his loue ; yet now at length,
There haue I danger where I lookt for ftrength ;
I would to God my blood had rather beene
Powr'd out, the offring of an enemy,   1370
Than practiz'd to be fhed by one of mine,
That one of mine fhould haue this infamy.
Haue I beene fo referu'd from feares, to fall
There where I ought not to haue fear'd at all !
Haue you fo oft aduif'd me to regard
The fafety which you faw me running from,
When with fome hote purfute I preffèd hard
My foes abroad ; to perifh thus at home !
   But now, that fafety only refts in you,
Which you fo oft haue wifht me looke vnto :   1380
And now vnto your bofomes muft I flye,
Without whofe will I will not wifh to liue :
And with your wils I cannot, 'leffe I giue
Due punifhment vnto this treachery.
   Amin. Attaras, bring the hatefull prifoner forth ;
This traytor, which hath fought t'vndoo vs all ;
To giue vs vp to flaugh[t]er, and to make
Our bloode a fcorne, here in this barbarous land ;

That none of vs fhould haue returnèd backe

Vnto our natiue country, to our wiues, 1390

Our aged parents, kindred, and our friends :

To make the body of this glorious hoft

A moft deformèd trunke without a head,

Without the life or foule to guide the fame.

    Cæn. O thou bafe traytor, impious paricide,

Who mak'ft me loath the blood that matcht with thine;

And if I might but haue my will, I vow,

Thou fhould'ft not die by other hand than mine.

    Alex. Fie, *Cænus,* what a barbarous courfe is this :

He firft muft to his accufation plead, 1400

And haue his triall, formall to our lawes ;

And let him make the beft of his bad caufe.

Philotas, here the Macedonians are,

To iudge your faﬅ, what language wilt thou vfe ?

    Phi. The Perfian language, if it pleafe your Grace :

For that, befide the Macedonians, here

Are many that will better vnderftand,

If I fhall vfe the fpeech your grace hath vf'd ;

Which was, I hold, vnto no other end,

But that the moft men here might vnderftand. 1410

    Alex. See how his natiue language he difdaines |

But let him fpeake at large, as he defires ;

So long as you remember he doth hate,

Befides the fpeech, our glory and the State. *Exit.*

    Phi. Blacke are the colours layd vpon the crime,

Wherewith my faith ftands charg'd, my worthy Lords ;

That as behind in fortune fo in time,

I come too late to cleere the fame with words :

My condemnation is gone out before

My innocency and my iuft defence ; 1420

And takes vp all your hearts, and leaues no doore
For mine excufe to haue an enterance ;
That deftitute of all compaffion, now,
Betwixt an vpright confcience of defart
And an vniuft difgrace, I know not how
To fatisfie the time, and mine owne heart.
Authority lookes with fo fterne an eye
Vpon this wofull bar, and muft haue ftill
Such an aduantage ouer mifery,
As that it will make good all that it will.   1430
   He who fhould onely iudge my caufe, is gone ;
And why he would not ftay, I do not fee,
Since when my caufe were heard, his pow'r alone
As well might then condemne as fet me free.
Nor can I by his abfence now be clear'd,
Whofe prefence hath condemn'd me thus vnheard.
And though the grieuance of a prifoners toong
May both fuperfluous and difgracefull feeme,
Which doth not fue, but fhewes the Iudge his wrong :
Yet pardon me, I muft not difefteeme   1440
My rightfull caufe for being defpif'd, nor muft
Forfake my felfe, though I am left of all. _
Feare cannot make my innocency vniuft
Vnto it felfe, to giue my truth the fall.
And I had rather (feeing how my fortune drawes)
My words fhould be deform`e`d than my caufe.
   I know that nothing is more delicate
Than is the fenfe and feeling of a State :
The clap, the bruit, the feare but of a hurt
In King's behalfs, thrufts with that violence   1450
The fubiećts will, to profecute report,
As they condemne ere they difcerne th'offence.

Eph. *Philotas,* you deceiue your felfe in this
That thinke to win compaffion and beliefe
B'impugning iuftice, and to make men geffe
We do you wrong out of our heat of griefe ;
Or that our place or paffion did lay more
On your misfortune, then your owne defert ;
Or haue not well difcern'd your fact before ;
Or would without due proofs your ftate fubuert.　1450
　Thefe are the vfuall theames of traytors tongues,
Who practife mifchiefs, and complaine of wrongs ;
Your treafons are too manifeftly knowne,
To mafke in other liuery then their owne.
　Crat. Thinke not, that we are fet to charge you here
With bare fufpitions, but with open fact,
And with a treafon that appeares as cleare
As is the fun, and know'n to be your act.
　Phi. What is this treafon? who accufes me?
　Crat. The proceffe of the whole confpiracy.　1460
　Phi. But where's the man that names me to be one?
　Crat. Here, this dead traytor fhewes you to be one
　Phi. How can he, dead, accufe me of the fame,
Whom, liuing, he nor did, nor yet could name ?
　Crat. But we can other teftimony fhow,
From thofe who were your chiefeft complices.
　Phi. I am not to b'adiudg'd in law, you know,
By teftimony, but by witneffes.
Let them be here produc'd vnto my face,
That can auouch m'a party in this cafe.
My Lords, and fellow Souldiers, if of thofe
Whom *Dymnus* nominated, any one

l. 1448, 'than ' ¹ : l. 1454, *ibid.* : l. 1468, ' *Non teftimonijs funt teftibus* '
(in margin).

Out of his tortures will a word difclofe
To fhew I was a party, I haue done.
Thinke not fo great a number euer will
Endure their torments, and themfelues accufe,
And leaue me out ; fince men in fuch a cafe, ftill
Will rather flander others than excufe.
Calamity malignant is, and he
That fuffers iuftly for his guiltineffe   1480
Eafes his owne affliction but to fee
Others tormented in the fame diftreffe.
And yet I feare not whatfoeuer they
By rackes and tortures can be forft to fay.
Had I beene one, would *Dymnus* haue conceal'd
My name, being held to be principall ?
Would he not for his glory haue reueal'd
The beft to him, to whom he muft tell all ?
Nay, if he falfly then had nam'd me one,
To grace himfelfe, muft I of force be one ?   1490
      Alas, if *Ceballinus* had not come to me,
And giuen me note of this confpiracy,
I had not ftood here now, but beene as free
From queftion, as I am [from] treachery :
That is the only cloud that thundereth
On my difgrace.   Which had I deem'd true,
Or could but haue diuin'd of *Dymnus* death,
Philotas had, my Lords, fat there with you.
My fault was, to haue beene too credulous :
Wherein I fhew'd my weakneffe, I confeffe.   1500
      Crat. Philotas, what, a Monarch, and confeffe
Your imperfections, and your weakneffe ?
      Phi. O *Craterus*, do not infult vpon calamity ;
It is a barberous grofneffe, to lay on

The weight of fcorne, where heauy mifery
Too much already weighs mens fortunes downe :
For if the caufe be ill I vndergo,
The law, and not reproch, muft make it fo.
   Cæn. There's no reproch can euer be too much
To lay on traytors, whofe deferts are fuch.   1510
   Phi. Men vfe the moft reproches, where they feare
The caufe will better proue than they defire.
   Cæn. But fir, a traytors caufe that is fo cleare
As this of yours, will neuer neede that feare.
   Phi. I am no traytor, but fufpected one
For not beleeuing a confpiracy :
And meere fufpect, by law, condemneth none ;
They are approuèd facts for which men die.
   Crat. The law, in treafons, doth the will correct
With like feuereneffe as it doth th'effect :   1520
Th'affection is the effence of th'offence ;
The execution only but the accidence ;
To haue but will'd it, is to haue done the fame.
   Phi. I did not erre in will, but in beliefe :
And if that be a traytor, then am I the chiefe.
   Crat. Yea, but your will made your beliefe confent
To hide the practife till th'accomplifhment.
   Phi. Beliefe turns not by motions of our will,
And it was but the euent that made that ill.
Some facts men may excufe, though not defend,   1530
Where will and fortune haue a diuers end.
Th'example of my father made me feare
To be too forward to relate things heard ;
Who writing to the King, wifht him forbeare
The potion his Phyfitian had prepar'd :

l. 1535, ' potions ' for ' portions ' (misprint).

1490

For that he heard *Darius* tempted had
His faith, with many talents, to be vntrue :
And yet his drugs in th'end not prouing bad,
Did make my fathers care feeme more than due :
For oft, by an vntimely diligence,   1540
A bufie faith may giue a Prince offence.
So that, what fhall we do ? If we reueale
We are defpif'd ; fufpeĉted if conceale.
And as for this, where euer now thou be,
O *Alexander*, thou haft pardon'd me :
Thou haft already giuen me thy hand,
The earneft of thy reconcilèd heart ;
And therefore now O let thy goodneffe ftand
Vnto thy word, and be thou as thou wert.
If thou beleeu'dft me, then I am abfolu'd ;   1550
If pardon'd me, my fetters are diffolu'd.
What haue I els deferu'd fince yefter night ;
When at thy table I fuch grace did find ?
What hainous crime hath fince beene brought to light,
To wrong my faith, and to diuert thy mind ?   •
That from a reftfull, quiet, moft profound
Sleeping, in my misfortunes made fecure
Both by thy hand and by a confcience found,
I muft be wak't for gyues, for robes impure ;
For all difgrace that on me wrath could lay ;   1560
And fee the worft of fhame, ere I faw day ;
When I leaft thought that others cruelty
Should haue wrought more than thine owne clemency ?
    Crat. Philotas, whatfoeuer gloffe you lay
Vpon your rotten caufe, it is in vaine :
Your pride, your carriage, euer did bewray

1. 1559, 'gyues' ¹, ², for '23 'giues'—accepted.

Your difcontent, your malice, and difdaine :
You cannot palliat mifchiefe, but it will
Th'row all the faireft couerings of deceit
Be alwayes feene.   We know thofe ftreames of ill 1570
Flow'd from that head that fed them with conceit.
You fofter malecontents ; you entertaine
All humors ; you all factions muft embrace ;
You vaunt your owne exployts ; and you difdaine
The Kings proceedings, and his ftile difgrace ;
You promife mountaines, and you draw men on,
With hopes of greater good than hath been feene ;
You bragg'd of late, that fomething would be done
Whereby your Concubine fhould be a Queene.
And now we fee the thing that fhould be done;   1580
But, God be praif'd, we fee you firft vndone.
    Phi. Ah, do not make my nature if it had
So pliable a fterne of difpofition,
To turne to euery kindneffe, to be bad,
For doing good to men of all condition.
Make not your charity to interpret all
Is done for fauour, to be done for fhow,
And that we, in our bounties prodigall,
Vpon our ends, not on mens needs beftow.
Let not my one dayes errour make you tell,   1590
That all my life-time I did neuer well ;
And that becaufe this falles out to be ill,
That what I did, did tend vnto this ill.
It is vniuft to ioyne t'a prefent fact
More of time paft, than it hath euer had
Before to do withall, as if it lackt
Sufficient matter els to make it bad.
I do confeffe indeed I wrote fomething

Againſt this title of the ſonne of *Ioue*,
And that not of the King, but to the King   1600
I freely vſ'd theſe words out of my loue :
And thereby hath that dangerous liberty
Of ſpeaking truth, with truſt on former grace,
Betrai'd my meaning vnto enmity,
And draw'n an argument of my diſgrace :
So that I ſee, though I ſpeake what I ought,
It was not in that manner as I ought.
　And God forbid, that euer ſouldiers words
Should be made liable vnto miſdeeds ;
When fainting in their march, tir'd in the fight,   1610
Sicke in their tent, ſtopping their wounds that bleeds ;
Or haut and iolly after conqueſt got,
They ſhall out of their heate vſe words vnkinde ;
Their deeds deſerue, to haue them rather thought
The paſſion of the ſeaſon, than their minde :
For ſouldiers ioy, or wrath, is meaſureleſſe,
Rapt with an inſtant motion : and we blame,
We hate, we prayſe, we pity in exceſſe,
According as our preſent paſſions frame.
Sometimes to paſſe the Ocean we would faine,   1620
Sometimes to other worlds, and ſometimes ſlacke
And idle, with our conqueſts, entertaine
A ſullen humor of returning backe :
All which conceits one trumpets ſound doth end,
And each man running to his ranke doth loſe
What in our tents diſlikt vs, and we ſpend
All that conceiuèd wrath vpon our foes.
And words, if they proceede of leuity,
Are to be ſcorn'd, of madneſſe, pitied ;

　　　l. 1612, 'haut' of ¹, ², = proud, corrects '23 'haue.'

If out of malice or of iniury, 1630
To be remifs'd or vnacknowledgèd :
For of themfelues, they vanifh by difdaine,
But if purfude, they will be thought not vaine.

 Crat. But words, according to the perfon, way ;
If his defignes are haynous, fo are they :
They are the tinder of fedition ftill,
Wherewith you kindle fires, inflame mens will.

 Phi. Craterus, you haue th'aduantage of the day
The law is yours, to fay what you will fay :
And yet doth all your gloffe but beare the fence 1640
Only of my misfortune, not offence.
Had I pretended mifchiefe to the King,
Could not I haue effeɛted it without
Dymnus ? Did not my free acceffe bring
Continuall meanes t'haue brought the fame about ?
Was not I, fince I heard the thing difcride,
Alone, and arm'd, in priuate with his Grace ?
What hindred me, that then I had not tride
T'haue done that mifchiefe, hauing time and place ?

 Crat. Philotas, euen the Prouidence aboue, 1650
Proteɛtreffe of the facred ftate of Kings ;
That neuer fuffers treachery to haue
Good counfell ; neuer in this cafe but brings
Confufion to the aɛtors ; did vndo
Your hearts in what you went about to do.

 Phi. But yet defpaire, we fee, doth thruft men on,
Se'ing no way els, t'vndo ere be vndon.

 Crat. That fame defpaire doth likewife let me[n] fall
In that amaze, they can do nought at all.

 Phi. Well, well, my Lords, my feruice hath made
   know'n 1660

III.   I I

The faith I owe my Souereigne, and the State ;
Philotas forwardneffe hath euer fhow'n
Vnto all nations, at how high a rate
I priz'd my King, and at how low my blood,
To do him honour and my country good.   [are ;
   Eph. We blame not what y'haue been, but what you
We accufe not here your valour, but your fact ;
Not to haue beene a leader in the warre,
But an ill fubiect in a wicked act ;
Although we know, thruft rather with the loue   1670
Of your owne glory, than with duty lead,
You haue done much ; yet all your courfes proue
You tide ftill your atchieuements to the head
Of your owne honour, when it hath beene meet
You had them layd downe at your Souereignes feet.
God giues to Kings the honour to command,
To fubiects, all their glory to obay ;
Who ought in time of war as rampiers ftand,
In peace as th'ornaments of State aray.
The King hath recompens'd your feruices   1680
With better loue than you fhew thankfulneffe.
By grace he made you greater than you were
By nature, you receiu'd that which he was not tide
To giue to you : his gift was far more deere
Than all you did, in making you imployd.
But fay your feruice hath deferu'd it all,
This one offence hath made it odious all :
And therefore here in vaine you vfe that meane,
To plead for life, which you haue cancell'd cleane.
   Phi. My Lord, you far miftake me, if you deeme
I plead for life ; that poore weake blaft of breath, 1690

     l. 1683—'23 erroneously inserts 'he' after 'nature.'

From which fo oft I ran with light efteeme,
And fo well haue acquainted me with death :
No, no, my Lords, it is not that I feare ;
It is mine honour that I feeke to cleare ;
And which, if my difgracèd caufe would let
The language of my heart be vnderftood,
Is all which I haue euer fought to get,
And which,—O leaue me now, and take my blood ;
Let not your enuy go beyond the bound   1700
Of what you feeke : my life ftands in your way ;
That is your ayme, take it ; and do not wound
My reputation with that wrong, I pray.
If I muft needs be made the facrifice
Of enuy, and that no oblation will
The wrath of Kings, but only blood, fuffice,
Yet let me haue fome thing left that is not ill.
Is there no way to get vnto our liues,
But firft to haue our honour ouerthrowne ?
Alas, though grace of Kings all greatneffe giues, 1710
It cannot giue vs vertue, that's our owne.
Though all be theirs our hearts and hands can do,
Yet that by which we do is only ours.
The trophees that our blood erects vnto
Their memory, to glorifie their pow'rs,
Let them enioy : yet onely to haue done
Worthy of grace, let not that be vndone ;
Let that high fwelling riuer of their fame
Leaue humble ftreames, that feed them yet their name.
    O my deare father, didft thou bring that fpirit, 1720
Thofe hands of vallour, that fo much haue done
In this great worke of *Afia*, this to merit,

l. 1692, ' oft ' from ¹,², is dropped by '23.

By doing worthily, to be vndone ?
And haft thou made this purchafe of thy fword,
To get fo great an Empire for thy Lord,
And fo difgrac'd a graue for thee and thine,
T'extinguifh by thy feruice all thy line ?
　One of thy fonnes by being too valourous,
But fiue dayes fince,—yet O well,—loft his breath ;
Thy dear *Nicanor* th'halfe arch of thy houfe;　　1730
And here now the other at the barre of death,
Stands ouercharg'd with wrath in far worfe cafe
And is to be confounded with difgrace ;
Thy felfe muft giue th'acquitance of thy blood,
For others debts, to whom thou haft done good :
Which, if they would a little time afford,
Death would haue taken it without a fword.
Such the rewards of great imployments are,
Hate killes in peace, whom Fortune fpares in warre.
And this is that high grace of Kings we feeke,　　1740
Whofe fauour and whofe wrath confumes alike.
　Eph. Lo here the mifery of Kings, whofe caufe
How euer iuft it be, how euer ftrong,
Yet in refpect they may, their greatneffe drawes
The world to thinke they euer do the wrong.
But this foule fact of yours, you ftand vpon
Philotas, fhall, befide th'apparency
Which all the world fees plaine, ere we haue done
By your owne mouth be made to fatisfie
The moft ftiffe partialift that will not fee.　　1750
　Phi. My mouth will neuer proue fo falfe (I truft)
Vnto my heart, to fhew it felfe vniuft ;
And what I here do fpeake, I know, my Lords ,
I fpeake with mine owne mouth, but other where

What may be fayd, I fay, may be the words
Not of my breath, but fame that oft doth erre ;
Let th'oracle of *Ammon* be inquir'd
About this faƈt ; who, if it fhall be true,
Will neuer fuffer thofe who haue confpir'd
Againſt *Ioues* fonne, t'efcape without their due,   1760
But will reueale the truth : or if this fhall
Not feeme conuenient, why then lay on all
The tortures that may force a tongue to tell
The fecret'ſt thought that could imagine ill.

 Bel. What need we fend to know more than we know ?
That were to giue you time to acquant your friends
With your eſtate, till fome combuſtion grow
Within the campe, to haſten on your ends,
And that the gold and all the treafury
Committed to your fathers cuſtody   1770
In *Medea*, now might arme his defp'rat troups
To come vpon vs, and to cut our throats.
What, fhall we aſke of *Ioue*, that which he hath
Reueal'd already ?   But let's fend to giue
Thanks, that by him the King hath fcap't the wrath
Of thee, difloyall traytor, and doth liue.

 Guar. Let's teàre the wretch in pieces, let vs rend
With our owne hands the traitrous paricide.

 Alex. Peace, *Belon*, filence, louing fouldiers :
You fee, my Lords, out of your iudgements graue,   1780
That all excufes fickly colours haue,
And he that hath thus falfe and faithleffe beene
Muſt find out other gods and other men
Whom to forfweare, and whom he may deceiue ;
No words of his can make vs more beleeue

  l. 1778, ' traitrous ' of ¹ and 'traytrous ' ² corrects '23 ' traytors.'

His impudence : and therefore, feeing tis late,
We, till morning, do difmiffe the Court.

ACTVS. V. CHORVS : Græcian *and* Perſian.

Perſian.

WEll, then I fee there is fmall difference   1790
     Betwixt your ſtate and ours, you ciuill **Greeks,**
You great contriuers of free gouernments;
Whoſe ſkill the world from out all countries ſeeks.
Thoſe whom you call your Kings, are but the fame
As are our Souereigne tyrants of the Eaſt ;
I fee they only differ but in name,
The effeƈts they ſhew, agree, or neere at leaſt.
Your great men here, as our great Satrapaes,
I fee layd proſtrate are with baſeſt ſhame,
Vpon the leaſt ſuſpeƈt or iealouſies   1800
Your Kings conceiue, or others enuies frame ;
Only herein they differ, That your prince
Proceeds by forme of law t'effeƈt his end ;
Our Perſian Monarch makes his frowne conuince
The ſtrongeſt truth : his ſword the proceſſe ends
With preſent death, and makes no more ado :
He neuer ſtands to giue a gloſſe vnto
His violence, to make it to appeare
In other hew than that it ought to beare,
Wherein plaine dealing beſt his courſe commends : 1810
For more h'offends who by the law offends.
What need hath Alexander *ſo to ſtriue*
By all theſe ſhewes of forme, to find this man
Guilty of treaſon, when he doth contriue
To haue him ſo adiudg'd? Do what he can,

He muſt not be acquit, though he be cleere,
Th'offender, not th'offence, is puniſht heere,
And what auailes the fore-condemn'd to ſpeake?
How euer ſtrong his cauſe, his ſtate is weake.

    Græ. *Ah, but it ſatisfies the world, and we*   1820
Thinke that well done which done by law we ſee.

    Per. *And yet your law ſerues but your priuate ends,*
And to the compaſſe of your pow'r extends:
But is it for the maieſty of Kings,
To ſit in iudgement thus themſelues, with you?

    Græ. *To do men iuſtice, is the thing that brings*
The greateſt maieſty on earth to Kings.

    Per. *That, by their ſubalternate miniſters*
May be perform'd as well, and with more grace:
For, to command it to be done, infers   1830
More glory than to do. It doth imbaſe
Th'opinion of a pow'r t'invulgar ſo
That ſacred preſence, which ſhould neuer go,
Neuer be ſeene, but euen as gods, below,
Like to our Perſian King in glorious ſhow;
And who, as ſtarres affixèd to their ſpheare,
May not deſcend to be from what they are.

    Græ. *Where Kings are ſo like gods, there ſubiects are*
          not men.

    Per. *Your king begins this courſe, and what will you*
          be then?

    Græ. *Indeed ſince proſperous fortune gaue the raine*
To head-ſtrong pow'r and luſt, I muſt confeſſe,   1841
We Græcians haue loſt deeply by our gaine,
And this our greatneſſe makes vs much the leſſe:
For by th'acceſſion of theſe mighty States,
Which Alexander *wonderouſly hath got,*

He hath forgot himſelfe and vs, and rates
His ſtate aboue mankind, and ours at nought.
This hath thy pompe (O feeble Aſia) *wrought ;*
Thy baſe adorings hath transform'd the King
Into that ſhape of pɾide, as he is brought   1850
Out of his wits, out of acknowledging
From whence the glory of his greatneſſe ſprings,
And that it was our ſwords that wrought theſe things.
How well were we within the narrow bounds
Of our ſufficient yeelding Macedon,
Before our Kings inlarg'd them with our wounds,
And made theſe ſallies of ambition !
Before they came to giue the regall law
To thoſe free States which kept their crownes in aw !
They by theſe large dominions are made more,   1860
But we become far weaker than before.
What get we now by winning, but wide minds
And weary bodies, with th'expence of blood ?
What ſhould ill do, ſince happy fortune findes
But miſery, and is not good though good ?
Action begets ſtill action, and retaines
Our hopes beyond our wiſhes, drawing on
A neuer ending circle of our paines,
That makes vs not haue done, when we haue done.
What can giue bounds to Alexanders *ends,*   1870
Who counts the world but ſmall, that call's him great ?
And his deſires beyond his pray diſtends,
Like beaſts, that murder more than they can eat !
When ſhall we looke his trauels will be done,
That 'tends beyond the Ocean and the Sunne ?
What diſcontentments will there ſtill ariſe
In ſuch a Campe of Kings, to inter-ſhocke

Each others greatneſſe ; and what mutinies
Will put him from his comforts, and will mocke
His hopes, and neuer ſuffer him to haue 1880
That which he hath of all which Fortune gaue ?
And from Philotas *blood (O worthy man)*
Whoſe body now rent on the torture lies,
Will flow that vaine of freſh conſpiracies,
As ouerflow him will, do what he can :
For cruelty doth not imbetter men,
But them more wary makes than they haue been.

    Per. *Are not your great men free from tortures then*
Muſt they be likewiſe rackt as other men ?

    Græ. *Treaſon affoords a priuiledge to none ;* 1890
Who like offends hath puniſhment all one.

S C E N A II. *Polidamas, Soſtratus.*

Polidamas.

FRiend *Soſtratus*, come, haue you euer know'n
    Such a diſtraᴄted face of Court, as now ?
Such a diſtruſtfull eye, as men are grow'n
To feare themſelues, and all ; and do not know
Where is the ſide that ſhakes not ; who lookes beſt
In this foule day, th'oppreſſor or th'oppreſt ?
What poſting, what diſpatches, what aduice ! 2000
What ſearch, what running, what diſcoueries !
What rumors, what ſuggeſtions, what deuice
To cleere the King, pleaſe people, hold the wife,
Re[ſ]t[r]aine the rude, cruſh the fuſpeᴄted ſort
At vnawares, ere they diſcerne th'are hurt !
So much the fall of ſuch a weighty Peere
Doth ſhake the State, and with him tumble downe

All whom his beames of fauours did vpbeare,
All who to reſt vpon his baſe were knowne :
And none, that did but touch vpon his loue,   2010
Are free from feare to periſh with his loue.
My ſelf (whom all the world haue know'n t'imbrace
Parmenio in th'intireneſſe of my heart,
And euer in all battels, euery chace
Of danger, fought ſtill next him on that part)
Was feazed on this laſt night, late in my bed
And brought vnto the preſence of the King,
To pay (I thought) the tribute of my head :
But O 'twas for a more abhorrèd thing !
I muſt redeeme my danger with the bloôd   2020
Of this deare friend, this deare *Parmenio's* blood ;
His life muſt pay for mine, theſe hands muſt gore
That worthy heart for whom they fought before.
    Soſt. What, hath the King commanded ſuch a deed,
To make the hearts of all his ſubieɛts bleed ?
Muſt that old worthy man *Parmenio* die ?
    Pol. O *Soſtratus*, he hath his doome to die,
And we muſt yeeld vnto neceſlity.
For comming to the King, and there receiu'd
With vnexpeɛted grace, he thus began :   2030
Polidamas, we both haue beene deceiu'd,
In holding friendſhip with that faithleſſe man
Parmenio, who, for all his glozing mine,
Thou ſeeſt hath ſought to cut my throat and thine ;
And thou muſt worke reuenge for thee and me :
And therefore haſt to *Media* ſpeedily,
Take theſe two letters here, the one from me
Vnto my ſure and truſty ſeruants there,

l. 2023, ' for ' of ¹, ² corrects '23 ʳ' from.'

The other fignèd with *Philotas* feale,
As if the fame t'his father written were: 2040
Carry them both, effeĉt what I haue fayd ;
The one will giue th'acceffe, the other ayd.
I tooke the letters, vow'd t'effeĉt the fame :
And here I go the inftrument of fhame.

    Soft. But will you charge your honor with this
        fhame ?

    Pol. I muft, or be vndone, with all my name :
For I haue left all th'adamantine ties
Of blopd and nature, that can hold a heart
Chain'd to the wor[l]d ; my brethren and allies,
The hoftages to caution for my part :   2050
And for their liues muft I difhonour mine ;
Els fhould the King rather haue turn'd this fword
Vpon my heart, than forft it impioufly,
(Hauing done all faire feruice to his Lord,
Now to be imploy'd in this foule villany).

    Thus muft we do who are inthrall'd to Kings,
    Whether they will iuft or vnlawfull things.
But now *Parmenio* ; O, me thinkes I fee
Thee walking in th'artificiall groue
Of pleafant *Sufis*, when I come to thee,   2060
And thou remembring all our ancient loue,
Haftes to imbrace me, faying, O my friend,
My deare *Polidamas*, welcome my friend :
Well art thou come, that we may fit and chat
Of all the old aduentures we haue run.
Tis long *Polidamas* fince we two met ;
How doth my fouereigne Lord, how doth my fon ?
When I vile wretch, whil'ft m'anfwere he attends
With this hand giue the letter ; this hand ends

His fpeaking ioy, and ftabb's him to the heart.   2070
And thus *Parmenio* thou rewarded art
For all thy feruice : thou that didft agree
For *Alexander* to kill *Attalus,*
For *Alexander* I muft now kill thee.
Such are the iudgements of the heauenly pow'rs :
We others ruines worke, and others ours.
 Cho. P. Why this is right, now *Alexander* takes
The courfe of pow'r ; this is a Perfian tricke.
This is our way, here publike triall makes
No doubtfull noife, but buries clamor quicke.   2080
 Græ. Indeed now *Perfia* hath no caufe to rue,
For you haue vs vndone, who vndid you.

NVNCIVS.

*T*His *worke is done, the fad Cataſtrophe*
 Of this great aċt of blood is finiſht now,
Philotas *ended hath the Tragedy.*
 Cho. *Now my good friend, I pray thee tell vs how.*
 Nun. *As willing to relate, as you to heare :*
A full-charg'd heart is glad to find an eare.
 The Councell being difmifs'd from hence, and gone, 2090
Still Craterus *plies the King, ſtill in his eare,*
Still whiſpering to him priuatly alone,
Vrging (it ſeem'd) a quicke difpatch of feare :
For they who ſpeake but priuatly to Kings,
Do feldome ſpeake the beſt and fitteſt things.
Some would haue had him forthwith ſton'd to death,
According to the Macedonian courfe,
But yet that would not fatisfie the breath
Of bufie rumour, but would argue force :

2070   ‘ *There muſt be ſome confeſſions m̀ade within,*   **2100**
      That muſt abroad more ſatisfaction win ;
      Craterus, *with* Cænus *and* Epheſtion
      Do mainly vrge to haue him torturèd ;
      Whereto the King conſents ; and thereupon
      They three are ſent to ſee't accompliſhèd.
      Racks, irons, fires, the griſely torturers
      Are hideouſly prepar'd before his face :
      Philotas *all vnmou'd, vnchang'd appeares,*
      As if he would deaths ouglieſt brow out-face,
2080   *And ſcorn'd the worſt of force, and aſkt them, Why* **2110**
      They ſtai'd to torture the Kings enemy ?
      Cho. *That part was acted well, God grant we heare*
      No worſe a Scene than this, and all goes cleare :
      So ſhould worth act, and they who dare to fight
      Againſt corrupted times, ſhould die vpright ;
      Such hearts Kings may diſſolue, but not defeat.
      A great man where he falles he ſhould lie great ;
      Whoſe ruine, like the ſacred carcaſes
      Of ſcattred Temples which ſtill reuerent lie,
      And the religious honour them no leſſe   **2120**
      Than if they ſtood with all their gallantry :
      But on with thy report.
      Nun. *Straight were hot irons appli'd to ſere his*
           ſleſh ;
      Then wreſting racks his comly body ſtraine ;
      Then iron whips, and then the racke afreſh ;
      Then fire againe, and then the whips againe ;
      Which he endures with ſo reſolu'd a looke,
      As if his mind were of another ſide
      Than of his body ; and his ſenſe forſooke
      The part of nature, to be wholy tide   **2130**

To honour ; that he would not once confent
So much as with a figh t'his punifhment.

    Cho. *Yet doth he like himfelfe, yet all is well,*
This argument no tyrant can refell ;
This plea of refolution winnes his caufe
More right than all, more admiration drawes :
For we loue nothing more, than to renowne
Men ftoutly miferable, highly downe.

    Nun. *But now ?*

    Cho. *We feare that But.   O, if he ought defcend,*
Leaue here, and let the Tragedy here end.   2141
Let not the leaft act now of his, at laft,
Marre all his act of life, and glory paft.

    Nun. *I muft tell all, and therefore giue me leaue :*
Swoll'n with raw tumors, vlcerèd with the ierks
Of iron whips, that flefh from bone had raz'd,
And no part free from wounds ; it erks
His foule to fee the houfe fo foule defaft,
Wherein his life had dwelt fo long time cleane,
And therefore craues he, they would now difmiffe • 2150
His grieuous tortures, and he would begin
To open all wherein h'had done amiffe.
Streight were his tortures ceaft : and after they
Had let him to recouer fenfe, he fayd,
Now Craterus, *Say what you will haue me fay :*
Wherewith, as if deluded or delaid,
Craterus *in wrath calles prefently againe*
To haue the tortures to be reapplied :
When, whatfoeuer fecret of his heart
Which had beene fore-conceiu'd but in a thought,   2160
What friend foeuer had but tooke his part

                    l. **2143**, ' glories ' ¹, ².

In common loue h'accuf'd ; and fo forgot
Himfelfe, that now he was more forward to
Confeffe, than they to vrge him thereunto ;
Whether affliction had his fpirits vndone,
Or feeing, to hide or vtter, all was one ;
Both wayes lay death : and therefore he would vie
Now to be fure to fay enough to die ;
And then began his fortunes to deplore,
Humbly befought them whom he fcorn'd before ;   2170
That Alexander *(where he ftood, behind*
A Trauers, out of fight) was heard to fpeake :
   I neuer thought, a man that had a mind
   T'attempt fo much, had had a heart fo weake !
   There he confeft, that one Hegelochus,
When firft the King proclaim'd himfelfe Ioues *fonne,*
Incens'd his fathers heart againft him thus,
By telling him, That now we were vndone,
If we endur'd, that he, which did difdaine
To haue beene Philips *fonne, fhould liue and raigne.*
He that aboue the ftate of man will ftraine   2181
His ftile, and will not be that which we are,
Not only vs contemnes, but doth difdaine
The gods themfelues, with whom he would compare.
We haue loft Alexander, *loft (faid he)*
The King, and fall'n on pride and vanity ;
And we haue made a god of our owne blood,
That glorifies himfelfe, neglects our good,
Intolerable is this impious deed
To gods, whom he would match, to men he would exceed.
   Thus hauing ouer night Hegelochus,   2191
Difcourf'd, my father fends next day
For me to heare the fame : and there to vs

All he had fayd to him he made him refay,
Suppofing, out of wine, the night before,
He might but idly raue. When he againe,
Far more inrag'd, in heat and paffion more,
Vrg'd vs to cleere the State of fuch a ftaine ;
Coniur'd vs to redeeme the Common-weale,
And do like men, or els as men conceale.   2200
      Parmenio *thought, whil'ft yet* Darius *ftood,*
This courfe was out of feafon, and thereby
Th'extinguifhing of Alexanders *blood*
Would not profit vs, but th'others pow'rs
Might make all th'Orient and all Afia *ours.*
That courfe we lik't, to that our counfell ftands,
Thereto we tide our oaths and gaue our hands.
And as for this, he faid, for Dymnus *plot,*
Though he were cleere, yet now he cleer'd him not.
And yet the force of racks at laft could do   2210
So much with him, as he confeft that too,
And fayd, that fearing Bactra *would detaine*
The King too long, he haft'ned on his ends,
Left that his father, Lord of fuch a traine
And fuch a wealth, on whom the whole depends,
Should, being agèd, by his death preuent
Thefe his defignes, and fruftrate his intent.
      Cho. *O would we had not heard his latter iarre :*
This all his former ftraines of worth doth marre.
Before this laft, his fpirits [ftout] commends,   2220
But now he is vnpitied of his friends.
      Nun. *Then was* Demetrius *likewife brought in place,*

l. 2214, In ¹, ², here, the following margin note is added—"Dum
inficiatus eft facinus crudeliter torqueri qui videbatur poft confeffionem
Philotas ne amicorum quidem mifericordiam meruit."

And put to torture, who denies the deed.
Philotas *he auerres it to his face ;*
Demetrius *ſtill denies.   Then he eſpide*
A youth, one Calin, *that was ſtanding by :*
Calin, *ſayd he, how long wilt thou abide*
Demetrius *vainly to auouch a lie ?*
   The youth, that neuer had beene nam'd before
In all his tortures gaue them cauſe to geſſe   2230
Philotas *car'd not now to vtter more*
Than had beene priuy to his practiſes.
And ſeeing they had as much as they deſir'd,
They with Demetrius *ſton'd him vnto death :*
And all whom Dymnus *nam'd to haue conſpir'd,*
With grieuous tortures now muſt loſe their breath :
And all that were alli'd, which could not flie,
Are in the hands of iuſtice now to die.
   Cho. *What, muſt the puniſhment arriue beyond*
Th'offence ? not with th'offender make an end ?   2240
   Nun. *They all muſt die who may be fear'd in time*
To be the heires vnto their kindreds crime.
All other puniſhments end with our breath,
But treaſon is purſu'd beyond our death.
   Cho. *The wrath of Kings doth ſeldome meaſure keepe ;*
Seeking to cure bad parts they lance too deepe.
When puniſhment, like lightning ſhould appeare,
To few mens hurt but vnto all mens feare.
Great elephants and lions murder leaſt ;
Th'ignoble beaſt is the moſt cruell beaſt.   2250
But all is well, if by the mighty fall
Of this great man, the King be ſafely freed :
But if this Hydra *of ambition ſhall*
Haue other heads to ſpring vp in his ſteed,

Then hath he made but way for them to rife,
Who will affault him with frefh treacheries.
The which may teach vs to obferue this ftraine,
To admire high hill's, but liue within the plaine.

The Apology.

THE wrong application, and mifconceiuing of this
Tragedy of *Philotas*, vrges me worthy Readers,
to anfwere for mine innocency, both in the choice of
the fubieft, and the motiues that long fince induced me
to write it ; which were firft the delight I tooke in the
Hiftory it felfe as it lay, and then the aptneffe, I faw it
had, to fall eafily into aft, without interlacing other
inuention then it properly yeelded in the owne circum-
ftances; which were fufficient for the worke, and a lawfull
reprefenting of a Tragedy.   Befides, aboue eight yeares
fince, meeting with my deare friend D. *Lateware*,
(whofe memory I reuerence) in his Lords Chamber and
mine, I told him the purpofe I had for *Philotas* ; who
fayd that himfelfe had written the fame argument,
and caufed it to be prefented in S^t. *Johns* Colledge in
Oxford; where as I after heard, it was worthily and
with great applaufe performed.   And though, I fayd,
he had therein preuented me, yet I would not defift,
whenfoeuer my Fortunes would giue me peace, / to try
what I could doe in the fame fubieft ; wherevnto both
hee, and who were prefent, incouraged me as to an

example worthy of note. And liuing in the Country,
about foure yeares fince, and neere halfe a yeare before
the late Tragedy of ours, (whereunto this is now moſt
ignorantly refembled) vnfortunately fell out heere in
England, I began the fame, and wrote three Acts there-
of,—as many to whom I then fhewed it can witneſſe,—
purpofing to haue had it prefented in Bath by certaine
Gentlemens fonnes, as a priuate recreation for the
Chriftmas, before the Shrouetide of that vnhappy dis-
order. But by reafon of fome occafion then falling 2290
out, and being called vpon by my Printer for a new
impreſſion of my workes, with fome additions to the
ciuill Warres, I intermitted this other fubiect. Which
now lying by mee, and driuen by neceſſity to make vfe
of my pen, and the Stage to bee the mouth of my
lines, which before were neuer heard to fpeake but in
filence, I thought the reprefenting fo true a Hiftory, in the
ancient forme of a Tragedy, could not but haue had an
vnreproueable paſſage with the time, and the better fort
of men ; feeing with what idle fictions, and groſſe follies, 2300
the Stage at this day abufed mens recreations. And
withall taking a fubiect that lay (as I thought), fo farre
from the time, and fo remote a ftranger from the climate
of our prefent courfes, I could not imagine that Enuy or
Ignorance could poffibly haue made it, to take any par-
ticular acquaintance with vs, but as it hath a generall
alliance to the frailty of greatneſſe, and the vfuall work-
ings of ambition, the perpetuall fubiects of bookes and
Tragedies.

And for *Philotas*, it is plaine, that his fathers great- 2310
neſſe opened firſt the way to *Alexanders* fufpition and
the enuy of the Nobility, and then his owne vanting

with difpifing the new title conferred by the Oracle
of *Ammon* vpon the King, begat the notion of his
diflike of the State ; and indeede *Alexanders* drawing
a pedegree from Heauen, with affuming the *Perfian*
magnificence, was the caufe that withdrew many, the
hearts of the Nobility and people from him ; and by
Philotas owne confeffion, was that which gaue a pur-
pofe to him and his father to haue fubuerted the King, 232
when he had eftablifhed *Afia*, and freed them from other
feares.

And this concealing of the treafon reuealed vnto
him, howfoeuer he excufed it, fhewed how much his
heart was alienated from his allegiancy. Which being
by *Epheftion* and *Craterus*, two the moft graue and
worthy Councellors of *Alexander* prouidently difcerned,
was profecuted in that manner, as became their neere-
neffe and deereneffe with their Lord and Maifter, and
fitting the fafety of the State, in the cafe of fo great an 233
afpirer : Who, had he not beene preuented (howfoeuer
popularly in the Army it might be otherwife deeméd)
he had no doubt turned the courfe of the gouernment
vpon his father or himfelfe, or elfe imbroyling it, made
it a monftrous body with many heads, as it afterwards
proued vpon the death of *Alexander*. For though the
affection of the multitude (whom he did mignion)—and
who, as I fayd, lookes ftill vpon mens fortunes not the
caufe,—difcerned not his ends; nor peraduenture him-
felfe, that knew not how large they might be, nor how 234
much his heart would hold, nor of what capacity would
be his ambition, if occafion were offered : Yet fome more
cleere-fighted, as if rayfed by a diuine prouidence to
put off that State, till the full period of diffolution,

(which after followed) was come, faw well, to how hie a
ftraine he had fet his hopes by his affeꞇed carriage.
And *Craterus*, who fo wifely purfued this bufineffe, is
deemed to haue beene one of the moft honeft men that
euer followed *Alexander* in all his aꞇions, and one that
was true vnto him euen after his death.   And for any 2350
refemblance, that thorough the ignorance of the Hiftory
may be applied to the late Earle of *Effex*, it can hold
in no proportion but only in his weakneffes, which I
would wifh all that loue his memory not to reuiue.
And for mine owne part, hauing beene perticularly
beholding to his bounty, I would to God his errors and
difobedience to his Souereigne, might be fo deepe
buried vnderneath the earth, and in fo low a tombe
from his other parts, that hee might neuer be
remembred   among   the   examples   of   2360
difloyalty   in   this   Kingdome,   or
paraleld   with   Forrèine   Con-
fpirators.

S A M.   D A N I E L.

FINIS.

l. 2268, 'we' I have corrected by 'which': l. 2314, 'and' by 'the,'
and also removed . (period) after 'Ammon': l. 2345, removed) after
'come' and placed it after 'followed': l. 2346, 'ftraine' for 'ftaine':
l. 2352, removed . (period) after '*Essex*': l. 2355, 'part' for 'parts': and
l. 2357, 'be' for 'by.'   See 'Memorial-Introduction—Biographical' in
Vol. I.; also 'Memorial-Introduction—Critical,' for further notices of
this 'Apology.'   G.

III.

THE VISION OF THE TWELVE GODDESSES.

1604.

NOTE.

A *unique* exemplar of the firſt edition of the present 'Shew' or Mask, is in the Bodleian (Malone 201), The following is the title-page :—

THE

VISION OF

the 12. Goddeſſes, preſented in a Maſke the 8. of Ianuary, at *Hampton* Court :

By the Queenes moſt excellent Maieſtie, and her Ladies.

LONDON

Printed by T. C. for *Simon Waterſon,* and are
to be ſold at his Sop [*sic*] in Pauls Church-
yard, at the Signe of the
Crowne. 1604.

I deemed it well personally to collate the text of the 4to of 1623 with the above. The result has been seven little corrections of misprints. I note these.—The 4to of 1623 (l. 40) repeats 'to *Proſerpina* riches, to *Macaria* felicitie,' and misspells ' Marcaria ' in the first ; l. 45 drops 'it' : l. 78 misreads 'the' for 'their' ; l. 94 drops 'with' ; l. 148 misprints 'lonatus' ; l. 166, 'protend' for 'portend' ; l. 187, 'wherein' for 'therein.' Opposite, as usual, is the title-page of 1623. The following is the title-page of a dainty volume which is the only modern reproduction of the 'Viſion' : " The Vision of the Twelve Goddesses, presented in a Maske the *eight of January, at Hampton* Court. By the Queenes most excellent Maiesty, *and her Ladies.* By Samuel Daniel.' The Introduction and Notes are excellent, albeit Mr. Law, its accomplished Editor, might have chosen better work of Daniel or others, to represent the Masks of the Jacobean era.· See 'Memorial-Introduction—Critical.' G.

THE
VISION OF
THE TVVELVE GOD-

deſſes, preſented in a Maske the
eight of January, at Hampton
Court.

By the Queenes moſt excellent Maieſty,
and her Ladies.

By Samvel Daniel.

LONDON,
Printed by Nicholas Okes,
for Simon Waterson.
1623.

THE
VISION OF
THE TVVELVE GODS

&c. presented in a Maske, the
... of January, at Hampton
Court.

By the Queenes most excellent Maiesty
and her Ladies.

By SAMVEL DANIEL

LONDON,
Printed by ...
...
1623.

TO THE RIGHT HONORABLE
the Lady *Lucie*, Counteſſe
of *Bedford*.

Madame.

N reſpeƈt of the vnmannerly preſump-
tion of an indiſcreet Printer, who
vvithout vvarrant hath divulged the
late ſhewe at Court, preſented the
eight of *Ianuary*, by the Queenes
Maieſtie and her Ladies; and the ſame 10
very diſorderly ſet forth : I thought
it not amiſſe, ſeeing it vvould other-
wiſe paſſe abroad, to the preiudice both of the Maſke
and the inuention, to deſcribe the whole forme thereof
in all points as it was then performed, and as the world
wel knows very worthily performed, by a moſt mag-
nificent Queene; whoſe heroicall ſpirit, and bounty onely
gaue it ſo faire an execution as it had. Seeing alſo
that theſe ornaments and delights of peace are in their
ſeaſon, as fit to entertaine the world, and deſerue to be 20
made memorable as well as the grauer aƈtions,—both of
them concurring to the decking and furniſhing of glory

and Maieftie, as the neceffary complements requifit for
State and Greatneffe.

And therefore firft I will deliuer the intent and fcope
of the proiect : Which was onely to prefent the figure
of thofe bleffings, with the wifh of their encreafe and
countinuance, which this mightie Kingdome now enioyes
by the benefite of his moft gracious Maieftie ; by whom
we haue this glory of peace, with the acceffion of fo 30
great ftate and power.   And to expreffe the fame, there
were deuifed twelue Goddeffes, vnder whofe Images
former times haue reprefented the feuerall gifts of
heauen, and erected Temples, Altars, and Figures vnto
them, as vnto diuine powers, in the fhape & name of
vvomen.   As vnto *Iuno* the Goddeffe of Empire and
regnorum præfedi, they attributed that bleffing of power.
To *Pallas*, Wifedome and Defence : to *Venus*, Loue
and Amity : to *Vefta*, Religion : to *Diana*, the gift of
Chaftitie : to *Proferpina* riches : to *Macaria*, felicitie : 40
to *Concordia*, the vnion of hearts : *Aftræa*, Iuftice :
Flora, the beauties of the earth : *Ceres* plenty : to
Tethis power by Sea.

And though thefe Images haue oftentimes diuers
fignifications, yet it being not our purpofe to reprefent
them, with all thofe curious and fuperfluous obferuations,
vve tooke them onely to ferue as Hierogliphicqs for our
prefent intention, according to fome one propertie that
fitted our occafion, without obferuing other their myfticall
interpretations ; wherein the authors themfelues are fo 50
irrigular and confufed, as the beft Mytheologers, vvho
will make fomwhat to feeme any thing, are fo vnfaithfull
to themfelues, as they haue left vs no certaine way at
all, but a tract of confufion, to take our courfe at aduen-

ture. And therefore owing no homage to their intricate
obferuations, vve vvere left at libertie to take no other
knowledge of them, then fitted our prefent purpofe, nor
were tied by any lawes of Heraldry to range them
otherwife in their precidencies, then they fell out to
ftand vvith the nature of the matter in hand. And 60
in thefe cafes it may vvell feeme *ingenerofum fapere
folum ex commentarijs quafi maiorum inuenta induftriæ
noftræ viam precluferit, quafi in nobis offæta fit vis naturæ,
nihil ex feparere,* or that there can be nothing done
authenticall, vnleffe vve obferue all the ftrict rules of
the booke.

And therefore we tooke their apteft reprefentations
that lay beft and eafieft for vs. And firft prefented the
Hieroglephick of Empire and Dominion, as the ground
and matter vvhereon this glory of State is built. Then 70
thofe bleffings and beauties that preferue and adorne
it : As armed policie, loue, Religion, Chaftitie, wealth,
happineffe, Concord, Iuftice, florifhing feafons, plenty :
and laftly power by fea, as to imbound and circle the
greatnes of dominion by land.

And to this purpofe vvere thefe Goddeffes thus pre-
fented in their proper and feuerall attyres, bringing in
their hands the particular figures of their power which
they gaue to the Temple of Peace, erected vpon foure
pillars, reprefenting the foure Vertues that fupported a 80
Globe of the earth.

Firft, *Iuno* in a fkie-colour mantle imbrodered with
gold, and figured with Peacocks feathers, wearing a
Crowne of gold on her head, prefents a Scepter.

2

Pallas (which was the perfon her Maieſtie chofe to reprefent) was attyred in a blew mantle, with a filuer imbrodery of all weapons and engines of war, with a helmet-dreſſing on her head, and prefents a Launce and Target.

3

Venus, in a Mantle of Doue-colour and filuer, imbrodred with Doues, prefented (in ſtead of her *Ceſtus*, the girdle of Amity) a Skarffe of diuers colours.

4

Veſta, in a white Mantle, imbrodred with gold-flames, with a dreſſing like a Nun, prefented a burning Lampe in one hand, and a Booke in the other.

5

Diana, in a greene Mantle, imbrodered with filuer halfe Moones, and a croiſſant of pearle on her head: prefents a Bow and a Quiuer.

6

Proferpina, in a blacke Mantle, imbrodered with gold-flames, with a crowne of gold on her head: prefented a Myne of gold-ore.

7

Macaria, the Goddeffe of Felicitie, in a Mantle of purple and filuer, imbrodered with the Figures of Plentie and Wifedome, (which concurre to the making of true happineffe) prefents a Cadaceum with the Figure of abundance.

Concordia, in a party coloured Mantle of Crimfon and White (the colours of *England* and *Scotland* ioyned) imbrodered with filuer, hands in hand, with a dreffing likewife of party coloured Rofes, a Branch whereof in a wreath or knot fhe prefented.

9

Aftræa, in a Mantle Crimfon, with a filuer imbrodery, Figuring the Sword and Balance (as the Characters of Iuftice) which fhe prefented.

10

Flora, in a Mantle of diuers colours, imbrodered with all forts of Flowers, prefents a Pot of Flowers.

11

Ceres, in Strawe colour and Siluer imbrodery, with eares of Corne, and a dreffing of the fame, prefents a Sickle.

12

Tethes, in a Mantle of Sea-greene, with a filuer imbrodery of Waues, and a dreffing of Reedes, prefents a Trident.

Now for the introducing this Shew : It was deuifed that the *Night*, reprefented in a blacke vefture fet with Starres, fhould arife from below, and come towards the vpper end of the Hall : there to waken her fonne *Somnus*, fleeping in his Caue, as the Proem to the Vifion. Which Figures when they are thus prefented

in humane bodies, as all Vertues, Vices, Paſſions,
Knowledges, and whatſoeuer Abſtraſts elſe in imagina-
tion are, vvhich vve vvould make viſible, vve produce
them, vſing humane aſtions, and euen *Sleepe* it ſelfe
(which might ſeeme improperly to exerciſe waking mo-
tions) hath been often ſhewed vs in that manner, with
ſpeech and geſture.   As for example :

Excuſit tandem ſibi ſe ; cubitoque leuatus
Quid veniat (cognouit enim) Scitatur.

Intanto ſoprauenne, & gli occhi chiuſe
A i Signori, & a i Sergenti il pigro Sonno.

And in another place :

Il Sonno viene, & Sparſo il corpo ſtanco
Col ramo intimo nel liquor di Lethe.

So there, *Sleepe* is brought in, as a body, vſing ſpeech
and motion : and it was no more improper in this
forme to make him walke, and ſtand, or ſpeake, then it
is to giue voyce or paſſion to dead Men, Ghoſts, Trees,
and Stones : and therefore in ſuch matters of Shewes,
theſe like Charaſters (in what forme ſoeuer they be   I
drawne) ſerue vs but to read the intention of vvhat vve
would repreſent ; as in this proieſt of ours, *Night &*
Sleepe vvere to produce a Viſion,—an effeſt proper to
their power, and fit to ſhadow our purpoſe, for that
theſe apparitions & ſhewes are but as imaginations,
and dreames that portend our affeſtions ; and dreames
are neuer in all points agreeing right with waking
aſtions : and therefore were they apteſt to ſhadow
whatſoeuer error might be herein preſented.   And

therefore vvas *Sleepe* (as hee is defcribed by *Philoftratus* 170 *in Amphirai imagine*) apparelled in a vvhite thin Vefture caft ouer a blacke, to fignifie both the day and the night, with wings of the fame colour, a Garland of Poppy on his head ; and in ftead of his yuoyrie and tranfparent horne, hee was fhewed bearing a blacke Wand in the left hand, and a white in the other, to effect either confufed or fignificant dreames, according to that inuocation of *Statius*.

———*Nec te totas infundere pennas*
Luminibus compello meis, hoc turba precatur,   180
Lætior, extremo me tange cacumine virgæ.

And alfo agreeing to that of *Sil. Ital.*
———*Tangens Lethea tempora Virga.*

And in this action did he here vfe his white Wand, as to infufe fignificant Vifions to entertaine the Specta-tors, and fo made them feeme to fee there a Temple with a *Sybilla* therein attending vpon the Sacrifices ; which done, *Iris* (the Meffenger of *Iuno*) defcends from the top of a Mountaine raifed at the lower end of the Hall, and marching vp to the Temple of Peace, giues 190 notice to the *Sybilla* of the comming of the Goddeffes, and withall deliuers her a Profpectiue, wherein fhe might behold the Figures of their Deities, and thereby defcribe them ; to the end that at their defcending, there might be no ftay or hinderance of their Motion, which was to be carryed vvithout any interruption, to the action of other entertainments that were to depend one of another, during the vvhole Shew : and that the eyes of the Spectators might not beguile their eares, as·

in fuch cafes it euer happens, vvhiles pompe and fplen- 200
dor of the fight takes vp all the intention vvithout
regard [to] vvhat is fpoken ; and therefore vvas it
thought fit their defcriptions fhould be deliuered by
the *Sybilla*.

Which as foone as fhe had ended, the three *Graces*
in filuer Robes vvith vvhite Torches, appeared on the
top of the mountaine, defcending hand in hand before
the Goddeffes ; vvho likevvife followed three and three,
as in a number dedicated vnto Sanctity and an
incorporeall nature, vvhereas the *Dual, Hierogliphicè pro* 210
immudis accipitur.   And betweene euery ranke of God-
deffes, marched three Torch-bearers in the like feuerall
colours, their heads and Robes all dect with Starres ;
and in their defcending, the Cornets fitting in the
Concaues of the Mountaine, and feene but / to their
breafts, in the habit of *Satyres,* founded a ftately
March ; vvhich continued vntill the Goddeffes were
approached iuft before the Temple, and then ceafed,
when the Confort Muficke (placed in the *Cupula*
thereof, out of fight) began : whereunto the three 220
Graces retyring themfelues afide, fang, vvhiles the
Goddeffes one after an other vvith folemne pace afcended
vp into the Temple, and deliuering their prefents to
the *Sybilla* (as it vvere but in paffing by) returned
downe into the midft of the Hall, preparing themfelues
to their dance, vvhich (affoone as the *Graces* had ended
their Song) they began to the Muficke of the Violls
and Lutes, placed on one fide of the Hall.

Which dance being performed with great maiefty
and Arte, confifting of diuers ftraines, fram'd vnto 230
motions circular, fquare, triangular, vvith other propor-

tions exceeding rare and full of variety; the Goddeffes made a paufe, cafting themfelues into a circle, whilft the *Graces* againe fang to the Muficke of the Temple, and prepared to take out the Lords to dance. With whom after they had performed certaine Meafures, Galliards, and Curranto's, *Iris* againe comes and giues notice of their pleafure to depart: whofe fpeech ended, they drew themfelues againe into another fhort dance, with fome few pleafant changes, ftill retyring them 240 toward the foote of the Mountaine, which they afcended in that fame manner as they came downe, whilft the Cornets taking their Notes from the ceafing of the Muficke below, founded another delightfull March.

And thus Madame, haue I briefly deliuered, both the reafon and manner of this Mafke; as well to fatisfie the defire of thofe who could not well note the carriage of thefe paffages, by reafon (as I fayd) the prefent pompe and fplendor entertain'd them otherwife (as that which is moft regardfull in thefe Shewes) 250 wherein (by the vnpartiall opinion of all the beholders Strangers and others) it was not inferiour to the beft that euer was prefented in Chriftendome; as alfo to giue vp my account hereof vnto your Honour, whereby / I might cleere the reckoning of any imputation that might be layd vpon your iudgement, for preferring fuch a one, to her *Maiefty* in this imployment, as could giue no reafon for what was done.

· And for the captious Cenfurers, I regard not what they can fay, who commonly can do little elfe but fay; 260 and if their deepe iudgements euer ferue them to pro-duce any thing, they muft ftand on the fame Stage of Cenfure with other men, and peraduenture performe no

fuch great wonders as they would make vs beleeue :
and I comfort my felfe in this, that in Court I know
not any (vnder him, who acts the greateft parts) that is
not obnoxious to enuy, and a finifter interpretation.
And whofoeuer ftriues to fhew moft wit about thefe
Pun[c]tillos of Dreames and fhewes, are fure ficke of a
difeafe they cannot hide, and would faine haue the 270
world to thinke them very deeply learned in all
mifteries whatfoeuer. And peraduenture they thinke
themfelues fo ; which if they do, they are in a farre
worfe cafe then they imagine ; *Non poteft non indoctus
effe qui fe doctum credit.* And let vs labour to fhew
neuer fo much fkill or Arte, our weakneffes and ignor-
ance will be feene, whatfoeuer couering vve caft ouer it.
And yet in thefe matters of fhewes (though they be
that which moft entertaine the vvorld) there needs no
fuch exact fufficiency in this kind.] For, *Ludit iftis* 280
animus, non proficit. And therefore, Madame, I will no
longer idlely hold you therein, but refer you to the
fpeeches, and fo to your better delights, as one vvho
muft euer acknowledge my felfe efpecially bound vnto
your Honour.

SAM: DANIEL.

The Night *reprefented, in a blacke Vefture fet with
Starres, comes and wakens her Sonne* Somnus *(fleep-
ing in his Caue) with this Speech.*

Wake darke *Sleepe,* roufe thee from out
   this Caue,
Thy Mother *Night* that bred thee in
   her wombe
And fed thee firft vvith filence and
   vvith eafe,
Doth here thy fhadowing operations
   craue :
And therefore wake my Sonne, awake, and come,
Strike vvith thy Horny vvand, the fpirits of thefe
That here expect fome pleafing nouelties :   10
And make their flumber to beget ftrange fights,
Strange vifions and vnvfuall properties.
Vnfeene of latter Ages, ancient Rites,
Of gifts diuine, vvrapt vp in myfteries :
Make this to feeme a Temple in their fight,
Whofe maine fupport, holy Religion frame :
And [1] *Wifdome,* [2] *Courage,* [3] *Temperance,* and [4] *Right,*
Make feeme the Pillars that fuftaine the fame.

Shadow fome *Sybill* to attend the Rites,
And to defcribe the Powers that fhall refort,   20
With th'interpretation of the benefits
They bring in clouds, and what they do import.
Yet make them to portend the true defire
Of thofe that vvifh them waking, reall things :
Whilft I will hou'ring, here a-loofe retire
And couer all things vvith my fable Wings.

Somnus.

DEare Mother *Night*, I your commandement
          Obey, and Dreames t'interpret Dreames will
          make,
As / vvaking curiofity is wont ;   30
Though better dreame a fleep, then dreame awake.
And this white horny Wand fhall vvorke the deed ;
Whofe power doth Figures of the light prefent :
When from this fable *radius* doth proceed
Nought but confufed fhewes, to no intent.
Be this a Temple ; there *Sybilla* ftand,
Preparing reuerent Rites with holy hand ;
And fo bright vifions go, and entertaine
All round about, vvhilft I'le to fleepe againe.

Iris, *the Meſſenger of the Goddeſſes difcending from the* 40
Mount, where they were aſſembled, (dect like the Raine-
bow) fpake as followeth.

I The daughter of Wonder (now made the Meffenger
          of Power), am here difcended, to fignifie the com-
ming of a Cœleftiall prefence of Goddeffes, determined
to vifit this faire Temple of Peace, vvhich holy hands

and deuout defires, haue dedicated to unity and concord.
And leauing to fhew themfelues any more in *Samos,*
Ida, Paphos, their ancient delighting places of *Greece,*
and *Afia,* made now the feats of Barbarizme and fpoyle, 50
vouchfafe to recreat themfelues vpon this *Wefterne*
Mount of mighty BRITTANNY; the Land of ciuill
Mufick and of reft, and are pleafed to appeare in
the felfe-fame Figures wherein antiquity hath formerly
cloathed them, and as they haue bin caft in the imagi-
nation of piety, who hath giuen mortall fhapes to the
gifts and effects of an eternall power, for that thofe
beautifull Caracters of fenfe were eafier to be read then
their myfticall *Ideas,* difperfed in that wide and incom-
prehenfible volume of Nature.   60

And well haue mortall men apparelled all the *Graces,*
all the *Bleffings,* all *Vertues,* with that fhape wherein
themfelues are much delighted, and which worke the
beft Motions, and beft reprefent the beautie of heauenly
Powers.

And therefore reuerent Propheteffe, that here atten-
deft vpon / the deuotions of this Place, prepare thy felfe
for thofe Rytes that appertaine to thy function, and the
honour of fuch Deities; and to the end thou mayft
haue a fore-notion what Powers, and who they are that 70
come, take here this Profpectiue, and therein note and
tell vvhat thou feeft : for well mayeft thou there obferue
their fhadowes, but their prefence will bereaue thee of
all, faue admiration and amazement; for who can looke
vpon fuch Powers and fpeake?   And fo I leaue thee.

Sybilla, *hauing receiued this Meffage, and the Profpectiue,*
vfeth thefe words.

VVHat haue I feene ? where am I ? or do I fee
at all ? or am I any where ? was this *Iris*,
(the Meffenger of *Iuno*) or elfe but a fantafme or imagi-
nation ? will the diuine Goddeffes vouchfafe to vifit this
poore Temple ?   Shall I be bleft, to entertaine fo great
Powers ? it can be but a dreame : yet fo great Powers
haue bleft as humble roofes, and vfe, out of no other
refpeƈt, then their owne gracefulnes, to fhine vvhere
they will.   But what Profpeƈtiue is this ? or what fhall
I herein fee ?   Oh admirable Powers ! what fights are
thefe ?

Iuno.

FIrft, here Imperiall *Iuno* in her Chayre,   90
With Scepter of command for Kingdomes large :
Defcends all clad in colours of the Ayre,
Crown'd with bright Starres, to fignifie her charge.

Pallas.

NExt, War-like *Pallas*, in her Helmet dreft   .
With Lance of vvinning, Target of defence :
In vvhom both Wit and Courage are expreft,
To get with glory, hold vvith Prouidence.

Venus. /

THen louely *Venus* in bright Maiefty,
Appeares with milde afpeƈt, in Doue-like hue : 100
With th'all combining Skarffe of Amity.
T'ingird ftrange Nations with affeƈtions true.

Vefta.

NExt Holy *Vefta*, with her flames of Zeale
Prefents her felfe, clad in white Purity :

Whofe booke, the foules fweet comfort, doth reueale
By the euer-burning Lampe of Piety.

Diana.

THen chafte *Diana*, in her Robes of greene,   110
     With weapons of the Wood her felfe addrefts   .
To bleffe the Forrefts, where her power is feene,
In peace vvith all the vvorld but Sauage beafts.

Proferpina.

NExt rich *Proferpina*, vvith flames of gold,
     Whofe ftate although within the earth, yet fhe
Comes from aboue, and in her hand doth hold
The Myne of wealth, with cheerefull Maiefty.

Macaria.

THen all in purple Robes, rich Happineffe   120
     Next her appeares, bearing in either hand,
Th'Enfignes both of wealth and wits, t'expreffe
That by them both, her Maiefty doth ftand.

Concordia.

NExt all in party-coloured Robes appeares,
     . In white and crimfon, gracefull *Concord*, dreft
With knots of Vnion, and in hand fhe beares
The happy ioynèd Rofes of our reft.

Aftrea./

CLeare-eyed *Aftrea*, next, with reuerent brow   130
     Clad in Cæleftiall hue, (which beft fhe likes)
Comes with her Ballance, and her fword to fhew
That firft her iudgement weighs before it ftrikes.

Flora.

THen cheereful *Flora*, all adorn'd with ftowers,
      Who cloathes the earth with beauty and delight
In thoufand fundry fuits, whilft fhining houres
Will fkarce afford a darkneffe to the night.

Ceres.

NExt plenteous *Ceres* in her Harueft weede,   140
      Crown'd with th'increafe of what fhe gaue to
         keepe,
To gratitude and faith: in whom we read,
Who fowes on Vertue fhall with glory reape.

Tethis.

LAftly comes *Tethis*, *Albions* faireft loue˘
      Whom fhe in faithfull Armes deignes t'embrace,
And brings the Trydent of her Power, t'approue
The kinde refpe&t fhe hath to do him grace.

      Thus haue I read their fhadowes, but behold !
      In glory, where they come as Iris *told.*   150

The three Graces, *comming to the vpper part of the Hall*
   fang this Song, while the Goddeffes deliuered their pre-
   fents.

Gratia funt [1] *dantium,* [2] *reddentium,* [3] *& promerentium.*

                    1

DEfert, Reward, and Gratitude,
      The *Graces* of Societie :

Doe here with hand in hand conclude
The bleſſed chaine of Amitie :
 For we deſerue, we giue, we thanke,   160
 Thanks, Gifts, Deſerts, thus ioyne in ranke.

2

We yeeld the ſplendant raijes of light,
Vnto theſe bleſſings that deſcend :
The grace vvhereof with more delight,
The vvell diſpoſing doth commend ;
 Whilſt Gratitude, Rewards, Deſerts,
 Pleaſe, winne, draw on, and couple hearts.

3

For worth and power and due reſpect,   170
Deſerues, beſtowes, returnes with Grace :
The meed, reward, the kinde effect,
That giue the world a cheerefull face,
 And turning in this courſe of right,
 Make Vertue moue with true delight.

The Song being ended, and the Maſkers *in the miadeſt
of the Hall, diſpoſing themſelues to their Daunce :*
Sybilla *hauing placed their ſeuerall preſents on the
Altar, vttereth theſe words.*

O Powers of powers, grant to our vowes we pray   180
  That theſe faire bleſſings which we now erect
In Figures left vs here, in ſubſtance may
Be thoſe great props of glory and reſpect.
[1] Let Kingdomes large, [2] let armèd policie,
[3] Milde loue, [4] true zeale, [5] right ſhooting at the white

Of braue difignes : [6] let wealth, [7] felicitie,
[8] Iuftice, [9] and concord, [10] pleafure, [11] plenty, [12] *might*
And power by Sea, with Grace proportionate,
Make glorious both the Soueraigne and his State.

After this the Mafkers *danced their owne meafures,.* [1]
which being ended, and they ready to take out the
Lords, the three Graces *fang.*

VV Hiles worth with honour make their choife
For meafured motions ordred right,
Now let vs likewife giue a voyce,
Vnto the touch of our delight.

For comforts lock't vp without found,
Are th'vnborne children of the thought :
Like vnto Treafures neuer found
That buried lowe are left forgot.   2

Where words, our glory doth not fhew,
(There) like braue actions without Fame :
It feemes as Plants not fet to grow,
Or as a Tombe without a Name.

The Mafkers *hauing ended their dancing with the Lords,*
Iris *giues warning of their departure.*

Iris.

A S I was the ioyfull Meffenger to notifie the com-
ming, fo am I now the fame of the departure
of thefe diuine powers. Who hauing cloathed them- 2
felues with thefe apparances, doe now returne backe
againe to the Spheres of their owne being from whence

they came.   But yet, of my felfe, this / much I muſt
reueale, though againſt the warrant of a Meſſenger ;
who I know had better to faile in obedience then in
preſumption, that theſe Deities by the motion of the
all-directing *Pallas*, the glorious Patroneſſe of this
mighty Monarchy, deſcending in the Maieſtie of their
inuiſible eſſence, vpon yonder Mountaine, found there,
the beſt, (and moſt worthily the beſt) of LADIES, dis- 220
porting with her choyſeſt Attendants ; whoſe formes
they preſently vndertooke, as delighting to be in the
beſt-built-Temples of Beauty and Honour.   And in
them vouchſafed to appeare in this manner, being
otherwiſe no obiects for mortall eyes.   And no doubt,
but that in reſpect of the perſons vnder whoſe beauti-
full couerings they haue thus preſented themſelues,
theſe Deities will be pleaſed the rather at their inuoca-
tion (knowing all their deſires to be ſuch) as euermore
to grace this glorious Monarchy with the Reall effects 230
of theſe bleſſings repreſented.

> *After this, they fell to a ſhort departing*
> *dance, and ſo aſcend the Mountayne.*

FINIS.

IV,

THE QVEENES ARCADIA.

1606.

NOTE.

The first edition of 'The Queenes Arcadia' was published in 1606. An exemplar (probably *unique*) is among the Malone books in the Bodleian (200). The following is its title-page :—

THE

QVEENES

ARCADIA.ǀ

A Paſtorall Trage-comedie
preſented to her Maieſtie and her
Ladies, by the Vniuerſitie of
Oxford in Chriſts Church,
in Auguſt laſt.

1605.

AT LONDON.

Printed by *G. Eld*, for *Simon Waterſon*,
1606.

This was followed by reprints in the 'Certaine Small Workes' of 1607, 1609 and 1611. Collation shows that, except trivial orthographical alterations, the original text was adhered to ; but it must be stated here that the errata lists of the 'Certaine Small Workes' are simply departures from the original 4to of 1606, and that the 4to of 1623 is moſt of all culpable, as witness these restorations and corrections from the Author's own text of 1606. See p. 211 for title-page, as usual, from the 4to of 1623. G.

Line	5, 'knowſt'	1606,	'knoweſt'	1623.
,,	26, 'maladine'	,,	'maladies'	,,
,,	28, 'made'	ı	'may'	.
,,	39, 'do'		'to'	
,,	92, 'Carinus'	,,	'Carnius'	,,
,,	93, 'fond'	,,	'found'	,,

1606,	'Lees'	1623.
,,	'the'	,,
،	'figne'	
،	'pack'	
	'them'	
,,	'ioyning'	,,
,,	'doe'	,,
rs' ,,	'Impreffitors'	,,
,,	'bonds'	,,
،	dropped out	,,
	'powers'	،
	'one'	،
،	'from'	،
،	'commend'	،
,, .	dropped out	،
،	'and'	،
,,	'fociety'	,,
,,	'ftarkle'	,,
ne dropped out by		,,
1606,	dropped out	،
,,	'the'	،
،	'extremity'	،
،	dropped out	،
،	'Away'	،
،	'no'	،
،	'when that'	،
،	'tell me'	،
،	dropped out	,,
،	'this'	،
،	'ftarres'	
،	'fo faith'	,,
،	'Elixit'	,,
، ،،	'Hypocratis'	,,
، ،	'Auicon'	,,
,,	'booke'	,,
,,	'fends'	،،
،،	'not'	
،	'furely'	
،	'lay'	
،	'pelight'	
،	'her'	,,

14

Line 1368, 'what'   1606, 'that'   1623.
 ,, 1368, 'fecret'   ,, 'fecrets'   ,,
 ,, 1409, 'a lone'   ,, 'alone'   ,,
 ,, 1438, 'on'   ,, dropped out   ,,
 ,, 1468, 'in accents'   ,, 'in th' accents'   ,,
 ,, 1827, 'thy'   , 'the'   ,,
 ,, 1873, 'perceiu'd'   ,, 'perceiue'   ,,
 ,, 1983, 'thee'   . 'the'
 ,, 2131, 'holpe'   , 'helpt'
 ,, 2158, 'affections'   ,, 'affection'   ,,
 ,, 2236, 'reportes'   ,, 'report'   ,,
 ,, 2241, 'Acryfius'   ,, 'Aryfius'   ,,
 ,, 2325, 'too'   , 'to'
 ,, 2389, 'hath'   , 'haue'
 ,, 2402, 'Of'   ,, 'O'
 ,, 2479, 'feete'   'feele'
 ,, 2547, 'diflinkt'   ,, 'miflikt'   ,,
 ,, 2562, 'then'   , 'their'   ,,
 ,, 2570, 'happie'   ,, dropped out   ,,

The critical Reader will perceive that this large list, in nearly every instance, makes nonsense of the place, in the 4to of 1623. The following corrections of both 1606 and 1623 I have made :—

Line 974, 'frame' for 'forme.' See l. 974.
 ,, 983, 'cuftomary' for 'conftumary.'
 ,, 1026, 'is' for 'are.'
 ,, 1080, '*Alc.*' inserted.
 ,, 1165, 'is' for 'in.'
 ,, 2028, 'clouer' for 'clauer.'
 ,, 2120, 'haft' for 'hafte.'
 ,, 2285, a second '*Erg.*' removed.
 ,, 2565, 'rendes' for 'reades.'

Two misprints of 1606 are corrected in 1623—viz., l. 1402, 'dead' for 'deed' : l. 1970, 'this' for 'thus.' Line 310, 'debauflment,' misprinted 'debanflment' in all the texts : l. 532, 'from' misprinted in all 'for.' Obvious mistakes of letters, as 'n' for 'u' and the like, occur in both—all silently put right.   G.

THE
QVEENES
ARCADIA.

A Paſtorall Trage-Comedie pre-
ſented to her Maieſty and her
Ladies, by the Vniuerſity of
Oxford *in Chriſts Church, in*
Auguſt. 1605.

By Samvel Daniel.

LONDON,
Printed by Nicholas Okes,
for Simon Waterson.
1623.

The Names of the Actors.

MELIBÆUS.
ERGASTUS. } two ancient *Arcadians.*

COLAX, a corrupted traueller.

TECHNE, a fubtle wench of *Corinth.*

AMYNTAS.
CARINUS. } the louers of *Cloris.*

CLORIS.

PALÆMON.
SILUIA. } Iealous Louers.

MIRTILLUS.

DORINDA.

AMARILLIS, in loue with *Carinus.*

DAPHNE, abufed by *Colax.*

ALCON, a Quack-faluer.

LINCUS, a Petty-fogger.

MONTANUS, the father of *Amyntas.*

ACRYSIUS, the father of *Cloris.*

To the Queenes moſt excellent Maieſtie.

*T*Hat which their zeale, whoſe onely zeale was bent
    To ſhew the beſt they could that might delight
Your royall minde, did lately repreſent
Renownèd Empreſſe to your Princely ſight :
Is now the offring of their humbleneſſe,
Here conſecrated to your glorious name ;
Whoſe happy preſence did vouchſafe to bleſſe
So poore preſentments, and to grace the ſame :
    And though it be in th'humbleſt ranke of words,
And in the loweſt region of our ſpeach,   10
Yet is it in that kinde, as beſt accords
With rurall paſſions ; which vſe not to reach
Beyond the groues and woods, where they were bred :
And beſt become a clauſtrall exerciſe,
Where men ſhut out retyr'd, and ſequeſtred
From publike faſhion, ſeeme to ſympathize
With innocent, and plaine ſimplicity :
And liuing here vnder the awfull hand
Of diſcipline, and ſtrict obſeruancy,
Learne but our weakeneſſes to vnderſtand,   20

And therefore dare not enterprize to ſhow
In lowder ſtile the hidden myſteries,
And arts of Thrones ; which none that are below
The Sphere of action, and the exercife
Of power can truely ſhew : though men may ſtraine
Conceipt aboue the pitch where it ſhould ſtand,
And forme more monſtrous figures then containe
A poſſibility, and goe beyond
The | nature of thoſe managements ſo farre,
As oft their common decency they marre :   30
Whereby the populaſſe (in whom ſuch ſkill
Is needleſſe) may be brought to apprehend
Notions, that may turne all to a taſt of ill
What euer power ſhall do, or might intend :
And thinke all cunning, all proceeding one,
And nothing ſimple, and ſincerely done :
Yet the eye of practiſe, looking downe from hie
Vpon ſuch ouer-reaching vanity,
Sees how from error t'error it doth flote,
As from an vnknowne Ocean into a Gulfe :   40
And how though th' Woolfe, would counterfeit the Goate,
Yet euery chinke bewrayes him for a Woolfe.
   And therefore in the view of ſtate t'haue ſhow'd
A counterfeit of ſtate, had beene to light
A candle to the Sunne, and ſo beſtow'd
Our paines to bring our dimneſſe vnto light.
For maieſty, and power, can nothing ſee
Without it ſelfe, that can ſight-worthy be.
And therefore durſt not we but on the ground,
From whence our humble Argument hath birth,   50
Erect our Scene ; and thereon are we found,
And if we fall, we fall but on the earth,

From whence we pluckt the flowers that here we bring ;
Which if at their firſt opening they did pleaſe,
It was enough, they ſerue but for a ſpring :
The firſt ſent is the beſt in things as theſe.
A muſicke of this nature on the ground,
Is euer wont to vaniſh with the ſound.
But yet your royall goodneſſe may raiſe new,
Grace but the Muſes they will honour you. 60

Chi non fa, non falla.

THE QVEENES
ARC·ADIA.

ACTVS. I. SCENA. I.

Ergaſtus. Melibæus.

Ow is it *Melibæus* that we finde
  Our Country, faire *Arcadia*, ſo much
    chang'd
  From what it was ; that was thou
    knowſt of late,
  The gentle region of plaine honeſty,
  The modeſt ſeat of vndiſguiſed truth,
  Inhabited with ſimple innocence :
And now, I know not how, as if it were
Vnhallowed, and dieſted of that grace,　　　 10
Hath put off that faire nature which it had,
And growes like ruder countries, or more bad.
　Mel. Indeed *Ergaſtus* I haue neuer knowne
So vniuerſall a diſtemperature,

In all parts of the body of our ftate,
As now there is ; nor euer haue we heard
So much complaining of difloyalty,
Among'ft your yonger Nymphes, nor euer found
Our heardfmen fo deluded in their loues,
As if there were no faith on either fide.   20
We neuer had in any age before
So many fpotleffe Nymphes, fo much diftain'd
VVith blacke report, and wrongfull infamy ;
That few efcape the tongue of malice free.

    Erg. And me thinkes too, our very aire is chang'd,
Our wholefome climate growne more maladiue ;
The fogges, and the Syrene offends vs more
(Or we made thinke fo), then they did before.
The windes of Autumne, now are fayd to bring
More noyfomneffe, then thofe do of the Spring :   30
And all of vs feele new infirmities,
New Feuers, new Catarres, oppreffe our powers ;
The milke wherewith we cur'd all maladies,
Hath either loft the nature, or we ours.

    Mel. And we that neuer were accuftomed
To quarrell for our bounds, how do we fee
Montanus and *Acryfius* interftriue
How farre their feuerall Sheep-walkes fhould extend,
And cannot be agreed do what we can :
As if fome vnderworking hand ftrake fire,   40
To th'apt inkindling tinder of debate,
And foftred their contention and their hate.

    Erg. And me thinkes too, the beauty of our
        Nymphes
Is not the fame, as it was wont to be.
That Rofie hew, the glory of the Cheeke,

Is either ftolne, or elfe they haue forgot,
To blufh with fhame, or to be pale with feare:
Or elfe their fhame doth make them alwayes blufh;
For alwayes doth their beauties beare one hew,
And either Nature's falfe, or that vntrue.   50

 Mel. Befides their various habits grow fo ftrange,
As that although their faces certaine are,
Their bodies are vncertaine euery day,
And alwayes differing from themfelues fo farre,
As if they fkorn'd to be the fame they are.

 And all of vs are fo transform'd, that we
Difcerne not an *Arcadian* by th'attyre;
Our ancient Paftorall habits are defpif'd,
And all is ftrange, hearts, clothes, and all difguif'd.

 Erg. Indeed vnto our griefe we may perceiue,   60
The whole complection of *Arcadia* chang'd,
Yet cannot finde the occafion of this change:
But let vs with more wary eye obferue
Whence the contagion of thefe cuftomes rife,
That haue infected thus our honeft plaines,
With cunning difcord, idle vanity,
Deceiptfull wrong, and caufleffe infamy;
That by th'affiftance of our grauer Swaines,
We now at firft, may labour to preuent
The further courfe of mifchiefes, and reftore   70
Our late cleane woods, to what they were before.

 Mel. Content *Ergaftus*, and euen here will be
A place conuenient for fo fit a worke:
For here our Nymphs, and heardfmen on this Greene,
Do vfually refort, and in this Groue
We may obferue them beft, and be vnfeene.

ACT. I. SCEN. II.

Colax.   Techne.

COme my deare *Techne*, thou and I muſt plot
    More cunning proiects yet, more ſtrange
    deſignes   80
Amongſt theſe ſimple groſſe *Arcadians* here,
That know no other world, but their owne plaines ;
Nor yet can apprehend the ſubtle traines
We lay, to mocke their rurall ignorance.
But ſee, here comes two of their amorous Swaines
In hote contention ; let vs cloſe conuay
Our ſelues, here vnderneath this couerture,
And ouer heare their paſſionate diſcourſe.
    Tech. Colax, this place well ſuch a purpoſe fits ;
Let vs ſit cloſe, and faith, it ſhall goe hard,   90
Vnleſſe we make ſome profit by their wits.

Carinus.   Amyntas.

Car. Now fond *Amyntas*, how cam'ſt thou poſſeſt
With ſuch a vaine preſumption, as thou art,
To thinke that *Cloris* ſhould affect thee beſt,
When all *Arcadia* knowes I haue her heart ?
    Am. And how *Carinus* canſt thou be ſo mad,
T'imagine *Cloris* can, or doth loue thee,
When by ſo many ſignes as I haue had,
I finde her whole affection bent to me ?   100
    Car. What are thoſe ſignes by which you come to
        caſt,
And calculate the fortune of your hopes ?
    Am. More certaine ſignes then thou canſt euer ſhew.
    Car. But they are more then ſignes, that I can ſhew.

Am. Why let each then produce the beſt he can,
To proue which may be thought the likelieſt man.
   Car. Content *Amyntas,* and do thou begin.
   Am. And I am well contented to begin.
Firſt if by chance, whil'ſt ſhe at Barley-breake
With other Nymphes, do but perceiue me come,   110
Streight lookes her cheeke with ſuch a Roſie red,
As giues the ſetting Sunne vnto the Weſt
When morrow tempeſts are prefigurèd.
   Car. Euen ſo that hew prognoſticates her wrath,
Which brings to thee the ſtormy windes of ſighes.
   Am. And if I finde her with her fellow Nymphes
Gathering of flowers by ſome ſweet Riuers ſide,
At my approach ſhe ſtraight way ſtands vpright,
Forgets her worke, and downe lets ſlide her lap,
And out fall all her flowers, vpon the ground.   120
   Car. So doth the ſilly ſheepe forget to feed,
When it perceiues the greedy Wolfe at hand.
   Am. And if ſhe meet but with my dog, ſhe takes
And ſtrokes him on the head, playes with his eares,
Spits in his mouth, and claps him on the backe,
And ſays, come, come *Melampus* go with me.
   Car. She may loue what is thine, but yet hate thee.
   Am. Whilſt at a Chryſtall ſpring the other day,
She waſht her louely face, and ſeeing me come,
She takes vp water with her dainty hand,   130
And with a downe-caſt looke beſprinckles me.
   Car. That ſhewes that ſhee vvould gladly quench in
      thee
The fire of loue, or elſe like loue doth beare,
﹐As did the *Delian* Goddeſſe, vvhen ſhe caſt
Diſdainefull vvater on *Acteons* face.

Am. As *Siluia*, one day, fate vvith her alone,
Binding of certaine choice felected hearbes
To her left arme, againft bewitching fpels,
(And I at the inftant comming) fhee perceiu'd
Her pulfe vvith farre more violence to beat   140
(As fh'after told me) then it did before.

Car. The like is felt vvhen natures enemy,
The hatefull feauer, doth furprife our powers.

Am. And euen but yefternight, fhe going before
With other maides, and feeing me following her,
Lets fall this dainty Nofegày, hauing firft
Beftow'd a kiffe thereon, to th'end I might
Receiue it fo, and with it doe the like.

  Car. Poore withred fauours, they might teach thee
          know,
That fhee efteemes thee, and thy lóue as light   150
As thofe dead flowers, fhee vvore but for a fhow
The day before, and caft away at night.

Am. Now friend *Carinus*, thou that muttereft fo .
At thefe plaine fpeaking figures of her loue,
Tell by vvhat fignes thou doeft her fauours proue ?

Car. Now filly man, doeft thou imagine me
So fond to blab the fauours of my loue ?

Am. Was't not a pact agreed twixt thee & me ?

Car. A pact to make thee tell thy fecrecy.

Am. And haft thou then betrayd my eafie truft, 160
And dallied with my open fimpleneffe ?

Car. And fitly art thou feru'd, that fo wilt vaunt
The imagin'd fauours of a gentle Nymph ;
And this is that vvhich makes vs feele that dearth
Of grace, t'haue kindnes at fo hie a rate.
This makes them vvary how they doe beftow

The leaft regard of common curtefie,
When fuch as you, poore, credulous, deuout,
And humble foules, make all things miracles
Your faith conceiues, and vainely doe conuert   170
All fhadowes to the figure of your hopes.

   Am. Carinus now thou doeft me double wrong,
Firft to deride my eafie confidence,
And then t'vpbrayd my truft, as if my tongue
Had heere prophan'd faire *Cloris* excellencie
In telling of her mercies, or had fin'd
In vttering th'honour of a modeft grace
Beftowing comfort, in fo iuft a cafe.

   Car. Why man, thou haft no way deferu'd her loue.

   Am. Defert I cannot vrge, but faith I can ;   180
If that may haue reward, then happy man.

   Car. But you know how I fau'd her from the hands
Of that rude Satyre, vvho had elfe vndone
Her honour vtterly ; and therefore ought
My loue of due, raigne foueraigne in her thought.

   Am. But how that free, and vnfubdued heart,
Infranchif'd by the Charter of her eyes,
Will beare the impofition of a due
I doe not fee, fince loue knew neuer Lord
That could command the region of our will.   190
And therefore vrge thy due, I for my part,
Muft plead compaffion, and a faithfull.heart.

   Car. Plead thou thy faith, whilft I will get thy loue,
For you kinde foules doe feldome gracefull proue.

   Am. The more vnkind they, who fhould better way
Our honeft vowes, and loue for loue repay ;
But oft they beare the penance of their will,
And for the wrong they doe, they fpeed as ill.

SCEN. III.

Colax.   Techne.   200

Col. Alas poore fooles, how hotely they contend
Who fhall poffeffe a prey that's yet vngot.
But *Techne*, I muft by thy helpe foreftall
The mart of both their hopes, and whilft they fhall
Purfue the Ayre, I muft furprife their gaine.   [*game ?*]
And fitly now, thou maift occafion take
By thefe aduantages difcouered here,
T'impreffe in *Cloris* tender heart that touch
Of deepe diflike of both their vanteries,
As may conuert her wholly vnto me.   210
    Tec. Why will you then *Dorindas* loue forfake,
For whom you traueld fo, and made me take
Such labour to intice her to your loue ?
    Col. Tufh *Techne*, we defire not what we haue
But what we would ; our longings neuer ftay
With our attaynings, but they goe beyond.
    Tec. And vvhy ? *Dorinda* is as faire as fhe.
    Col. That I confeffe, but yet that payes not me,
For *Cloris* is another, and tis that,
And onely that, vvhich, *Techne*, I defire.   220
Some thing there is peculiar, and alone
To euery beauty, that doth giue an edge
To our defires, and more vve vvill conceiue
In that vve haue not then in that vve haue.
And I haue heard, abroad vvhere beft experience
And vvit is learnd, that all the faireft choyce
Of vvoemen in the vvorld, ferue but to make
One perfeft beauty, vvhereof each brings part.
One hath a pleafing fmile, and nothing elfe :

Another but fome filly Mole to grace   230
Th'aire of a difproportion'd face ;
Another pleafes not but vvhen fhe fpeakes,
And fome in filence onely gracefull are :
Some till they laugh, we fee, feeme to be faire,
Some haue their bodies good, their geftures ill,
Some pleafe in Motion, fome in fitting ftill,
Some are thought louely, that haue nothing faire,
Some againe faire that nothing louely are.
So that we fee how beauty doth confift
Of diuers peeces, and yet all attract,   240
And therefore vnto all my loue afpires ;
As beauty varies, fo doth my defires.

   Tec. Ah but yet *Colax* doe not fo much wrong
Vnto a Nymph, now when thou haft fubdu'd
And won her heart, and knowft fhe holdft thee deare.

   Col. Tufh, wrong is as men thinke it, and I fee
It keepes the world the beft in exercife
That elfe would languifh, and haue nought to doe.
Difcord in parts, makes harmon' in the whole.
And fome muft laugh, whilft other fome condole. 250
And fo it be not of the fide we are,
Let others beare it ; what neede we to care?
And now *Dorinda* fomething hath to doe,
Now, fhe may fit, and thinke, and vexe and plot
For eafe, and ioying of her full delight
Would but haue dull'd her fpirits, and marrd her quite.

   Tec. Alas, yet I muft pitty her, poore foule
In this diftreffe, I being on my felfe
Of the frayle corporation, and doe know
That fhe will take it very grieuoufly.   260
And yet in troth fh'is feru'd but well inow,

III.   15

That would negleƈt *Mirtillus* honeſt loue,
And truſt ſtrong proteſtations, and new othes ;
Be wonne with garded words, and gawdy clothes.

   Col. Well, well, *Dorinda* ſhall not waile alone,
She ſhall haue others to confort her mone :
For ſince my laſt returne from *Telos* Court
I haue made twenty of their coyeſt Nymphs
Turne louers, with a few proteſting words
And ſome choyce complementall periuries ;   270
I made *Palæmon*, to ſuſpeƈt the faith
Of his chaſt *Siluia*, and chaſt *Siluia* his ;
In hope thereby to worke her loue to me.
I wrought coy *Daphne* to infringe her vow
Made to *Menalcas* ; and I told her how
Thoſe ſetters which ſo heauily were laid
Vpon our free affeƈtions, onely were
But cuſtomary bands, not naturall.
And I thinke *Techne* thou haſt done thy part
Here, in this gentle region of kind hearts,   280
Since thou cam'ſt hither, for I ſee thou thriu'ſt.

   Tec. Indeed whilſt I in *Corinth* did remaine,
I hardly could procure the meanes to liue,
There were ſo many of my trade, that ſold
Complexions, dreſſings, tiffanies and tyres ;
Deuiſors of new faſhions and ſtrange wyers,
Bedbrokers, Night wormes, and Compoſitors ;
That though I knew theſe arts as well as they
Yet being ſo many we could get ſmall pay.
Here, who but *Techne* now is all in all ?   290
Techne is ſent for, *Techne* onely ſhewes
New ſtrange deuiſes to the choyceſt Nymphes :
And I thinke *Techne* teaches them thoſe trickes,

As they will not forget againe in haft.
I haue fo opened their vnapt conceits
Vnto that vnderftanding of themfelues,
As they will fhew in time they were well taught,
If they obferue my rules, and hide a fault.

   Col. Ah well done *Techne.* Thus muft thou and I
Trade for our profit with their ignorance,   300
And take our time, and they muft haue their chance.
But pray thee *Techne,* doe not thou forget
To lay a traine for *Cloris.* So adue.

   Tec. Colax I will not, and the rather too,
For that I beare a little leaning loue
To fweet *Amyntas* ; for me thinkes he feemes
The louelieft Shepheard all *Arcadia* yeelds,
And I would gladly intercept his loue.

SCEN. IIII.

Melibæus. Ergaftus.   310

SO this is well ; Here's one difcouery made ;
   Here are the heads of that diftemperature,
From whence thefe ftrange debaufhments of our
   Nymphes
And vile deluding of our Shepheards fprings :
Here is a monfter, that hath made his lufts
As wide as is his will, and left his will
Without all bounds, and cares not whom he wrongs,
So that he may his owne defires fulfill ;
And being all foule himfelfe, would make all ill,
This is that *Colax* that from forraine lands,   320
Hath brought home that infection that vndoes
His countrey goodneffe, and impoyfons all.

His being abroad would marre vs quite at home :
Tis ſtrange to ſee, that by his going out,
He hath out-gone that natiue honeſty,
Which here the breeding of his countrey gaue.
For here I doe remember him a child,
The ſonne of *Nicoginus* of the Hill ;
A man though low in fortune, yet in minde
High ſet ; a man ſtill practiſing   330
T'aduance his forward ſonne beyond the traine
Of our *Arcadian* breed ; and ſtill me thought
I ſaw a diſpoſition in the youth,
Bent to a ſelfe conceited ſurlineſſe,
With an inſinuating impudence.

    Erg. A man the fitter made for Courts abroad
Where I would God he had remainèd ſtill,
With thoſe looſe-liuing wanton Sybarites,
Where luxurie, had made her outmoſt proofe.
From whence I heare he comes, and hither brings 340
Their ſhames, to brand vs with the like reproach.

    And for this other viper which you ſaw,
I doe remember how ſhe came of late
For ſuccour to theſe parts, and ſought to teach
Our younger maides to dreſſe, and trie our Flaxe,
And vſe the Diſtaffe, and to make a hem,
And ſuch like ſkill, being ſkill enough for them ;
But ſince I ſee ſhe hath preſum'd to deale
In points of other ſcience, different farre
From that plaine Art of honeſt huſwifery,   350
And as it ſeemes hath often made repaire
Vnto the neighbour Cities round about ;
From whom ſhe hath theſe ſtrange diſguiſes got
T'abuſe our Nymphes, and as it ſeemes deſires

To fute their mindes as light as their attires;
But we fhall foone preuent this growing plague
Of pride and folly, now that fhe defcry
The true fymptoma of this malady ;
And by this ouerture thus made we truft
We fhortly fhall difcouer all the reft.   360

ACT. II. SCEN. I.

Siluia. Cloris.

O *Cloris*, here haue thou and I full oft
    Sate and beene merry, in this fhady Groue.
Here haue we fung full many a Rundelay,
Told Riddles, and made Nofegayes, laught at loue,
And other paffions, whilft my felfe was free,
From that intollerable mifery,
Whereto affection now inuaffels me.
Now *Cloris* I fhall neuer more take ioy   370
To fee, or to be feene, with mortall eye ;
Now forrow muft be all my company.
    Clo. Why *Siluia*, whence fhould all this griefe arife ?
    Sil. I am vndone *Cloris*, let that fuffice.
    Clo. Tell me fweet *Siluia*, how comes that to paffe ?
    Sil. O *Cloris* if thou be as once I was
Free, from that miferable plague of loue,
Keepe thee fo ftill ; let my affliction warne
Thy youth, that neuer man haue power to moue
Thy heart to liking ; for beleeue me this,   380
They are the moft vnfaithfull impious race
Of creatures on the earth ; neuer beleeue
Their proteftations, nor their vowes, nor teares :
All is deceit ; none meanes the thing he fweares.

Truſt a mans faith ? nay rather will I goe
And giue my ſelfe a prey to ſauage beaſts ;
For all they ſeeke, and all they labour for,
Is but t'vndoe vs ; and when that is done,
They goe and triumph on the ſpoile the'haue won.
Truſt men, or take compaſſion when they grieue,   390
O *Cloris* 'tis to cheriſh and relieue
The frozen Snake, which with our heat once warmd,
Will ſting vs to the heart in recompence ;
And O no maruell tho the Satyre ſhund
To liue with man, when he perceiu'd he could,
With one and the ſame breath blow heat and cold.
Who would haue euer thought *Palæmons* othes
Would haue prou'd falſe ? who would haue iudgd **the**
    face
That promiſ'd ſo much faith, and honeſty
Had beene the viſor but of treachery ?   400
    Clo. Is't poſſible *Palæmon* ſhould b'vntrue ?
    Sil. Tis poſſible, *Palæmon* is vntrue.
    Clo. If it be ſo, deare *Siluia*, I thinke then
That thou ſaiſt truth, there is no truſt in men.
For I proteſt I neuer ſaw a face
That promiſ'd better of a heart then his,
And if he faile, whoſe faith then conſtant is ?
    Sil. O *Cloris*, if thou didſt but know how long,
And with what earneſt ſuite, he ſought my loue ;
What vowes he vſ'd, what othes, what teares among ;   410
What ſhewes he made, his conſtancy to prooue,
You would admire : and then againe to ſee
How I although I lou'd him with my heart
Stood out, and would by no means vrgèd be,
To ſhew the leaſt affeſtion of my part.

For I had heard that, which (O now too well)
I finde, that men were cunning, and would not
Regard the thing that eafily was got.
   Clo. Siluia, indeed and I haue heard fo too.
   Sil. And therefore I would try him, and not feeme 420
His vowes, nor proteftations to efteeme :
At length one day, here in this felfe-fame place,
(Which I fhall euer, and good caufe I haue
To thinke on whilft I liue) walking with me,
After he had vrgèd me moft earneftly :
O *Siluia*, faid he, fince nor oath, nor vow,
Nor teares, nor prayers, haue the power to moue,
Nor all that I can doe, can make thee know
How true a heart, I offer to thy loue ;
I muft try fome way elfe to fhew the fame,   430
And make thy vndifcerning wilfull youth
Know, though too late, (perhaps vnto thy fhame)
Thy vvayward error, and my conftant truth :
When thou maift figh, and fay in griefe of minde,
Palæmon lou'd, and *Siluia* vvas vnkinde.
With that vvringing my hand, he turnes away,
And though his teares vvould hardly let him looke,
Yet fuch a looke did through his teares make way,
He fhew'd how fad a farewell there he tooke.
And vp towards yonder craggy rocke he goes, 440
His armes incrofs'd, his head downe on one fide,
With fuch a mournfull pace, as fhewd his woes
Way'd heauier then his paffions could abide :
Faine vvould I haue recald him backe, but fhame,
And modeftie could not bring forth his name :
And faine vvould I haue followed, yet me thought
It did not fit the honour of a maide

To follow one, yet ſtill I ſent from me,
T'attend his going, feare, and a carefull eye.
    At length vvhen he vvas gotten to the top,   450
I might perceiue how vvith infolded armes,
And lookes vp bent to heauen, he ſtands and turnes
His vvofull face vnto the other ſide,
Whereas that hideous fearefull downfall is:
And ſeem'd as if he vvould haue throwne him off:
And as I thought, vvas now vpon the point:
When my affrighted powers could hold no more,
But pitty breaking all thoſe bands of ſhame,
That held me back, I ſhrikd, and ran, God knowes,
With all the ſpeede my feeble feete could make,   460
And clammering vp at length (vvith much adoe)
Breathleſſe, I got, and tooke him by the hand,——
And glad I had his hand, and vvas not come
Too late to haue it,—and I puld him backe:
But could not ſpeake one vvord ; no more did he:
Senſe ſeem'd to faile in him, and breath in me.
And on before I vvent, and led him on,
And downe conducted him into this plaine,
And yonder loe, vnder that fatall tree,——
Looke *Cloris* there, euen in that very place,——   470
We ſate vs downe, my arme about his necke ;
Which *Ioue* thou know'ſt held neuer man before:
There onely did my teares conferre vvith his,
Words we had none : it vvas inough to thinke
For paſſion vvas too buſie now vvithin,
And had no time to come abroad in ſpeech,
And though I vvould haue ſpoken, yet me thought
I ſhould not, but my ſilence told him this,
That told too much, that all I was was his.

Clo. Well *Siluia*, I haue heard fo fad a tale,   480
As that I grieue to be a woman borne,
And that by nature we muft be expof'd
Vnto the mercy of vnconftant men :
But what faid then *Palæmon* in the ende ?
   Sil. Oh what he faid, and what deepe vowes he
        made ?
When ioy and griefe, had let his fenfes loofe ;
Witneffe O gentle tree vnder whofe fhade,
We fate the while ; witneffe, if euer maide
Had more affurances by oathes of man.
And well may you beare witneffe of this deede,   490
For in a thoufand of your barkes he hath
Incaru'd my name, and vnder wrote his vowes :
Which will remaine fo long as you beare bowes.
But *Cloris*, learne this leffon well of mee ;
Take heed of pitty ;—pitty was the caufe
Of my confufion : pitty hath vndone
Thoufands of gentle natures, in our fexe ;
For pitty is fworne feruant vnto loue :
And this be fure, where euer it begin
To make the way, it lets your maifter in.   500
   Clo. But what affurance haue you of his fraud ?
It may be you fufpect him without caufe.
   Sil. Ah *Cloris*, *Cloris*, would I had no caufe !
He who beheld him wrong me in thefe woods,
And heard him courting *Nifa*, and proteft
As deepe to her, as he had done to me,
Told me of all his wicked treachery,
   Clo. Pray, who was that ? tell me good *Siluia*, tell.
   Sil. Why it was *Colax*, one I know full well
Would not report vntruths to gaine the world ;   510

A man of vertue, and of worthy parts.
He told me all, and more then I will fhew ;
I would I knew not halfe of that I know.
  Ah had he none but *Nifa*, that bafe trull,
The fcorne and ieft of all *Arcadia* now
To ferue his lufts, and falfifie his vow ?
Ah had it yet beene any elfe, the touch
Of my difgrace, had neuer beene fo much ;
But to [be] left for fuch a one as fhe,
The ftale of all, what will folke thinke of me ?   520
Cloris in troth, it makes me fo much loath
My felfe, loath thefe woods, and euen hate the day,
As I muft hide my griefes out of the way :
I will be gone, *Cloris*, I leaue thee here,
I cannot ftay ; and prethee, *Cloris*, yet
Pitty thy poore companion *Siluias* care,
And let her fortune make thee to beware.
  Clo. Siluia adue, the Gods relieue thy woes,
Since men thus faile, and loue no pitty fhowes,   .

SCEN. II.   530

Cloris.   *Techne.*

Loue ? nay, I'me taught from louing whilft I llue,
    Siluia, thy counfell hath lockt vp my heart
So faft from loue, as let them figh, and grieue,
And pine, and waile who vvill, I for my part
Will pitty none of all this race of men.
I fee vvhat fhowes foeuer they pretend,
Their loue is neuer deadly ; none of thefe
That languifh thus haue dide of this difeafe
That euer I could heare ; I fee all do   540

Recouer foone, that happen thereinto.
And if they did not, there were no great hurt ;
They may indure, they are of ftronger powers ;
Better their hearts fhould ake, then they break ours.
    Well, had I not beene thus forewarnd to day,
Out of all queftion, I had fhortly falne,
Into the melting humour of compaffion too ;
That tender pitty that betrayes vs thus.
For fomething I began to feele, me thought,
To moue vvithin me, when as I beheld   550
Amyntas walke, fo fadly, and fo pale ;
And euer where I went, ftill in my way,
His lookes bent all to me, his care of mee :
Which well I faw, but would not feeme to fee.
But now he hath his arrent, let him goe,
Pitty fhall neuer cure that heart of his
T'vndoe mine owne ; the griefe is beft where tis.
    Tec. What, *Cloris*, all alone, now fie for fhame,
How ill doth this become fo faire a face,
And that frefh youth to be without your loue ?   560
    Clo. Loue, *Techne* ? I haue here as many loues
As I intend to haue, whilft I haue breath.
    Tec. Nay that you haue not, neuer hault with me ;
For I know two at leaft poffeffors be
Of your kinde fauours, as themfelues doe boaft.
    Clo. Boft of my fauours, no man rightly can ;
And otherwife, let them doe what they can.
    Tec. No *Cloris*, did not you the other night
A gallant Nofegay to *Amyntas* giue ?
    Clo. I neuer gaue him Nofegay in my life.   570
    Tec. Then truft me *Cloris* he doth wrong you much ;
For he produc'd it there in open fight,

vaunted to *Carinus*, that you firſt
ciſſe the ſame, then gaue it vnto him,
tolde too how farre gone you were in loue ;
t paſſion you would vſe, when he was by ;
you would ieſt with him, and wantonly
water in his face ; call his dogge yours,
ſhew him your affeƈtions by your eye.
then *Carinus* on the other ſide   580
ſaunts, that ſince he had redeemed you
of the Satyres hands, he could command
· loue and all ; that you were onely his.
and much more, I heard them I proteſt,
out of you ; how truly you know beſt.
'o. *Techne*, their idle talke, ſhall not vexe me ;
ow the ground I ſtand on, and how free
ieart, and I, inioy our liberty ;
if *Amyntas*, hath interpreted
lookes according to his owne conceit,   590
iath miſtooke the text, and he ſhall finde
t difference twixt his comment, & my minde.
for his Noſegay, it ſhall make me take
: care hereafter how I ſcatter flowers :
iim preſerue it well, and let him make
i of his gaines, he gets no more of ours.
hus had I beene ſeru'd, had I reueal'd
leaſt regard of common courteſie
ich as theſe : but I doe thanke the gods
ie reſeru'd me, from that vanitie :   600
:uer I ſuſpeƈted this to be
veine of men, and this now ſettles me.
for *Carinus*, let him vaunt what good
id for me, he can but haue againe

My hearty thankes, the payment for his paine ;
And that he fhall, and ought in womanhood.
And as for loue, let him goe looke on her
That fits, and grieues, and languifhes for him,
Poore *Amarillis* ; who affects him deare,
And fought his loue with many a wofull teare.   610
And well deferues a better man then he :
Though he be rich *Lupinus* fonne, and ftands
Much on his wealth, and his abilitie :
She is witty, faire, and full of modeftie.
And were fhe of my minde, fhe rather would
Pull out her eyes, than that fhe would be feene,
To offer vp fo deare a facrifice
To his wilde youth, that fcornes her in that wife.
   Tec. Cloris in troth, I like thy iudgement well,
In not affecting of thefe home-bred Swaines,   620
That know not how to manage true delight ;
Can neither hide their loue, nor fhew it right.
Who would be troubled with groffe ignorance,
That vnderftands not truely how to loue ?
No *Cloris*, if thou didft but know, how well
Thou art efteem'd, of one that knowes indeed
How to obferue thy worth, and his owne wayes ;
How to giue true delight, how to proceed
With fecrecy, and wit, in all affayes,
Perhaps you might thinke one day of the man.   630
   Clo. What, is this creature then you praife, a man ?
   Tec. A man ? yes *Cloris*, what fhould he be elfe ?
   Clo. Nought elfe, it is enough he be a man.
   Tec. Yea and fo rare a man as euer yet
Arcadia bred, that may be proud fhe bred
A perfon of fo admirable parts ;

A man that knowes the world, hath feene abrod,
Brings thofe perfections that doe truly moue ;
A gallant fpirit, an vnderftanding loue.
O if you did but know how fweet it were,   640
To come vnto the bed of worthineffe,
Of knowledge, of conceits,—where ftrange delights
With ftrange difcourfes ftill fhall entertaine
Your pleafed thoughts with frefh varietie,—
Ah you would loath to haue your youth confin'de,
For euer more betweene the vnfkilfull armes
Of one of thefe rude vnconceiuing Swaines,
Who would but feeme a trunke without a minde ;
As one that neuer faw but thefe poore plaines,
Knowes but to keepe his fheepe, and fet his fold,   650
Pipe on an Oaten Reede fome Rundelayes,
And daunce a Morrice on the holy dayes.
And fo fhould you be alwayes fweetly fped
With ignorance, and two fooles in a bed.
But with this other gallant fpirit you fhould
Be fure to ouerpaffe that tedioufneffe,
And that faciety which cloyes this life,
With fuch a variable cheerefulneffe,
As you will bleffe the time t'haue beene his wife. 659
   Clo. What, hath this man you thus commend, a name?
   Tec. A name ? why yes, no man but hath a name :
His name is *Colax* ; and is one I fweare
Doth honour euen the ground whereon you tread,
And oft, and many times God knowes,
Hath he with tender paffion, talkt of you ;
And faid, Well, there is one vvithin thefe vvoods
(Meaning by you) that yet of all the Nymphes
Mine eyes haue euer feene vpon the earth,

In all perfections doth exceede them all.
For all the beauties in that glorious Court   670
Of *Telos*, vvhere I liu'd, nor all the Starres
Of *Greece* befide, could fparkle in my heart
The fire of any heate, but onely fhee.
Then vvould he ftay, and figh ; and then againe :
Ah vvhat great pitty fuch a creature fhould,
Be tide vnto a clogge of ignorance ;
Whofe body doth deferue to be imbrac'd,
By the moft mighty Monarch vpon earth.
Ah that fhe knew her vvorth, and how vnfit
That priuate woods fhould hide that face, that wit.
   Thus hath he often faid, and this I fay,   681
Obferue him vvhen you vvill, you fhall not fee
From his hye fore-head to his flender foote,
A man in all parts, better made then he.
   Clo. *Techne*, me thinkes, the praifes that you giue
Shewes your owne loue ; and if he be that man
You fay, 'tvvere good you kept him for your felfe.
   Tec. I muft not loue impoffibilities ;
Cloris, he vvere a moft fit man for you.
   Clo. For me ? alas *Techne* you moue too late. 690
   Tec. Why haue you paft your promife t'any yet ?
   Clo. Yes fure, my promife is already paft.
   Tec. And if it be, I truft you are fo wife
T'vnpaffe the fame againe for your owne good.
   Clo. No, that I may not when it is once paft.
   Tec. No *Cloris*, I prefume that wit of yours
That is fo pierfiue, can conceiue how that
Our promife muft not preiudice our good :
And that it is no reafon that the tongue,
Tie the whole body to eternall wrong,   700

Clo. The Tongue is but the Agent of the heart,
And onely as commiffioner allowd
By reafon, and the will, for the whole ftate,
Which warrants all it fhall negotiate.

Tec. But prithee tell me to what rufticke Swaine
You pafs'd your word to caft away your felfe?

Clo. No, I haue paft my word to faue my felfe
From the deceiptfull, impious periuries
Of treacherous men, and vow'd vnto my heart
Vntill I fee more faith then yet I fee,　　　　710
None of them all fhall triumph ouer me.

Tec. Nay then, and be no otherwife, tis well;
We fhall haue other time to talke of this.
But *Cloris* I haue fitted you in faith,
I haue here brought, the moft conceipted tyre,
The rareft dreffing euer Nymph put on;
Worth ten of that you weare; that, now me thinkes
Doth not become you; and befides, tis ftale.

Clo. Stale why? I haue not worne it fcarce a
　　　moneth.　　　　　　　　　　　　　　•

Tec. A moneth? why you muft change them twife
　　　a day:　　　　　　　　　　　　　720
Hold hither *Cloris*, this was not well laid;
Here is a fault, you haue not mixt it well
To make it take, or elfe it is your hafte
To come abroad fo foone into the Ayre.
But I muft teach you to amend thefe faults,
And ere I fhall haue done with you, I thinke,
I fhall make fome of thefe inamored youthes
To hang themfelues, or elfe runne madde for loue,
But goe, let's trie this dreffing I haue brought.

SCEN. III.   730

Palæmon. Mirtillus.

MIrtillus, did *Dorinda* euer vow,
Or make thee any promife to be thine?
Mir. *Palæmon* no, fhe neuer made me vow,
But I did euer hope fhe would be mine;
For that I had deliuered vp my youth,
My heart, my all, a tribute to her eyes,
And had fecur'd her of my conftant truth,
Vnder fo many faithfull fpecialties,
As that although fhe did not graunt againe,   740
With any fhew the acquittance of my loue,
Yet did fhee euer feeme to entertaine
My affections, and my feruices t'approoue;
Till now of late I know not by what meane,
(Ill fare that meane) fhe grew to that difpight,
As fhe not onely clowds her fauours cleane,
But alfo fcorn'd to haue me in her fight;
That now I am not for her loue thus mou'd,
But onely that fhe will not be belou'd.
Pal. If this be all th'occafion of thy griefe,   750
Mirtillus, thou art then in better cafe
Then I fuppof'd, and therefore cheere thy heart;
And good caufe too, being in the ftate thou art,
For if thou didft but heare the Hiftory
Of my diftreffe, and what part I haue fhar'd
Of fad affliction, thou wilt then foone fee
There is no mifery vnleffe compar'd.
For all Arcadia, all thefe hills, and plaines,
Thefe holts, and woods and euery Chriftall fpring,
Can teftifie my teares, and tell my flames,   760

III.   16

And with how cleane a heart, how cleere a faith
Palæmon louèd *Siluia*, and how long.
And when confum'd with griefe, and dri'd with care,
Euen at the point to facrifice my life
Vnto her cruelty, then lo fhe yeelds,
And was content for euer to be mine :
And gaue m'affurance vnderneath her hand,
Sign'd with a faithfull vow, as I conceiu'd,
And witneffèd with many a louely kiffe,
That I thought fure I had attain'd my bliffe.   770
And yet (aie me) I got not what I got,
Siluia I haue, and yet I haue her not.
    Mir. How may that be, *Palæmon* pray thee tell ?
    Pal. O know *Mirtillus* that I rather could
Runne to fome hollow caue, and burft and die
In darknes, and in horror, then vnfold
Her fhamefull ftaine, and mine owne infamy.
But yet it will abroad, her impudence
Will be the trumpet of her owne difgrace,
And fill the wide and open mouth of fame   780
So full, as all the world fhall know the fame.
    Mir. Why, what is *Siluia* falfe, or is fhe gone ?
    Pal. *Siluia* is falfe and I am quite vndone.
    Mir. Ah out alas, who euer would haue thought
That modeft looke, fo innocent a face,
So chaft a blufh, that fhame-faft countenance,
Could euer haue told how to wantonife ?
Ah what fhall we poore louers hope for now
Who muft to win, confume, and hauing wonne
With hard and much adoe, muft be vndone?   790
    Pal. Ah but *Mirtillus* if thou didft know who
Is now the man, her choice hath lighted on,

How would'ſt thou wonder? for that paſſes all ;
That I abhore to tell, yet tell I ſhall ;
For all that would will ſhortly know't too well :
It is baſe *Thirſis*, that wild hare-braine youth
Whom euery milk-maid in *Arcadia* ſkornes :
Thyrſis is now the man with vvhome ſhe walkes
Alone, in thickets, and in groues remote.
Thvrſis is all in all, and none but he ;   800
With him ſhe dallies vnder euery tree.
Truſt women? ah *Mirtillus*, rather truſt
The Summer windes, th'Oceans conſtancy ;
For all their ſubſtance is but leuity.
Light are their wauing vailes, light their attires,
Light are their heads, and lighter their deſires :
Let them lay on vvhat couerture they will
Vpon themſelues, of modeſty and ſhame,
They cannot hide the woman with the ſame.
Truſt women ? ah *Mirtillus* rather truſt   810
The falſe deuouring Crocodiles of *Nile* ;
For all they worke is but deceipt and guile :
What haue they but is fain'd ? their haire is fain'd,
Their beauty fain'd, their ſtature fain'd, their pace,
Their ieſture, motion, and their grace is fain'd :
And if that all be fain'd without, vvhat then
Shall we ſuppoſe can be ſincere within ?
For if they doe but vveepe, or ſing, or ſmile,
Smiles, teares, and tunes, are ingins to beguile ;
And all they are, and all they haue of grace,   820
Conſiſts but in the outſide of a face.
O loue and beauty, how are you ordain'd
Like vnto fire, vvhoſe flames farre off delight,
But if you be imbrac'd conſume vs quite ?

Why cannot vve make at a lower rate
A purchafe of you, but that we muſt giue
The treaſure of our hearts, and yet not haue
What we haue bought ſo dearely for all that ?
O *Siluia* if thou needs wouldſt haue beene gone,
Thou ſhould'ſt haue taken all away of thee ;   830
And nothing left to haue remain'd with me.
Thou ſhould'ſt haue carried hence the portraiture
VVhich thou haſt left behind within my heart,
Set in the table-frame of memory,
That puts me ſtill in minde of what thou wert,
VVhilſt thou wert honeſt, and thy thoughts were pure;
So that I might not thus in euery place,
VVhere I ſhall ſet my carefull foote, conferre
VVith it of thee, and euermore be told,
That here ſate *Siluia* vnderneath this tree ;   840
And here ſhe walkt, and lean'd vpon mine arme ;
There gathered flowers, and brought them vnto me ;
Here by the murmurs of this ruſling ſpring,   .
She ſweetly lay, and in my boſome ſlept ;
Here firſt ſhe ſhewd me comforts when I pinde ;
As if in euery place her foote had ſtept,
It had left *Siluia* in a print behind.
But yet, O theſe were *Siluias* images,
Then whilſt her heart held faire, and ſhe was chaſte ;
Now is her face all ſullied with her faſt ;   850
And why are not thoſe former prints defac'd ?
VVhy ſhould ſhe hold, ſtill in the forme ſhe was,
Being now deform'd, and not the ſame ſhe was ?
O that I could *Mirtillus* locke her out
Of my remembrance, that I might no more
Haue *Siluia* here, vvhen ſhe will not be here.

Mir. But good *Palæmon*, tell vvhat proofes haſt thou
Of her diſloyalty, that makes thee ſhow
Theſe heauy paſſions, and to grieue ſo much?
 Pal. Mirtillus, proofes that are alas too plaine; 860
For *Colax*, one thou knowſt can well obſerue
And iudge of loue ; a man both ſtaid, and wiſe,
A gentle heardſman, out of loue, and care
He had of me, came and reported all ;
And how he ſaw them diuers times alone,
Imbracing each the other in the woods.
Beſides ſhe hath of late with ſullaine lookes,
That ſhew'd diſliking, ſhunn'd my company,
Kept her a looſe ; and novv I thinke to day,
Is gone to hide her quite out of the vvay. 870
 But *Siluia* though thou go and hide thy face,
Thou canſt not hide thy ſhame, and thy diſgrace ;
No ſecret thicket, groue, nor yet cloſe grot,
Can couer ſhame, and that immodeſt blot.
Ah didſt thou lend thy hand in kind remorſe
To ſaue me from one death, to giue m'a worſe ?
Had it not yet beene better I had died,
By thy vnſpotted honeſt cruelty,
Then now by thy diſgracèd infamy ?
That ſo I might haue carried to my graue 880
The image of chaſte *Siluia* in my heart,
And not haue had theſe notions, to ingraue
A ſtainèd *Siluia* there, as now thou art ?
Ah yes, it had beene better farre, I prooue,
T'haue periſht for thy loue, then vvith thy loue.
 Mir. Ah good *Palæmon*, ceaſe theſe ſad com-
   plaints,
And moderate thy paſſions ; thou ſhalt ſee

She may returne, and thefe reports be found
But idle fictions on vncertaine ground.

    Pal. Mirtillus I perceiue my tedious tale,   890
Begins to be diftaftefull to thine eare ;
And therefore will I to fome defert vale,
To fome clofe groue to waile, where none fhall heare
But beafts, and trees, whofe fenfe I fhall not tyre
VVith length of mone ; for length is my defire.
And therefore, gentle Sheepheard, now adieu,
And truft not women, for they are vntrue.

    Mir. Adue *Palæmon*, and thy fad diftreffe,
Shall make me weigh *Dorindas* loffe the leffe :
For if I fhould be hers, and fhe prooue fo,   900
Better to be mine owne and let her go.

SCEN. IV.

Ergaſtus.   *Melibæus.*

NOw *Melibæus* ; who would haue fuppos'd
    That had not feene thefe impious paffages,
That euer monftrous wretch could haue expos'd
T[w]o honeft hearts to thefe extremities,
T'attaine his wicked ends ? by hauing wrought
Firft in, vnto their eafie confidence
A way, by an opinion to be thought,   910
Honeft, difcreet, of great experience.

    Whereby we fee open-fac't villanie
Without a mafke, no mifchiefe could haue done ;
It was the couerture of honefty,
That laid the fnare, whereby they were vndone,
And that's the ingine that confounds vs all ;
That makes the breach whereby the world is fackt,

And made a prey to cunning, when we fall
Into the hands of wife diſhoneſty :
Whenas our weake credulity is rackt	920
By that opinion of ſufficiency,
To all the inconuenienceṣ that guile,
And impious craft can praⅽtiſe to beguile.

And note but how theſe cankers alwayes feaze
The choyſeſt fruits with their infeⅽtions ;
How they are ſtill ordainèd to diſeaſe,
The natures of the beſt compleⅽtions.

Mel. Tis true. And what an inſtrument hath he
To be the Agent of his villany ?	[there got,
How truely ſhe negotiats, and doth plot,	930
To vndermine fraile imbecillity.
How ſtrong, theſe ſpirits combine them in a knot,
To circumvent plaine open honeſty ?

And what a creature there is to conuerſe
With feeble maydes ; whoſe vveaknes ſoone is led
VVith toyes, and new diſguiſes, to reuerſe
The courſe wherein by cuſtome they vvere bred ?
And then what fitneſſe too her trade affoords,
To trafficke with the ſecrets of their heart,
And cheapen their affeⅽtions vvithˊfaire words,	940
VVhich vvomen ſtraight to women vvill impart ?
And then to ſee how ſoone example vvill
Diſperſe it ſelfe, being met with our deſire ?
How ſoone, it vvill inkindle others ill,
Like *Neptha* that takes fire by ſight of fire ?
So that vnleſſe we runne vvith all the ſpeed
VVe can, to quench this new ariſing flame
Of vanity, and luſt, it will proceed
T'vndoe vs, ere vve ſhall perceiue the ſame :

How farre already is the mifchiefe runne,   950
Before vve fcarfe perceiu'd it was begunne ?

ACT III.   SCEN.   I.

Alcon.   Lincus.

VVHat my friend *Lincus?* now in troth well
        met.
  Lin. VVell met good *Alcon,* this fals happily
That we two thus incounter all alone,
VVho had not any conference fcarfe this moneth.
  Al. In troth I long'd to heare how you proceed
In your new practife here among thefe fwaines ;
For you and I muft grace each others arte :   960
Though you knew me, vvhen I in *Patras* dwelt,
And waited on a poore Phifitions man,
And I knew you a Pronotories boy,
That wrote Indentures at the towne-houfe-doore ;
Yet are you here now a great man of law,
And I a graue Phifition full of fkill ;
And here we two are held the only men :
But how thriue you in your new practife now ?
  Lin. Alcon, in troth, not any thing to fpeake ;
For thefe poore people of *Arcadia* here   970
Are foone contented each man with his owne,
As they defire no more, nor will be drawne
To any conteftation ; nor indeed
Is there yet any frame compof'd, whereby
Contention may proceed in practicke forme ?
For if they had this frame once, to contend,
Then would they brawle and wrangle without end.
For then might they be taught, and councell'd how

To litigate perpetually, you know ;
And fo might I be fure to doe fome good ;   980
But hauing here no matter whereupon
To furnifh reall actions, as elfe where ;
No tenures, but a cuftomary hold
Of what they haue from their progenitors
Common, without indiuiduitie ;
No purchafings, no contracts, no comerfe,
No politique commands, no feruices,
No generall affemblies but to feaft,
And to delight themfelues with frefh paftimes ;
How can I hope that euer I fhall thriue ?   990
    Alc. Ift poffible that a focietie
Can with fo little noyfe, and fweat fubfift ?
    Lin. It feemes it may, before men haue transform'd
Their ftate of nature in fo many fhapes
Of their owne managements, and are caft out
Into confufion, by their knowledges.
And either I muft packe me hence, or elfe
Muft labour wholly to diffolue the frame
And compofition, of their ftrange. built ftate ;
Which now I feeke to doe, by drawing them   1000
To appr'hend of thefe proprieties
Of *mine and thine,* and teach them to incroch
And get them ftates apart, and priuate fhares.
And this I haue already fet a worke
If it vvill take ; for I haue met with two
The apteft fpirits the countrey yeelds, I know,
Montanus and *Acryfius* ; vvho are both
Old, and both cholericke, and both peruerfe,
And both inclinable to Auarice ;
And if their quarrell hold, as tis begun   1010

I doe not doubt but all the reſt vvill on ;
And if the vvorſt ſhould fall, if I could gaine
The reputation but to arbitrate,
And ſway their ſtrifes, I vvould get vvell by that.

Alc. Tis maruell that their long and eaſie peace
That foſters plenty, and giues nought to doe,
Should not vvith them beget contention too,
As vvell as other vvhere vve ſee it doth.

Lin. This peace of theirs is not like others peace ;
Where craft laies traps t'inrich himſelfe with wiles,
And men make prey of men, and riſe by ſpoiles. 1021
This rather ſeemes a quiet then a peace :
For this poore corner of *Arcadia* here,
This little angle of the vvorld you ſee,
Which hath ſhut out of doore, all t'earth beſide,
And is bard vp with mountaines, and with rocks ;
Haue had no intertrading with the reſt
Of men, nor yet will haue, but here alone,
Quite out of fortunes way, and vnderneath
Ambition, or deſire, that weighes them not,   1030
They liue as if ſtill in the golden age,
When as the world was in his pupillage.

But for mine owne part, *Alcon*, I proteſt
I enuy them that they thus make themſelues,
An euerlaſting holy day of reſt,
Whiles others worke ; and I doe thinke it fit
Being in the world, they ſhould be of the world,
And if that other ſtates ſhould doe ſo too
As God forbid, what ſhould we Lawyers doe ?
But I hope ſhortly yet ; we ſhall haue here   1040
As many of vs as are other where :
And we ſhall ſweat, and chafe, and talke as loud,

Brawle our felues hoarfe, as well as they doe
At *Patras, Sparta, Corinth,* or at *Thebes* ;
And be as arrogant and euen as proud ;
And then twill be a world, and not before :
But how doft thou with thy profeffion frame ?

   Alc. No man can wifh a better place then this
To pra&ctife in my arte ; for here they will
Be ficke for company, they are fo kinde.   1050
I haue now twenty Pacients at this time,
That know not vvhat they ayle ; no more doe I :
And they haue Phyficke all accordingly.
Firft *Phillis* got running at Barley-breake
A little cold, vvhich I vvith certaine drugs
Adminiftred, vvas thought to remedie ;
Doris faw that how *Phillis* Phyficke wrought
(For *Phillis* had told her, fhe neuer tooke
So delicate a thing in all her life
That more reuiu'd her heart, and clear'd her blood ;)
Doris would needs be ficke too, and take fome. 1061
Melina feeing that, fhe would the like,
And fo fhe had the very fame receit ;
For to fay troth, I haue no more but that,
And one poore pill I vfe for greater cures.
But this is onely fweet and delicate,
Fit for young women, and is like th'hearbe Iohn,
Doth neither good nor hurt ; but that's all one :
For if they but conceiue it doth, it doth ;
And it is that Phyfitians hold the chiefe   1070
In all their cures, *conceit, and ftrong beliefe :*
Befides I am a ftranger come from farr
Which doth adde much vnto opinion too.
For who now but th'*Arabian* or the *Iew*

In forraine lands, are held the onely men,
Although their knowledge be no more then mine.
   Lin. Tis true friend *Alcon,* he that hath once got
Th'Elixir of opinion, hath got all,
And h'is th'man that turnes his braffe to gold.
   Alc. Then can I talke of *Gallen, Auerrois,*   1080
Hypocrates, Rafis, and *Auicen,*
And bookes I neuer read, and vfe ftrange fpeach
Of Symptons, Cryfis, and the Critique dayes ;
Eclegmats, Embrochs, Lixiues, Cataplafmes ;
Of Trochifes, Opiats, Apophilegmatifmes ;
With all the hideous tearmes Arte can deuife
T'amufe weake, and admiring ignorance.
   Lin. And that is right my tricke ; I ouerwhelme
My praƈtife too, with darknes, and ftrange words ;
With Paragraphs, Conditions, Codicilles,   1090
Acceptilations, aƈtions recifforie,
Noxall, and Hypothecall, and inuolue
Domefticke matter in a forraine phrafe.
   Alc. Then am I as abftrufe and myfticall,
In Careƈteer, and giuing my receit,
Obferuing th'odde number in my pills,
And certaine houres to gather and compound
My fimples, and make all t'attend the Moone.
Then doe I fhew the rare ingredients
I vfe for fome great cures, when need requires ;   1100
The liuer of a Wolfe, the Lyons gall,
The left fide of a Moles, the Foxes heart,
The right foote of a Tortufe, Dragons blood ;
And fuch ftrange fauage ftuffe, as euen the names
Are phyficke of themfelues, to moue a man.
And all the drugs I vfe, muft come from farre,

Beyond the Ocean, and the Sunne at leaſt,
Or elſe it hath no vertue Phyſicall ;
Theſe home-bred ſimples doe no good at all.
    Lin. No, no, it muſt be forraine ſtuffe, God wot, 1110
Or ſomething elſe that is not to be got.
    Al. But now in faith I haue found out a tricke,
That will perpetually ſo feede their rheumes,
And entertaine their idle weakneſſes,
As nothing in the vvorld could doe the like ;
For lately being at *Corinth*, 'twas my chance
T'incounter with a Sea-man, new-arriu'd
Of *Alexandria*, vvho from *India* came,
And brought a certaine hearbe wrapt vp in rowles,
From th'Iſland of *Nicoſia*, where it growes :   1120
Infuſ'd I thinke in ſome peſtiferous iuice.
(Produc'd in that contagious burning clime,
Contrarious to our nature, and our ſpirits)
Or elſe ſteep'd in the fuming ſap, it ſelfe
Doth yeeld, t'inforce th'infeɔting power thereof;
And this in powder made, and fir'd, he ſuckes
Out of a little hollow inſtrument
Of calcinated clay, the ſmoake thereof :
Which either he conuayes out of his noſe,
Or downe into his ſtomacke vvith a vvhiffe.   1130
And this he ſaid a wondrous vertue had,
To purge the head, and cure the great Catarre,
And to dry vp all other meaner rhumes ;
Which when I ſaw, I ſtraight vvay thought how vvell
This new fantaſticall deuiſe would pleaſe
The fooliſh people here growne humorous.
And vp I tooke all this commoditie,
And here haue taught them how to vſe the ſame.

Lin. And it is eafie to bring in the vfe
Of any thing, though neuer fo abfurd,   1140
When nations are prepar'd to all abufe,
And th'humour of corruption once is ftird.
   Alc. Tis true, and now to fee with what a ftrange
And gluttonous defire, th'exhauft the fame ;
How infinite, and how infatiably,
They doe deuour th'intoxicating fume,
You vvould admire ; as if their fpirits thereby
Were taken, and inchanted, or transformd,
By fome infufèd philter in the drug.
   For vvhereas heretofore they vvonted vvere,   1150
At all their meetings, and their feftiualls,
To paffe the time in telling vvitty tales,
In queftions, riddles, and in purpofes,
Now doe they nothing elfe, but fit and fucke,
And fpit, and flauer, all the time they fit ;
That I goe by, and laugh vnto my felfe,
And thinke that this wil one day make fome worke.
For me or others ; but I feare it vvill
B'another age will finde the hurt of this.
But fure the time's to come when they looke backe
On this, vvill vvonder vvith themfelues to thinke 1160
That men of fenfe could euer be fo mad,
To fucke fo groffe a vapour, that confumes
Their fpirits, fpends nature, dries vp memorie,
Corrupts the blood, and is a vanitie.
   Lin. But *Alcon* peace, here comes a patient, peace.
   Al. *Lincus*, there doth indeed, therefore away ;
Leaue me alone, for I muft now refume
My furly, graue, and Doctorall afpect.
This wench I know ; tis *Daphne*, who hath wrong'd

Her loue *Menalcas*, and plaid faft and loofe   1170
With *Cola,x* who reueald the whole to me.

SCEN. II.

Daphne.   *Alcon.*

Good Doctor *Alcon*, I am come to craue
       Your counfell, to aduife me for my health ;
For I fuppofe, in troath, I am not well ;
Me thinkes I fhould be ficke, yet cannot tell :
Some thing there is amiffe that troubles me,
For which I would take Phificke willingly.   1180

Alc. Welcome, faire Nymph, come let me try your
I cannot blame you t'hold your felfe not well.   [pulfe ;
Something amiffe quoth you, here's all amiffe ;
Th'whole Fabricke of your felfe diftempred is ;
The Syftole, and Dyaftole of your pulfe,
Doe fhew your paffions moft hyftericall.
It feemes you haue not very carefull beene,
T'obferue the prophilactick regiment
Of your owne body, fo that we muft now
Defcend vnto the Therapheuticall ;   1190
That fo we may preuent the fyndrome
Of Symtomes, and may afterwards apply
Some analepticall Elexipharmacum,
That may be proper for your maladie :
It feemes faire nimph you dream much in the night.

Dap. Doctor, I doe indeed.

Alc.   I know you doe ;
Y'are troubled much with thought.

Dap. I am indeed.

Alc.   I know you are   1200
You haue great heauineffe about your heart.

Dap. Now truly fo I haue.

Alc.   I know you haue.
You wake oft in the night.

Dap.   In troath I doe.

Alc. All this I know you doe;
And this vnleffe by phyficke you preuent,
Thinke whereto it may bring you in the end ;
And therefore you muft firft euacuate
All thofe Colaxicall hote humours which   1210
Difturbe your heart, and then refrigerate
Your blood by fome Menalchian Cordials,
Which you muft take, & you fhal ftraight find eafe :
And in the morning I will vifit you.

Dap. I pray Sir, let me take of that you gaue,
To *Phillis* th'other day ; for that fhe faid,
Did comfort wonderfully, and cheere her heart.

Alc. Faire nimph, you muft, if you wil vfe my art,
Let me alone, to giue vvhat I thinke good ;
I knew what fitted *Phillis* maladie,   1220
And fo, I thinke, I know what will fit you.   *Exit.*

Daphne fola.

O what a wondrous fkil[lfu]l man is this ?
Why he knowes all ? O God, who euer thought
Any man liuing, could haue told fo right
A womans griefe in all points as he hath ?
Why, this is ftrange that by my very pulfe
He fhould know all I ayle, as well as I.
Befide I feare he fees too much in mee,
More then I would that any man fhould fee.   1230
Me thought (although I could not well conceiue
His words, he fpake fo learnèd and fo ftrange)

He faid I had mifruld my body much ;
As if he meant that in fome wanton fort,   1230
I had abuf'd my body with fome man :
O how fhould he know that ? what is my pulfe
Become the intelligencer of my fhame ?
Or are my lookes the index of my heart ?
Sure fo he faid, and me thought too, he nam'd
Menalcas, or elfe fomething very like ;
And likewife nam'd that cunning treacherous wretch
That hath vndone me, *Colax*, that vile Diuell ;
Who is indeed the caufe of all my griefe,
For which I now feeke Phyficke ; but O what   1240
Can Phyficke doe to cure that hideous wound
My lufts haue giuen my Confcience ? which I fee
Is that which onely is difeaf'd within,
And not my body now ; that's it doth fo
Difquiet all the lodging of my fpirits,
As keepes me waking ; that is it prefents
Thofe onely formes of terror that affright
My broken fleepes ; that, layes vpon my heart
This heauy loade that weighes it downe with griefe ;
And no difeafe befide : for which there is   1250
No cure I fee at all, nor no redreffe.
    Didft thou alleadge vile man to my weake youth,
How that thofe vowes I made vnto my loue
Were bands of cuftome, and could not lay on
Thofe manicles on nature, vvhich fhould keepe
Her freedome prifoner by our dome of breath ?
O impious wretch now nature giues the lye
To thy foule heart and tels my grieuèd foule,
I haue done vvrong, to falfifie that vow
I firft to my deare loue *Menalcas* made.   1260

III.   17

And fayes th'affurance and the faith is giuen
By band on earth, the fame is feal'd in Heauen.
　　And therefore now *Menalcas* can thefe eyes
That now abhorre to looke vpon my felfe,
Dare euer view that vvrongèd face of thine,
Who haft relide on this falfe heart of mine?

SCEN. III.

Colax.　　　*Techne.*

I ft poffible fweet *Techne*, what you fay,
　　That *Cloris* is fo witty, and fo coy?　　　　　1270
　　Tec. Tis as I tell you *Colax*, fh'is as coy
And hath as fhrewd a fpirit, as quicke conceipt,
As euer wench I brok'd in all my life.
　　Col. Then there's fome glory in attaining her;
Here now I fhall be fure t'haue fomething yet
Befides dull beauty, I fhall lie vvith wit;
For thefe faire creatures, haue fuch feeble fpirits,
And are fo languifhing, as giue no edge
To appetite, and loue, but ftuffes delight.
　　Tec. Well if you get her, then you fhall be fure 1280
To haue your vvifh; and yet perhaps that ftore
You find in her, may checke your longing more
Then all their wants, whom you haue tride before.
　　Col. How? if I get her; what doe you fuppofe,
I fhall not get her? that were very ftrange.
　　Tec. Yes fir, fhe may be got, but yet I know
Sh'will put you to the triall of your wit.
　　Col. Let me alone, could I find feafon fit
To talke with her in priuate, fhe vvere mine.
　　Tec. That feafon may you now haue very well; 1290
For *Colax*, fhe hath promif'd faithfully

This euening late to meete me at the caue
Of *Erycina*, vnderneath the hill;
Where I muſt fit her vvith a new attyre
Where vvith ſh's farre in loue; and th'other day
Thinking to try it at her fathers houſe,
(Whether I went vvith her to deale for you)
The old *Acryſius* was himſelfe at home,
VVhich did enforce vs to deferre our worke
Vntill this euening, that we might alone   1300
There out of ſight, more cloſely do the ſame:
Where while ſhe ſtayes (for I will make her ſtay
For me a while) you at your pleaſure may
Haue th'opportunity vvhich you deſire.

   Col. O *Techne*, thou haſt bleſt me; if I now
On this aduantage conquer not her mind,
Let me be loathèd of all vvoman-kind.
And preſently will I go ſute my ſelfe
As brauely as I can, go ſet my lookes,
Arme my diſcourſe, frame ſpeaches paſſionate,   1310
And action both, fit for ſo great a worke:
Techne a thouſand thankes, and ſo adieu.   *Ex.*

   Tec. Well *Colax*, ſhe may yet deceiue thy hopes,
And I perſwade my ſelfe ſhe is as like
As any ſubtile vvench was euer borne,
To giue as wiſe a man as you the ſkorne:
But ſee, where one whoſe faith hath better right
Vnto her loue then you, comes here forlorne
Like fortunes out-caſt, full of heauines.   1319

   Ah poore *Amyntas*, vvould thou knewſt how much
Thou art eſteem'd, although not vvhere thou wouldſt,
Yet vvhere thou ſhould haue loue in that degree,
As neuer liuing man had like to thee.

Ah fee how I, who fets for others loue,
Am tooke my felfe, and intricated here
With one, that hath his heart another where?
But I vvill labour to diuert the ftreame
Of his affections, and to turne his thoughts
From that coy *Cloris*, to the liberty
Of his owne heart, vvith hope to make him mine. 1330

SCEN. IIII.

Techne.   Amyntas.

NOw fie *Amyntas*, why fhould you thus grieue
  For a moft foolifh vvay-ward girle, that fcornes
Your honeft loue, and laughes at all you doe ;
For fhame *Amyntas* let her go as fh'is.
You fee her vaine, and how peruerfly fet ;
Tis fond to follow vvhat we cannot get.
 Am. O *Techne, Techne*, though I neuer get,
Yet will I euer follow vvhilft I breath,   1340
And if I perifh by the vvay, yet fhall
My death be pleafing that for her I die.
And one day fhe may hap to come that way,
(And be it, O her way) where I fhall lye ;
And with her proud difdainefull foote fhe may
Tread on my tombe, and fay, loe where he lies,
The tryumph, and the conqueft of mine eyes.
And though I loofe my felfe, and loofe my teares,
It fhall be glory yet that I was hers.
VVhat haue I done of late, fhould make her thus 1350
My prefence with that ftrange difdaine to flye,
As if fhe did abhorre my company ?
Cloris God knowes, thou haft no caufe therefore,
Vnleffe it be for louing more, and more.

Why, thou wert vvont to lend me yet an eare, [heare.
And though thou wouldft not helpe, yet wouldft thou
 Tec. Perhaps fhe thinkes thy heat will be allayd,
The fire being gone, and therefore doth fhe well
Not to be feene there vvhere fhe vvill not aide.
 Am. Alas fhe knowes no hand but hers can quench
That heat in me, and therefore doth fhe vvrong 1361
To fire my heart, and then to runne away ;
And if fhe would not aide, yet might fhe eafe
My carefull foule, if fhe vvould but ftand by
And only looke vpon me while I die.
 Tec. Well well *Amyntas*, little doeft thou know
With vvhom that cunning vvanton forts her felfe.
Whil'ft thus thou mourn'ft, and vvith what fecret wiles
She vvorkes, to meet her louer in the vvoods ;
With whom in groues, and caues fhe dallying fits, 1370
And mockes thy paffions and thy dolefull fits.
 Am. No *Techne*, no, I know that cannot be,
And therefore do not vvrong her modefty ;
For *Cloris* loues no man, and that's fome eafe
Vnto my griefe, and giues a hope that yet
If euer foft affection touch her heart,
She will looke backe, and thinke on my defert.
 Tec. If that be all, that hope is at an end ;
For if thou wilt this euening but attend
And walke downe vnder *Erycinas* groue,   1380
And place thy felfe in fome clofe fecret bufh,
Right oppofite vnto the hollow caue
That lookes into the vally, thou fhalt fee
That honefty, and that great modefty.
 Am. If I fee *Cloris* there, I know I fhall
See nothing elfe vvith her, but modefty.

Tec. Yes fomething els will grieue your heart to fee:
But you muft be content, and thinke your felfe
Are not the firft that thus haue bin deceiu'd,
With faire appearing out-fides, and miftooke   1390
A wanton heart, by a chaft feeming looke.
But I coniure you by the loue you beare
Vnto thofe eyes which make you (as you are
Th'example of compaffion to the world)
Sit clofe and ·be not feene in any cafe.

Am. Well *Techne*, if I fhall fee *Cloris* there
It is enough, then thither will I goe
Who will go any where to looke on her.
And *Cloris* know, I do not go to fee,
Any thing elfe of thee, but only thee.   1400

Tec. Well go and thinke yet of her honeft care,
VVho giues the note of fuch a fhamefull deed ;
And iudge *Amyntas*, when thou fhalt be free,
VVho more deferues thy loue, or I or fhe.

S C E N. V.

Melibæus.   Ergaftus.

NOw what infernall proiects are here laid,
    T'afflict an honeft heart, t'expofe a maide,
Vnto the danger of a lone affault,
To make her to offend, without her fault.   1410

Er. And fee what other new appearing fpirits
Would raife the tempefts of difturbances
Vpon our reft, and labour to bring in
All the whole Ocean of vnquietneffe,
To ouerwhelme the poore peace we liue in ?
How one would faine inftruct, and teach vs how
To cut our throates with forme, and to contend

VVith artificiall knowledge, to vndoo
Each other, and to brabble without end.
As if that nature had not tooke more care   1420
For vs, then we for our owne felues cañ take ;
And makes vs better lawes then thofe we make.
And as if all that fcience ought could giue
Vnto our bliffe, but only fhewes vs how
The better to contend, but not to liue.
And euermore we fee how vice doth grow
With knowledge, and brings forth a more increafe,
When fkilfull men begin, how good men ceafe.
And therefore how much better do vve liue,
With quiet ignorance, then vve fhould do   1430
With turbulent and euer vvorking fkill,
Which makes vs not to liue, but labour ftill.
   Mel. And fee that other vaine fantafticke fpirit,
Who vvould corrupt our bodies too likewife,
As this our mindes, and make our health to be,
As troublefome as fickneffe, to deuife,
That no part of vs euer fhould be free ;
Both forraging on our credulity,
Take ftill th'aduantage of our weakeneffes ;
Both cloath their friuolous vncertainties   1440
In ftrange attires, to make it feeme the leffe.

ACTVS. IV. SCENA. I.

Techne. Amyntas.

A*Myntas* muft come backe I know this vvay,
    And here it will be beft for me to ftay ;
Andhere, indeed he comes, poore man I fee
All quite difmay'd : and now ile worke on him.

Come, vvho tels troth *Amyntas*, vvho deceiues
Your expe&ation now, *Cloris*, or I ?

Am. Peace *Techne* peace, and do not interrupt 1450
The griefe that hath no leafure to attend
Ought but it felfe, and hath fhut vp vvith it
All other fenfe in priuate clofe within,
From doing any thing, but onely thinke.

   Tec. Thinke ? whereon fhould you think ? y'haue
        thought enough
And too too much, on fuch a one as fhe,
Whom now you fee y'haue tride her honefty :
And let her goe proud girle accordingly ;
There's none of thefe young vvanton things that know
How t'vfe a man, or how to make their choyfe, 1460
Or anfwere mens affe&ions as they ought ;
And if y'will thinke, thinke fh'is not worth a thought.

   Am. Good *Techne*, leaue me ; for thy fpeech and fight
Beare both that difproportion to my griefe,
As that they trouble trouble, and confound
Confufion in my forrowes, vvhich doth loath
That found of words, that anfweres not the tone
Of my difprayers in th'accents of like mone.
And now hath forrow no vvorfe plague I fee
Then free and vnpartaking company ; 1470
Who are not in the fafhion of our vvoes,
And whofe affe&ion do not looke likewife
Of that comple&ion as our miferies :
And therefore pray thee leaue me, or elfe leaue
To fpeake, or if thou fpeake let it not be
To me, or elfe let me, not anfwere thee.

   Tec. Well I fay nothing, you know vvhat y'haue
      feene.

`Am.` Tis true, I do confeffe that I haue feene
The vvorft the world can fhew me, and the worft
That can be euer feene vvith mortall eye.   1480
I haue beheld the whole of all wherein
My heart had any intereft in this life ;
To be difrent and torne from of my hopes,
That nothing now is leaft, why I fhould liue :
That oftage I had giuen the world, which was
The hope of her, that held me to hold truce
With it, and with this life is gone ; and now
Well may I breake with them, and breake I will
And rend that paƈt of nature, and diffolue
That league of blood that ties me to my felfe.   1490
For *Cloris*, now hath thy immodefty
Infranchiz'd me, and made me free to dye :
VVhich otherwife I could not left it might
Haue beene fome ftaine and fome difgrace to thee.
    Ah was it not enough for this poore heart
T'indure the burden of her proud difdaine,
That weigh'd it to the earth, but it muft
Be crufht thus vvith th'oppreffion of her ftaine ?
The firft vvound yet though it were huge and wide,
Yet was it cleanely made, it feftred not ;   1500
But this now giuen, comes by a poyfoned fhot,
Againft all lawes of honor that are pure,
And rankles deadly, is vvithout all cure.
    Ah how fhe blufht vvhen as fhe iffued forth
VVith her inamor'd mate out of the caue !
And well then might fhe blufh at fuch a deed,
And with how vvild a looke fhe cafts about
Her fearefull eyes ! as if her loathfome finne
Now comming thus into the open fight,

VVith terror did her guiltineffe affright ;   1510
And vp fhe treades the hill vvith fuch a pace,
As if fhe gladly would haue out gone fhame,
Which yet for all her hafting, after came.
   And at their comming forth, me thought I heard
The villaine vfe my name, and fhe returne
The fame againe in very earneft fort ;
Which could be for no good I know to me,
But onely that perhaps it pleaf'd her then
To caft me vp by this way of her mouth
From off her heart, left it might ftuffe the fame. '1520
   But *Cloris* know thou fhalt not need to feare,
I neuer more fhall interrupt thy ioyes
With my complaints, nor more obferue thy waies ;
And O I would thy heart could be as free
From finne and fhame, as thou fhalt be from me.
I could (and I haue reafon fo to do)
Reuenge my wrong vpon that wicked wretch,
Who hath furpriz'd my loue, and robb'd thy fhame ;
And make his blood th'oblation of my wrath
Euen at thy feete, that thou might'ft fee the fame 1530
To expiate, for this vniuftice done,
But that the fact examin'd would difplay
Thy infamy abroad vnto the world,
Which I had rather die then once bewray.
And *Techne* pray-thee, tell her thus from me,—
But yet, ah tell it foftly in her eare,
And be thou fure no liuing creature heare.—
That her immodefty hath loft this day ;
Two the moft honeft guardians of her good
She had in life, her honour, and my blood.   1540
   Tec. Now I may fpeake, I truft, you fpeake to me.

Am. No not yet *Techne*, pray-thee ftay a while,—
And tell her too, though fhe fpares not her fhame,
My death fhall fhew, that I refpe&t her fame.

Tec. Then now I may.

Am. O *Techne* no not yet.—
And bid her not forget *Amyntas* faith,
Though fhe defpifèd him ; and one day yet
She may be toucht with griefe, and that ere long,
To thinke on her difhonour, and his wrong :   1550
Now *Techne* I haue done, and fo farewell.

Tec. But ftay *Amyntas*, now muft I begin.

Am. I cannot ftay *Techne*, let goe your hold ;
It is in vaine I fay, I muft be gone.

Tec. Now deare *Amyntas*, heare me but one word.—
Ah he is gone, and in that fury gone,
As fure he vvill in this extremity
Of his difpaire, do violence to himfelfe :
And therefore now vvhat helpe fhall I deuife
To ftay his ruine ? fure there is no meanes   1560
But to call *Cloris*, and perfwade with her
To follovv him, and to preuent his death ;
For though this pra&tife vvas for mine owne good,
Yet my deceipts vfe not to ftretch to blood.
But now I know not vvhere I fhould finde out
That cruell mayde ; but I muft caft about.

SCEN. II.

Amarillis. Dorinda.

DOrinda, you are yet in happy cafe,
    You are belou'd, you need not to complaine; 1570
'Tis I haue reafon onely to bewaile

My fortunes, who am caſt vpon diſdaine,
And on his rockey heart that wrackes my youth
With ſtormes of ſorrowes and contemnes my truth ;
'Tis I that am ſhut out from all delight
This vvorld can yeeld a mayd, that am remou'd
From th'onely ioy on earth, to be belou'd :
Cruell *Carinus* ſkornes this faith of mine,
And lets poore *Amarillis* grieue and pine.

   Do. Tis true indeed you ſay, I am belou'd,   1580
Sweete *Amarillis*, and perhaps much more
Then I vvould be : plenty doth make me poore ;
For now my heart, as if deuided ſtands
Betwixt two paſſions, loue and pitty both,
That draw it either way vvith that maine force,
As that I know not vvhich to yeeld vnto :
And then feare in the midd'ſt, holds m'in ſuſpence,
Leſt I loſe both by mine improuidence.

   Ama. How may that be *Dorinda* ? you know this,
You can enioy but one, and one there is   1590
Ought to poſſeſſe your heart, and loue a lone :
Who hunts two Hares at one time, catches none.

   Do. I muſt tell you deare friend the whole diſcourſe
From vvhom I cannot any thing conceale ;
Arcadia knowes, and euery Shepheard knowes
How much *Mirtillus* hath deſeru'd of me,
And how long time his woefull ſute hath laine,
Depending on the mercie of mine eyes ;
For whom I doe confeſſe, pitty hath beene
Th'Atturny euermore that ſtands and pleades   1600
Before my heart the iuſtice of his cauſe,
And ſaies he ought haue loue, by loues owne lawes.
But now the maiſter ſou'raigne Lord of hearts,

That great commander, and that tyrant Loue,
Who muſt haue all according to his will,—
Whom pitty onely vſhers, goes before,
As lightning doth the thunder,—he ſayes no,
And vvill that *Colax* onely haue my heart ;
That gallant heardſman full of ſkill and arte,
And all experience of Loues myſteries ;   1610
To whom I muſt confeſſe me to haue giuen
The earneſt of my loue ; but ſince that time
I neuer ſaw the man ; vvhich makes me much
To wonder that his dealing ſhould be ſuch :
For either Loue, hath (in reſpeƈt that I
Deſpiſèd haue the true and honeſt faith,
Of one that lou'd me with ſincerity),
Made me the ſpoyle of falſhood and contempt,
Or elſe perhaps the ſame is done to trye
My reſolution, and my conſtancy.   1620
        But yet I feare the worſt, and feare I may,
Leſt he now hauing got the viƈtory,
Cares for no more : and ſeeing he knowes my loue
Turnes towards him, he turnes his backe to me.
So that I know not vvhat vvere beſt reſolue,
Either to ſtand vnto the doubtfull faith
Of one that hath ſo dangerouſly begun,
Or elſe returne t'accept *Mirtillus* loue,
Who vvill perhaps when mine begins, haue done :
So that inwrapt in this diſtraƈted toyle   1630
I vexe, and know not vvhat to do the vvhile.
And therefore *Amarillis* I thinke ſure
(Se'ing now how others loue in me hath prou'd)
You are moſt happy not to be belou'd.

SCEN. III.

Cloris.   *Amarillis.*   *Dorinda.*

N Ow here betweene you two, kind louing foules,
    I know there can be no talke but of loue ;
Loue muſt be all the fcope of your difcourfe.
Alas poore hearts, I vvonder how you can   1640
In this deceiptfull vvorld thinke of a man.
For they doe nothing but make fooles of you,
And laugh vvhen they haue done, and prooue vntrue.

   Am. Well *Cloris* vvell, reioyce that you are free ;
You may be toucht one day as vvell as we.

   Clo. Indeed and I had like to this laſt night,
Had I not lookt vvith fuch an angry eye,
And frown'd fo fowre, that I made loue afeard.
There vvas a fellow needes forfooth would haue
My heart from me vvhether I would or not,   1650
And had as great aduantage one could haue ;
I tell you that he had me in a Caue.

   Do. What, in a Caue ? *Cloris* how came you there ?

   Clo. Truely *Dorinda* I vvill tell you how :
By no arte magique, but a plaine deuife
Of *Techne,* vvho would trie her wit on me ;
For fhe had promif'd me, to meete me there
At fuch an houre, and thither bring vvith her
A new ftrange dreffing fhe had made for me,
Which there clofe out of fight, I fhould trie on : 1660
Thither vvent I poore foole, at th'houre decreed,
And there expecting *Technes* company,
In rufhes fleering *Colax* after me ;
Whom fure fhe fent of purpofe to the place.
And there with his affected apifh grace

And ſtrainèd ſpeach, offring to ſeaze on me,
·Out ruſht I from him, as indeed amaz'd
At his ſo ſodaine and vnexpeſted ſight.
And after followes he, vowes, ſweares, proteſts
By all the gods, he neuer lou'd before   1670
Any one liuing in the world but me ;
And for me onely, would he ſpend his life.

    Do. Alas, and what am I forgotten then ?
Why theſe were euen the words he ſpake to me.

    Clo. And then inueighes againſt *Amyntas* loue,
Vantes his owne parts, and his great knowledges ;
And all ſo idle, as, in troth me thought
I neuer heard a man (more vainely talke,
For ſo much as I heard) for vp the hill
I went with ſuch a pace, and neuer ſtayd   1680
To giue regard to anything he ſayd :
As at the laſt I ſcarſe had left him breath
Sufficient to forſweare himſelfe withall.

    Do. Ah what hath then my ſilly ignorance done
To be deceiu'd, and mockt by ſuch a one ?

    Clo. And when I had recouered vp the hill,
I fairely ran away and left my man
In midd'ſt of his coniuring periuries ;
All empty to returne with mighty loſſe
Of breath and labour, hauing caſt away   1690
Much fooliſh paines in tricking vp himſelfe
For this exploit, and goes without his game ;
Which he in hope deuour'd before he came ;
I, I, too, miſt my dreſſing by this meanes.

    But I admire how any woman can
Be ſo vnwiſe to like of ſuch a man !
For I proteſt I ſee nought elſe but froth,·

And fhallow impudence, affe&ed grace,
And fome few idle pra&ife complement :
And all the thing he is without he is,   1700
For affe&ion ftriues but to appeare,
And neuer is of Subftance, or Sincere.
And yet this dare of falfhood hath beguil'd
A thoufand foolifh vvenches in his dayes.   [theirs.
     Do. The more vvretch he, and more hard hap was
     Clo. Why do you figh *Dorinda*? are you toucht
VVith any of thefe paffages of mine?
     Do. No truly not of yours, but I haue caufe
In my particular that makes me figh.
     Clo. Well, vvell, come one to put vs from this talke ;
Let vs deuife fome fport to paffe the time.   1711
     Am. Faith I haue no great lift to any fport.
     Do. Nor I in troth, tis fartheft from my minde.
     Clo. Then let vs tell old tales, repeate our dreames,
Or any thing rather then thinke of loue.
     Am. And now you fpeake of dreames, in troth laft
I vvas much troubled with a fearefull dreame.   [night
     Do. And truely *Amarillis* fo was I.
     Clo. And now I do remember too, I had
A foolifh idle dreame, and this it was :   1720
     Me thought the faireft of *Montanus* lambs,
And one he lou'd the beft of all his flocke,
VVas fingled out, and chac'd b'a cruell curre,
And in his hot purfuit makes towards me,
(Me thought) for fuccour, and about me ran,
As if it beg'd my ayde to haue his life ;
Which I long time deferr'd, and ftill lookt on,
And would not refcue it, vntill at length
I faw it euen quite wourried out of breath.

And panting at my feete, and could no more :   1730
And then me thought, I tooke it vp from death,
And cherifht it with me, and brought it backe
Home to *Montanus,* who vvas glad to fee
The poore recouer'd creature thus reftor'd ;
And I my felfe was greatly pleaf'd, me thought,
That by my hand fo good a deed vvas wrought ;
And *Amarillis* now tell vs your dreame ?
 Am. Me thought as I in *Eremathus* walkt,
A fearefull vvoolfe rufht forth from out a brake,
And towards me makes with open hideous iawes. 1740
From whom I ranne with all the fpeed I could,
T'efcape my danger, and t'ouertake
One vvhom I faw before, that might lend ayde
To me diftreft ; but he me thought did runne
As faft from me, as I did from the beaft.
I cride to him (but all in vaine) to ftay ;
The more I cride, the more he ranne away ;
And after I, and after me the woolfe,
So long, as I began to faint in minde ;
Seeing my defpaire before, my death behind :   1750
Yet ranne I ftill, and loe, me thought, at length
A little he began to flacke his pace ;
Which I perceiuing, put to all my ftrength
And ranne, as if defire had wing'd my heeles ;
And in the end me thought recouer'd him.
But neuer woman felt more ioy,—it feem'd,—
To ouertake a man, then did I him,
By whom I fcapte the danger I was in ;
That when I wak'd, as prefently I awak'd,
Toucht with that fudaine ioy, which my poore heart
God knowes, had not beene vi'd vnto of late :   1761
III.   18

I found my felfe all in a moyft faint fweate,
VVhich that affrighting horrour did beget ;
And though I were deliu'red of my feare,
And felt this ioy, yet did the trembling laft
Vpon my heart, when now the feare was paft.

  Clo. This *Amarillis* may your good portend,
That yet you fhall haue comfort in the end.

  Am. God grant I may, it is the thing I want. 1769

  Clo. And now *Dorinda* tell vs what you dream't.

  Do. I dream't, that hauing gone to gather flowers,
And weary of my worke, repofing me
Vpon a banke neere to a Riuers fide,
A fubtile Serpent lurking in the graffe,
Came fecretly, and feizèd on my breaft ;
Which, though I faw, I had no power to ftirre,
But lay me ftill, till he had eate away
Into my bofome, whence he tooke my heart ;
And in his mouth carrying the fame away,
Returnes me thought againe, from whence he came ;
Which I perceiuing prefently arofe,   1781
And after it moft wofully I went,
To fee if I could finde my heart againe :
And vp and downe, I fought but all in vaine.

  Clo. In troth 'tis no good lucke to dreame of Snakes ;
One fhall be fure t'heare anger after it.

  Do. And fo it may be I haue done to day.

  Clo. Indeed, and I haue heard it neuer failes.

SCEN. IIII.

Techne. Cloris. Amarillis. Dorinda. 1790

COme, you are talking here in iollity,
  Whilſt I haue ſought you *Cloris* all about :
Come, come, good *Cloris* quickly come away.

  Clo. What is the newes ? what haue we now to doo ;
Haue you another Caue to ſend me too ?

  Tec. Ah talke no more of that, but come away,
As euer you will ſaue the wofull life
Of a diſtreſſèd man that dies for you.

  Clo. Why what doth *Colax* whom you ſent to me
Into the Caue, faint now vvith his repulſe ?   1800

  Tec. ·I ſent him not, you would ſo wiſely goe,
In open ſight, as men might ſee you goe,
And trace you thither all the way you went.
But come, ah t'is not he, it is the man
You ought to ſaue : *Amyntas* is the man
Your cruelty, and rigor hath vndone :
O quickly come, or it vvill be too late ;
For 'twas his chance, and moſt vnluckely,
To ſee both you and *Colax*, as you came
Out of the Caue, and he thinkes verily   1810
You are poſſeſt by him ; which ſo confounds
His ſpirits, and ſinkes his heart, that ſure h'is runne
T'vndoe himſelfe ; and O I feare 'tis done.

  Clo. If it be done, my help will come too late ;
And I may ſtay, and ſaue that labour here.

  Am. Ah *Cloris* haſte away if it be ſo,
And doe not if thou haſt a heart of fleſh,
And of a woman, ſtay and trifle time ;
Goe runne, and ſaue thine owne ; for if he die,

'Tis thine that dies, his blood is fhed for thee ;   1820
And what a horror this will euer be
Hereafter to thy guilty confcience, when
Yeares fhall haue taught thee wit, and thou fhalt find
This deed inftampt in bloody Charaders,
Within the blacke records of thine owne thoughts ;
Which neuer will be raz'd whilft thou haft breath,
Nor yet will be forgotten by thy death.
Befides, wide Fame will trumpet forth thy wrong,
And thou fhalt be with all pofterity,
Amongft th'examples held of cruelty,   1830
And haue this fauage deed of thine be made
A fullen fubiect for a Tragedy,
Intitled *Cloris* ; that thereby thy name
May ferue to be an euerlafting fhame ;
And therefore go preuent fo foule a ftaine.
    Do. Ah go, go *Cloris*, hafte away with fpeede.
    Clo. Why, whether fhould I go ? I know not where
To finde him now, and if he do this deed,
It is his error, and no fault of mine ;
Yet pray thee *Techne*, which way went the man ? 1840
    Tec. Come *Cloris*, I will fhew which way he went,
In moft ftrange fury, and moft defperate fpeed ;
Still crying, *Cloris*, haft thou done this deed ?
    Clo. Why had not you ftaid, and perfwaded him ?
    Tec. I could not ftay him by no meanes I vf'd,
Though all the meanes I could deuife I vf'd.
    Clo. VVell, I will go, poore man to feeke him out
Though I can do him elfe no other good.
I know indeed he hath deferu'd my loue,
And if I would like any, fhould be him,   1850
So that I thought he would be true to me.

But thus my dreame may now chance come to paffe,
And I may happen to bring home indeed
Montanus fonne, *Amyntas* that deere Lambe
He loues fo well, and by my gracious deed,
He may efcape the danger he was in.
VVhich if I do, and thereby do inthrall
My felfe, to free anothers mifery,
Then will I fit and figh, and talke of loue
As well as you, and haue your company.   1860
For fomething I do feele begin to moue;
And yet I hope 'tis nothing elfe but feare;
Yet what know I that feare may hap to loue?
VVell *Techne*, come, I would not haue him yet
To perifh, poore *Amyntas*, in this fit.
    Ama. VVell *Cloris* yet he may, for ought I fee
Before you come, vnleffe you make more haft.
Ah cruell maide, fhe little knowes the griefe
Of fuch a heart that's defperate of reliefe;
Nor vnderftands fhe her owne happineffe,   1870
To haue fo true a louer as he is.
And yet I fee fh'is toucht, if not too late,
For I perceiu'd her colour come and goe;
And though in pride fhe would haue hid her woe,
Yet I faw forrow looke out at her eyes.
And poore *Amyntas* if thou now be gone,
Thou haft (like to the Bee that ftinging dies,
And in anothers wound left his owne life)
Tranfpierced by the death, that marble heart,
Which liuing thou couldft touch by no defert.   1880
And if thou fhalt efcape, thou haft furuiu'd
Her cruelty, which now repents her wrong,
And thou fhalt by her fauours be reuiu'd.

After the affliction thou haſt ſuffred long ;
Which makes me thinke, that time, and patience may
Intenerat at length the hardeſt heart,
And that I may yet after all my woe,
Liue t'ouertake *Carinus* mercy too.

 Do. And here this ſad diſtreſſe of ſuch a true
And conſtant louer ouercome with griefe   1890
Preſents vnto my guilty memory
The wrongs *Mirtillus* hath indur'd of me.
And O I would I knew now how he doth :
I feare he is not vvell ; I ſaw him not
Scarſe theſe three dayes ; I meruaile vvhere he is :
And yet vvhat need I meruaile, vvho haue thus
Chac'd him from me vvith frownes and vſage vile,
And fondly left the ſubſtance of his faith,
To catch the ſhadow of deceipt and guile ?

 Was *Colax* he I thought the onely man,   1900
And is he now prou'd to be ſuch a one ?
O that I euer lent an eaſie eare,
Vnto ſo falſe a wretches flatteries,
Whoſe very name I now abhorre to heare ;
And loath my ſelfe, for being ſo vnwiſe.
What ſhall I doe ſweet *Amarillis* now ?
Which way ſhall I betake me to recouer
The loſſe of ſhame, and loſſe of ſuch a louer ?

 Am. Indeed *Dorinda* you haue done him wrong,
But your repentance, and compaſſion now   1910
May make amends, and you muſt learne to do
As I long time haue done, indure and hope,
And on that turne of Fortunes Scene depend,
VVhen all extremities muſt mend, or end.

SCEN. V.

Melibæus. Ergaſtus.

VVEll, come *Ergaſtus*, we haue feene ynow,
    And it is more then time, that we prepare
Againſt this Hydra of confuſion now,
Which ſtill preſents new hideous heads of feare : 1920
And euery houre we fee begets new broyles,
And intricates our youth in deſperate toyles.
    And therefore let th'aduantage of this day,
Which is the great and generall hunting day
In *Eremanthus*, ſerue for this good deed :
And when we meete (as all of vs ſhall meet
Here in this place anone, as is decreed)
We will aduife our Shepheards to intermit
That worke, and fall to this imports vs more ;
To chaſe out theſe wilde miſchiefes that do lurke, 1930
And worſe infect, then th'*Erimanthian* Boare,
Or all Beaſts elfe ; which onely ſpoile our fields,
Whilſt theſe which are of more prodigious kinds,
Bend all their forces to deſtroy our mindes.
    Erg. And this occaſion will be very fit
Now to be tooke ; for one day loſt may loſe
More by example, then we ſhall reget
In thouſands ; for when men ſhall once diſcloſe
The way of ill that lay vnknowne before,
Scarce all our paines will euer ſtop it more.   1940
Man is a creature of a wilfull head,
And hardly is driuen, but eaſily is lead.

ACT. V. SCEN. I.

Amarillis. Carinus.

A H gentle *Lælaps*, pretty louing dogge,
　　Where haſt thou left thy maiſter? where is he, .
ıat great commander ouer thee and me?
ıou wert not wont be farre off from his feete,
ıd O no more would I, were he ſo pleaſ'd;
ıt would as well as thou goe follow him,　　　1950
ırough brakes and thickets, ouer cliffes and rocks
ı long as I had life to follow him,
ould he but looke vpon me with that eye
˙ fauour, as h'is vf'd to looke on thee.
ıou canſt be clapt and ſtrookt with that faire hand
ıat thruſts away my heart, and beates it backe
om following him, which yet it euer will;
ıd though he flye me, yet I muſt after ſtill:
ıt here he comes, me thought he was not farre.
Car. What meane you *Amarillis* in this ſort　　1960
　taking vp my dogge to marre my ſport?
Am. My deare *Carinus* thou doeſt much miſtake,
lo not marre thy ſport, tis thou marrſt mine,
d kilſt my ioyes with that hard heart of thine.
y dogge perhaps by ſome inſtinét doth know
w that I am his maiſters creature too,
d kindely comes himſelfe and fawnes on me
　ſhew what you in nature ought to doe?
Car. Fie *Amarillis*, you that know my minde
ıuld not me thinkes thus euer trouble me.　　1970
Am. What, it is troubleſome to be belou'd?
w is it then *Carinus* to be loath'd?
　had done like *Cloris*, ſkornd your ſute,

And fpurn'd your paffions, in difdainefull fort,
I had beene woo'd and fought, and highly priz'd,
But hauing n'other arte to winne thy loue,
Saue by difcouering mine, I am defpif'd
As if you would not haue the thing you fought,
Vnleffe you knew it were not to be got.
And now becaufe I lie here at thy feete,   1980
The humble booty of thy conquering eyes,
And lay my heart all open in thy fight,
And tell thee I am thine, and tell thee right ;
And doe not fute my lookes, nor clothe my words
In other colours, then my thoughts do vveare,
But doe thee right in all ; thou fkorneft me
As if thou didft not loue fincerity ;
Neuer did Cryftall more apparantly
Prefent the colour it contain'd within   1989
Then haue thefe eyes, thefe teares, this tongue of mine
Bewray'd my heart, and told how much I am thine.
   Car. Tis true I know you haue too much bewrayd,
And more then fits the honour of a mayd.
   Am. O if that nature hath not arm'd my breaft
With that ftronge temper of refifting proofe,
But that by treafon of my weake compleftion, I
Am made thus eafie to the violent fhot
Of paffion, and th'affeftion I fhould not :
Me thinkes yet you out of your ftrength and power,
Should not difdaine that weakenes, but fhould thinke
It rather is your vertue, as indeed   2001
It is, that makes me thus againft my kinde,
T'vnlocke my thoughts, and to let out my minde ;
When I fhould rather die and burft with loue,
Then once to let my tongue to fay, I loue.

And if your worthy parts be of that power
To vanquiſh nature, and I muſt be wonne,
Do not diſdaine the worke vvhen you haue done ;
For in contemning me you do diſpiſe
That power of yours which makes me to be thus. 2010
 Car. Now vvhat adoe is here with idle talke ?
And to no purpoſe ; for you know I haue
Ingag'd long ſince my heart, my loue and all
To *Cloris,* vvho muſt haue the fame and ſhall.
 Am. Why there is no ſuch oddes twixt her and me;
I am a Nymph, tis knowne, as well as ſhe.
There is no other difference betwixt vs twaine
But that I loue, and ſhe doth thee diſdaine.
No other reaſon can induce thy minde,
But onely that which ſhould diuert thy minde. 2020
I will attend thy flockes better then ſhe,
And dreſſe thy Bower more ſweet, more daintily,
And cheeriſh thee with Salets, and with Fruites,
And all freſh dainties that the ſeaſon ſutes,
I haue more ſkill in hearbes, then ſhe, by farre,
I know which nouriſh, which reſtoring are :
And I will finde Diċtamnus for thy Goates,
And ſeeke out Clouer for thy little Lambes,
And Tetriſoll to cheeriſh vp their Dammes ;
And this I know, I haue a better voyce 2030
Then ſhe, though ſhe perhaps may haue more arte ;
But, which is beſt, I haue the faithfull'ſt heart :
Beſides *Amyntas* hath her loue, I know,
And ſhe begins to manifeſt it now.
 Car. Amyntas haue her loue ? that were moſt
   ſtrange,
When he hath gotten that, you ſhall haue mine.

Am. O deere *Carinus*, let me reſt vpon
That bleſſed word of thine, and I haue done.

SCEN. II.

Mirtillus. Carinus. Amarillis. 2040

And ſpoil'd himſelfe, and lies in that weake caſe,
As we thinke neuer more to ſee his facè.
 Car. Mirtillus, I am ſorry t'heare ſo much :
Although *Amyntas* be competitor
In th'Empire of her heart, vvherein my life
Hath chiefeſt claime, I doe not wiſh his death :
But by vvhat chance, *Mirtillus* pray thee tell ?
 Mir. I will *Carinus*, though I grieue to tell. 2050
As *Tytirus, Menalcas*, and my ſelfe
Were placing of our toyles (againſt anon
That we ſhall hunt) below, within the ſtreight,
Twixt *Erimanthus*, and *Lycæus* mount,
We might perceeue vnder a ragged clife,
In that moſt vncouth deſart, all alone
Diſtreſſ'd *Amyntas* lying on the ground.
With his ſad face, turn'd cloſe vnto the rock,
As if he loathed to ſee more of the world,
Then that poore ſpace, which was twixt him and it :
His right hand ſtretcht along vpon his ſide, 2060
His left he makes the pillar to ſupport
His carefull head ; his Pipe he had hung vp
Vpon a Beach tree by, vvhere he likewiſe
Had plac'd his Sheep hooke, and his Knife, wherewith
He had incaru'd an wofull Elegy,

To fhew th'occafion of his mifery.
His dogge *Melampus* fitting by his fide,
As if he were partaker of his vvoe :
By vvhich we knew t'was he, and to him went ;   2070
And after vve had call'd and fhooke him vp,
And found him not to anfwere, nor to ftirre,
And yet his eyes abroad, his body warme ;
We took him vp, and held him from the ground.
But could not make him ftand by any meanes ;
And fincking downe againe, we fearcht to fee
If he had any vvound, or blow, or wrinch ;
But none could finde : at laft by chance we fpide
A little horne which he had flung afide,
Whereby we geft he had fome poyfon tooke.   2080
And thereupon vve fent out prefently
To fetch *Vrania* ; vvhofe great fkill in hearbes
Is fuch, as if there any meanes will be,——
As I feare none will be,——her onely arte
Muft ferue to bring him to himfelfe againe.

　　Car. Indeed *Vrania* hath bin knowne t'haue done
Moft defperate cures, and peraduenture may
Reftore him yet ; and I doe wifh fhe may.

　　Mir. But hauing there vf'd all the helpe we could,
And all in vaine, and ftanding by with griefe,   2090
(As we might well, to fee fo fad a fight :
And fuch an worthy Shepheard in that plight)
We might perceiue come running downe the hill,
Cloris and *Techne*, with what fpeed they could :
But *Cloris* had got ground, and was before,
And made more haft, as it concernd her more.
And nearer as fhe came, fhe fafter went,
As if fhe did defire to haue beene there

Before her feete, too flow for her fwift feare.
Aud comming to the place, fhe fuddenly   2100
Stopt, ftarts, and fhrikt, and hauing made fuch
    haft
T'haue fomething done, now could fhe nothing do :
Perhaps our prefence might perplex her too,
As being afham'd that any eye fhould fee
The new appearing of her naked heart,
That neuer yet before was feene till now.
   Car. And 'tis ill hap for me it was feene now.
   Mir. For we perceiu'd how *Loue* and *Modeftie*
With feu'rall Enfignes, ftroue within her cheekes
Which fhould be Lord that day, and chargèd hard
Vpon each other, with their frefh fupplies   2111
Of different colours, that ftill came, and went,
And much difturb'd her ; but at length diffolu'd
Into affeƈtion, downe fhe cafts her felfe
Vpon his fenfeleffe body, where fhe faw
The mercy fhe had brought was come too late :
And to him calles, O deare *Amyntas,* fpeake,
Looke on me, fweete *Amyntas,* it is I
That calles thee, I it is, that holds thee here,
Within thofe armes thou haft efteem'd fo deare.   2120
   And though that loue were yet fo young in her
As that it knew not how to fpeake, or what,
And that fhe neuer had that paffion prou'd,
Being firft a louer ere fhe knew fhe lou'd ;
Yet what fhe could not vtter, fhe fupplide,
With her poore bufie hands that rubb'd his face,
Chafd his pale temples, wrung his fingers ends,
Held vp his head, and puld him by the hands,
And neuer left her worke, nor euer ceaft.

Ama. Alas, the leaſt of this regard before,　　213
Might haue holpe all then, when 'twas in her power
T'haue ſau'd his heart, and to reuiue his minde.
Now for all this, her mercy is vnkinde ;
The good that's out of ſeaſon is not good.
There is no difference now twixt cruelty,
And the compaſſion that's not vnderſtood.

　　Mir. But yet at length, as if thoſe dainty hands,
Had had a power to haue awakened Death,
We might perceiue him moue his heauy eyes ;
Which had ſtood fixt all the whole time before :　214
And faſtens them directly vpon her.
Which when ſhe ſaw, it ſtrook her with that force,
As that it pierc'd through all the ſpirits ſhe had,
Made all the powers and parts of her ſhrinke vp,
With that convulſion of remorſe and griefe,
As out ſhe ſhrik'd, O deare, O my deare heart ;
Then ſhrikes againe, and then againe cryes out,
For now that looke of his did ſhake her more,
Then Death or any thing had done before ;　　·
That looke did read t'her new conceiuing heart,　215
All the whole tragicke Lecture of his loue ;
And his ſad ſuffrings ; all his griefes and feare ;
And now in th'end what he had done for her,
And with that powerfull force of mouing too,
As all the world of words could neuer doe.
　　Ah what a ſilly meſſenger is Speech
To be imploi'd in that great Embaſſie
Of our affections, in reſpect of th'eye ?
Ah 'tis the ſilent rhetoricke of a looke,
That works the league betwixt the States of hearts ;
Not words I ſee, nor knowledge of the booke,　216

Nor incantations made by hidden artes ;
For now this looke fo melts her into teares,
As that fhe powr'd them down like thunder drops ;
Or elfe did Nature taking pitty now
Of her diftreffe, imploy them in that ftore,
To ferue as vailes, and to be interpofde
Betwixt her griefe and her, t'impeach her fight,
From that full view of forrow thus difclofde,
  And now with this came in *Vrania* there,   2170
With other vvomen, to imploy their beft
To faue his life, if b'any meanes they can.
And fo vve came our vvay, being fent for now
About fome conference for our hunting fports ;
And with vs *Techne* comes, vvho is fuppofde,
T'haue beene a fpeciall caufe of much of this.
  Car. Alas this fad report doth grieue me much,
And I did neuer thinke, that *Cloris* had
So dearely lou'd him as I finde fhe doth ;
For by this act of hers I plainly fee,   2180
There will be neuer any hope for me.
  Ama. There may for me, if now *Carinus* thou
VVilt ftand but to thy vvord, as thou haft faid.
  Mir. Ah would to God *Dorinda* had bene there,
T'haue feene but *Cloris* act this vvofull part ;
It may be, it might haue deterr'd her heart
From crueltie, fo long as fhe had liu'd.
  Am. And I am glad *Carinus* hath but heard
So much this day ; for he may hap thereby
To haue fome feeling of my mifery ;   2190
But for *Dorinda*, neuer doubt at all,
She is more yours *Mirtillus* then you thinke.
  Mir. Ah *Amarillis*, I would that were true.

But loe where come our chiefeſt heardſmen now,
Of all *Arcadia*, we ſhall know more newes.

SCEN. III.

Melibæus, Ergaſtus, Montanus, Acriſius with other Arca-
dians, bringing with them Alcon, Lincus, Colax,
Techne, Piſtophœnax.

YOu gentle Shepheards and Inhabitors   2200
   Of theſe remote, and ſolitary parts
Of montaynous *Arcadia,* ſhut vp here
Within theſe Rockes, theſe vnfrequented Clifts,—
The walles and bulwarkes of our libertie,—
From out the noyſe of tumult, and the throng
Of ſweating toyle, ratling concurrencie ;
And haue continued ſtill the ſame and one
In all ſucceſſions from antiquitie ;
Whil'ſt all the ſtates on earth beſides haue made
A thouſand reuolutions, and haue rowl'd   2210
From change to change, and neuer yet found reſt,
Nor euer bettered their eſtates by change.
You, I inuoke this day in generall,
To doe a worke that now concernes vs all :
Leſt that we leaue not to poſteritie,
Th'*Arcadia* that we found continued thus
By our fore-fathers care who left it vs.
For none of you I know, whoſe iudgements graue
Can ought diſcerne, but ſees how much we are
Transformd of late, and changd from what we were ;
And vvhat diſtempers daily doe ariſe   2221
Amongſt our people, neuer felt before ;
At which I know you maruell, as indeed
You well **may** maruel, whence they ſhould proceed ;

And fo did good *Ergaſtus* here, and I,
Vntill we fet our felues more vvarily
To fearch it out; vvhich by good hap vve haue,
And found the authors of this vvickedneſſe.
Which diuels attyr'd here in the ſhape of men,
We haue produc'd before you, to the end   2230
You may take fpeedy order to fuppreſſe
Our growing follies, and their impiouſneſſe.

    Erg. Indeed   thefe   odious   wretches   which   you
       fee,
Are they who haue brought in vpon our reſt,
Thefe new and vnknowne mifchiefes of debate,
Of wanton pride, of fcandulous reportes,
Of vile deluding, chaſte and honeſt loues,
Of vndeferu'd fufpitious defperate griefes,
And all the fadneſſe we haue feene of late. *1*
    And firſt this man, this *Lincus* here you fee,   2240
Montanus you, and you *Acryſius* know,
With what deceit, and with what cunning arte,
He entertaind your ſtrifes, abufd you both;
By firſt perfwading you that you had right
In your demands, and then the right was yours;
And would haue made as many rights as men
Had meanes, or power, or will to purchafe them;
Could he haue once attain'd to his defires.
    Mon. We doe confeſſe our errour, that we were
Too eafily perfwaded by his craft,   2250
To wrangle for imagin'd titles; which
We here renounce, and quit for euermore.
    Acry. And we defire the memory thereof
May die with vs, that it be neuer knowne
Our feeble age hath fuch example ſhowne.

Erg. And now this other ftrange impoftor here,
This *Alcon*, who like *Lincus* hath put on,
The habite too of emptie grauitie,
To catch opinion, and conceit withall,
Seekes how to fet vs all at variance here   2260
With nature, as this other with our felues ;
And would confound her, working with his arte ;
And labours how to make our mindes firft ficke,
Before our bodies, and perfwade our health
It is not well ; that he may haue thereby
Both it and fickneffe euer vnder cure.
And forraine drugs brings to diftemper's here
And make vs like the wanton world abroad.

Mel. But here are two the moft pernitious fpirits
The world I thinke did euer yet produce;   2270
Colax and *Techne* ; two fuch inftruments
Of Wantonneffe, of Luft and treachery,
As are of power t'intice and to debaufh
The vniuerfall ftate of honefty.

Erg. But *Techne*, who is that ftands there by you ?
What, is your company increaft of late ?

Tec. Truely it is a very honeft man,
A friend of mine that comes to fee me here.

Erg. He cannot then but be an honeft man,
If he be one of your acquaintance fure.   2280

Mel. This man I found with them now fince you
Maintaining hote difpute with *Titerus*   [went,
About the rites and mifteries of *Pan.*

Erg. H'is like to be of their affociats then :
Techne, what is this fecret friend of yours ?

Tec. For-footh he is a very holy man.

Erg. A very holy man ? what is his name ?

Tec. Truely his name Sir is *Piſtophœnax.*

Erg. What, is he maſkt, or is that face his
   owne ?

Tec. He is not maſkt, tis his complexion ſure.   2290

Erg. Techne we cannot credite thy report.
Let one trie whether it be ſo or not :
O ſee a moſt deformèd ougly face,
Wherewith if openly he ſhould appeare,
He would deterre all men from comming neere.
And therefore hath that cunning wretch put on
This pleaſing viſor of apparency,
T'intice and to delude the world withall ;
So that you ſee with what ſtrange inginiers,
The proiect of our ruine is forecaſt,   2300
How they implanted haue their battery here,
Againſt all the maine pillors of our ſtate,
Our Rites, our Cuſtome, Nature, Honeſty.
T'imbroyle, and to confound vs vtterly,
Reckning vs barbarous ; but if thus their ſkill
Doth ciuilize, let vs be barbarous ſtill.

Mel. But now to ſhew the horrible effects
Of *Colax,* and of *Technes* practiſes,
(Beſides this laſt exploit they vvrought vpon
Amyntas, vvho, poore youth, lies now full weake: 2310
Vnder *Vranias* cure, vvhoſe ſkill we heare
Hath yet recall'd him to himſelfe againe)
We haue ſent out abroad into the vvoods,
For *Siluia* and *Palæmon,* two chaſt ſoules
Whom they haue tortur'd ſo vvith iealouſie
Of each the other, as they made them runne
A part, to languiſh ſeuerally alone ;
And we haue ſent for diuers others too,

Whofe hearts haue felt what impious craft can do :
And here they come, and now you fhall know all.   2320

SCEN. IV.

Palæmon. Mirtillus. Carinus. Siluia. Dorinda,
Amarillis. Daphne. Cloris. Amyntas.

COme good *Palæmon*, and good *Siluia* come,
      You haue indur'd too much, and too too long.
   Sil. Ah vvhy *Ergaftus* doe you fet our names
So neere together, when our hearts fo farre,
Are diftant from each other as they are ?
Indeed, whilft vve were one as once vve were,
And as we ought to be vvere faith obferu'd,   2330
Palæmon fhould not haue beene nam'd without
A *Siluia*, nor yet *Siluia* vvithout him ;
But now vve may *Ergaftus*, vve are two.
   Pal. Siluia, therein the greater wrong you doe.
   Sil. Palæmon, nay the greater vvrong you doe.
   Erg. Alas we know well where the wrong doth lie. ·
   Sil. I know you doe, and all the world may know.
   Pal. Siluia, you fee your fault cannot be hid.
   Sil. It is no fault of mine *Palæmon*, that
Your fhame doth come to be reuealèd here ;   2340
I neuer told it, you your felfe haue not
Conceal'd your worke fo clofely as you fhould.
   Pal. But there ftands one can tell what you haue beene.
   Sil. Nay, there he ftands can tell what you haue beene ;
And fure is now in publicke here produc'd
To teftifie your fhame, but not fet on
By me, I doe proteft ; who rather would

Haue di'd alone in fecret with my griefe
Then had your infamy difcouered here,
Wherein my fhame muft haue fo great a fhare.   2350

Pal. I haue not fought to manifeft your fhame,
Which *Siluia*, rather then haue done I would
Haue beene content t'indure the worft of deaths,
I hauing fuch an intreft in the fame.

Col. No *Siluia*, no *Palæmon*, I ftand here
Not t'accufe you, but t'accufe my felfe
Of wrong; you both, God knowes, are cleare ;
I haue abuf'd your apt credulitie,
With falfe reports of things that neuer were :
And therefore here craue pardon for the fame.   2360

Pal. Why *Colax*, did not *Siluia* entertaine
The loue of *Thyrfis* then as you told me ?

Col. *Palæmon* no, fhe neuer entertain'd
His loue, nor wrong'd you as I euer knew.

Sil. But *Colax* you faw how *Palæmon* did
With *Nifa* falfifie his vow to me.

Col. *Siluia*, by heauen and earth I fweare not I,
But onely fain'd it out of fubtiltie ;
For fome vngodly ends I had decreed.

Pal. O let not this be made fome cunning baite 2370
To take my griefes with falfe beliefe, for I
Had rather liue vvith forrow then deceipt,
And ftill t'be vndone, then to haue fuch reliefe.

Sil. Ah let not this deuife be wrought to guilde
My bitterneffe, to make me fwallow't now
That I might be another time beguilde
With confidence, and not truft vvhat I know.   ·

Pal. Ah *Siluia* now, how vvere I cleer'd of griefe,
Had I the power to vnbeleeue beliefe.

But ah my heart hath dwelt fo long in houfe   2380
With that firft tale, as this vvhich is come new,
Cannot be put in truft with my defire
So foone ; befides 'tis too good to be true.

    Sil. Could I *Palæmon* but vnthinke the thought
Of th'ill firft heard, and that it vvere not fo,
How bleft were I ? but loe I fee how doubt
Comes in farre eafier then it can get out.
And in thefe miferies of iealoufie,
Our eare hath greater credit then our eye.

    Mel. Stand not confuf'd, deare louers, any more, 2390
For this is now the certaine truth you heare,
And this vile vvretch hath done you both this vvrong.

    Pal. Ift poffible, and is this true you fay,
And do I liue, and doe I fee the day ?
Ah then come *Siluia*, for I finde this wound
That pierc'd into the center of my heart,
Hath let in loue farre deeper then it vvas.

    Sil. If this be fo, vvhy then *Palæmon* know,   .
I likewife feele the loue that vvas before
Moft in my heart, is now become farre more :   2400
And now O pardon me you worthy race
Of men, if I in paffion vttred ought
In preiudice of your moft noble fexe ;
And thinke it vvas m'agrieued errour fpake
It knew not vvhat, tranfported fo, not I.

    Pal. And pardon me you glorious company,
You ftarres of vvomen, if m'inraged heate
Haue ought profan'd your reuerent dignity ;
And thou bright *Pallas*, fou'raigne of all Nimphes,
The royall Miftreffe of our Paftorall Mufe,   2410
And thou *Diana* honour of the woods,

To whom I vow my fongs, and vow my felfe,
Forgiue me mine offence, and be you pleaf'd
T'accept of my repentance now therefore,
And grace me ftill ; and I defire no more.

Sil. And now I would that *Cloris* knew thus much,
That fo fhe might be vndeceiuèd too,
Whom I haue made beleeue fo ill of men :
But loe fee where fhe comes, and as it feemes
Brings her beliefe already in her hand,   2420
Preuents my act, and is confirm'd before.
Looke *Cloris* looke, my feares haue idle beene,
Palæmon loues me, there is truft in men.

Clo. And *Siluia* I muft now beleeue fo too,
Or elfe God helpe, I know not what to doe.

Pal. Looke here *Mirtillus* looke, what I told you
Is now prou'd falfe, and women they are true.

Mil. So I perceiue *Palæmon*, and it feemes
But vaine conceipt that other wife efteemes.

Mon. Alas here comes my deare reftorèd fonne, 2430
My louely child *Amyntas* here is come.

Acry. And here is *Cloris* my deare daughter come,
And lookes as if fhe were affrighted ftill,
Poore foule, with feare, and with her fudaine griefe.

Clo. Loe here *Montanus* I haue brought you home
Although with much a doe, your fonne againe ;
And forry am with all my heart that I,
Haue beene the caufe he hath indur'd fo much.

Mon. And I reftore him backe again to you
Deare *Cloris*, and doe vvifh you to forget   2440.
Your forrowes paft, and pray the Gods you may
From henceforth lead your life with happy ioy.

Acry. Doe *Cloris* take him, and I wifh as much.

Erg. Well then to make our ioyfull feſtiuals
The more complet, *Dorinda,* we intreate
You alſo to accept *Mirtillus* loue ;
Who we are ſure hath well deſeruèd yours.

Do. Although this be vpon ſhort warning, yet
For that I haue beene ſommonèd before
By mine owne heart and his deſerts to me,   2450
To yeeld to ſuch a motion, I am now
Content t'accept his loue, and wilbe his.

Mir. Dorinda, then I likewiſe haue my bliſſe,
And reckon all the ſufferings I haue paſt,
Worthy of thee to haue this ioy at laſt.

Mel. And you *Carinus,* looke on that good Nymph
Whoſe eye is ſtill on you, as if ſhe thought
Her ſuffring too, deſeru'd ſome time of ioy,
And now expeéts her turne, hath brought her lap
For comfort too whil'ſt Fortune deales good hap ; 2460
And therefore let her haue it now poore ſoule,
For ſhe is worthy to poſſeſſe your loue.

Car. I know ſhe is, and ſhe ſhall haue my loue,
Though *Colar* had perſwaded me before
Neuer t'accept or to beleeue the loue
Of any Nymph, and oft to me hath ſworne
How he had tri'd them all, and that none were
As men, beguild by ſhewes, ſuppoſ'd they were ;
But now I do perceiue his treachery,
And that they haue both loue and conſtancy.   2470

Ama. O deare *Carinus* bleſt be this good houre,
That I haue liu'd to ouertake at laſt
That heart of thine which fled from me ſo faſt.

Erg. And *Daphne* too me thinkes your heauy lookes
Shew how that ſomething is amiſſe with you.

Daß. Nothing amiffe with me, but that of late
I tooke a fall, which fomewhat grieues me yet.
   Erg. That muft aduife you *Daphne* from henceforth
To looke more warily vnto your feete ;
Which if you do, no doubt but all this will be well. 2480
   Mel. Then thus we fee the fadneffe of this day
Is ended with the euening of our ioy :
And now you impious fpirits, who thus haue raif'd
The hideous tempefts of thefe miferies,
And thus abuf'd our fimple innocence ;
We charge you all here prefent t'auoyd,
From out our confines ; vnder paine to be
Caft downe and dafht in pieces from thefe rockes,
And t'haue your odious carkafes deuour'd
By beafts, being worfe your felues then beafts to men. 2490
   Col. Well then come *Techne*, for I fee we two
Muft euen be forc'd to make a marriage too,
And goe to *Corinth*, or fome City neere,
And by our practife get our liuing there :
Which both together ioyn'd, perhaps we may :
And this is now the worft of miferies
Could come vnto me, and yet vvorthily,
For hauing thus abuf'd fo many Nymphes,
And vvrong'd the honour moft vnreuerently
Of vvomen, in that fort as I haue done, 2500
That now I am forft to vndergoe therefore,
The vvorft of Plagues : to marry vvith a W.
   Alc. But *Lincus*, let not this difcourage vs,
That this poore people iealous of their reft,
Exile vs thus ; for vve no doubt fhall finde
Nations enough, that vvill moft ready be
To entertaine our fkill, and cherifh vs.

And worthier people too, of fubtler fpirits,
Then thefe vnfafhion'd and vncomb'd rude fwaines.
   Lin. Yea and thofe Nations are farre fooner drawne
T'all friuolous diftractions then are thefe ;   2511
For oft vve fee, the groffe doe manage things,
Farre better then the fubtile ; cunning brings
Confufion fooner then doth ignorance.
   Alc. Yea, and I doubt not whil'ft there fhall be
       found
Fantafticke puling wenches in the world,
But I fhall florifh, and liue iollily,
For fuch as I by vvomen muft begin
To gaine a name, and reputation winne :
Which, vvhen we haue attain'd to, you know then 2520
How eafily the vvomen draw on men.
   Lin. Nor doe I doubt but I fhall likewife liue,
And thriue, where euer I fhall plant my felfe ;
For I haue all thofe helpes my fkill requires,
A wrangling nature, a contefting grace,
A clamorous voyce, and an audacious face.
And I can cite the law t'oppugne the law,
And make the gloffe to ouerthrow the text ;
I can alledge and vouch authority,
T'imbroyle th'intent, and fenfe of equity ;   2530
Befides, by hauing beene a Notary,
And vf'd to frame litigious inftruments
And leaue aduantages for fubtilty
And ftrife to worke on, I can fo deuife
That there fhall be no writing made fo fure
But it fhall yeeld occafion to conteft
At any time when men fhall thinke it beft ;
Nor be thou checkt vvith this *Piftophœnax,*

That at thy firſt appearing thou art thus
Diſcou'red here ; thou ſhalt along with vs,   2540
And take thy fortune too, as vvell as we.
   Piſt. Tuſh *Lincus*, this cannot diſcourage me,
For we that traffique with credulity
And with opinion, ſtill ſhall cheriſht be ;
But here your errour was to enter firſt
And be before me, for you ſhould haue let
Me make the way, that I might haue diſlinkt
That chaine of Zeale that holds in amity,
And call'd vp doubt in their eſtabliſht rites ;
Which would haue made you ſuch an eaſie way, 2550
As that you might haue brought in what you would,
Vpon their ſhaken and diſcattered mindes ;
For our profeſſion any thing refutes,
And all's vnſetled whereas faith diſputes.
   Mel. Now what a muttring keepe you there, away,
Begone I ſay, and beſt doe, whilſt you may,
And ſince we haue redeem'd our ſelues ſo well
Out of the bonds of miſchiefe, let vs all
Exile with them their ill example too;
Which neuer more remaines, as it begun,   2560
But is a wicked fire t' a farre worſe ſonne,
And ſtayes not till it makes vs ſlaues vnto
That vniuerſall Tyrant of the earth
Cuſtome, who takes from vs our priuiledge
To be our ſelues, rendes that great charter too
Of nature, and would likewiſe cancell man ;;
And ſo inchaines our iudgements and diſcourſe
Vnto the preſent vſances, that we
Muſt all our ſenſes thereunto refer.
Be as we finde our ſelues, not as we are,   2570

As if we had no other touch of truth
And reafon, then the nations of the times,
And place wherein we liue ; and being our felues
Corrupted, and abaftardizèd thus,
Thinke all lookes ill, that doth not looke like vs.
And therefore let vs recolleƈt our felues
Difperf'd into thefe ftrange confufèd ills,
And be againe *Arcadians*, as we were
In manners, and in habits as we were;
   And fo folemnize this our happie day   2580
   Of reftauration, with other feafts of ioy.

FINIS.

v.

TETHYS FESTIVALL.

1610.

NOTE.

⁊ For my exemplar of 'Tethys Feſtivall,' I am indebted to the Bodleian. That in the British Museum, though a dirty and stained copy, has the advantage over it of having prefixed a striking account of the great Ceremonial of which Daniel's 'Mask' formed only a slight part. Its title-page is as follows :—

The Order and Solemnitie of the

Creation of the High and mightie Prince

HENRIE, *Eldeſt Sonne to our ſacred*

Soueraigne, Prince of Wales, Duke of

Cornewall, Earle of Cheſter, &c.   As it was

celebrated in the Parliament Houſe, on

Munday the fourth of Iuune

laſt paſt.

Together with the Ceremonies of the

Knights of the Bath, and other

matters of ſpeciall regard, in-

cident to the ſame.

Wherunto is annexed the Royall Maſke, preſented

by the Queene and her Ladies, on Wedneſday

at night following.

Printed at Britaines Burſſe for *Iohn Budge*, and are
there to be ſold.   1610.   [4to.]

By some inadvertence 'Tethys Feſtivall' was not given in the 4to of 1623, and has fetched as high as £9 at book-sales.   Opposite is the title-page.   G.

TETHYS
FESTIVAL:
OR,
THE QVEENES
WAKE.

Celebrated at Whitehall, the fifth
day of June, 1610.

Deuifed by Samvel Daniel, one of
the Groomes of her Maiefties Honourable
priuie Chamber.

LONDON
Printed for *Iohn Budge*. 1610.

THE PREFACE TO THE READER.

OR fo much as fhewes and fpeĉtacles
of this nature, are vfually regiftred
among the memorable aĉts of the
time, beeing Complements of State,
both to fhew magnificence and to
celebrate the feafts to our greateft
refpeĉts : it is expeĉted (according
now to the cuftome) that I, beeing 10
imployed in the bufines, fhould publifh a defcription
and forme of the late Mafk, wherewithall it pleafed
the Queenes moft excellent Maieftie to folemnize the
creation of the high and mightie Prince Henry, Prince
of Wales, in regard to preferue the memorie thereof,
and to fatisfie their defires, who could haue no other
notice, but by others report of what was done.   Which
I doe not out of a defire to be feene in pamphlets, or of
forwardness to fhew my inuēction therin : for I thank
God, I labour not with that difeafe of oftentation, nor 20
affeĉt to be known to be the man *digitoque monftrarier*

hic eſt, hauing my name already wider in this kind then I deſire, and more in the winde then I would. Neither doe I feeke in the divulging hereof, to giue it other colours then thoſe it wore, or to make an Apologie of what I haue done : knowing, howſoeuer, it muſt paſſe the way of cenſure where / vnto I ſee all publications (of what nature ſoeuer) are liable. And my long experience of the world, hath taught me this, that neuer Remonſtrances nor Apologies could euer get ouer the ſtreame of opinion, to doe good on the other ſide, where contrarie affeƈtion and conceipt had to doe : but onely ſerued to entertaine their owne partialneſſe, who were fore-perſwaded ; and ſo was a labour in vaine. And it is oftentimes an argument of puſilanimitie, and may make *vt iudicium noſtrum, metus videatur*, and render a good cauſe ſuſpeƈted, by too much labouring to defend it ; which might be the reaſon that ſome of the late greateſt Princes of Chriſtendome would neuer haue their vndertakings made good by ſuch courſes, but with ſilence indured (and in a moſt wittie age) the greateſt batterie of paper that could poſſibly be made, & neuer once recharged the leaſt ordinance of a pen againſt it, counting it their glorie to do whileſt others talked. And ſhall we who are the poore Inginers for ſhadowes, & frame onely images of no reſult, thinke to oppreſſe the rough cenſures of thoſe, who notwithſtanding all our labour will like according to their taſte, or ſeeke to auoid them by flying to an Army of Authors, as idle as our ſelues ? Seeing there is nothing done or written, but incounters with detraƈtion and oppoſition ; which is an excellent argument of all our imbecillities & might allay our preſumption, when we fhall fee our greateft knowledges not to be fixt, but rowle according to the vncertaine motion of opinion, and controwleable by any furly fhew of reafon ; which we find is double edged and ftrikes euery way alike.   And therefore I do not fee why any man fhould rate his owne at that valew, and/ fet fo low prifes vpon other men's abilities.   *L'homme vaut l'homme,* a man is 6 worth a man, and none hath gotten fo high a ftation of vnderftanding, but he fhall find others that are built on an equall floore with him, and haue as far a profpe&t as he ; which when al is done, is but in a region fubie&t to al paffiõs and imperfe&tions.

  ⋅⋅And for thefe figures of mine, if they come not drawn in all proportions to the life of antiquity (from whofe tyrannie, I fee no reafon why we may not emancipate our inuentions, and be as free as they, to vfe our owne images) yet I know them fuch as were 70 proper to the bufines, and difcharged thofe parts for which they ferued, with as good correfpondencie, as our appointed limitations would permit.

  But in thefe things wherein the onely life confifts in fhew ; the arte and inuention of the Archite&t giues the greateft grace, and is of moft importance : ours, the leaft part and of leaft note in the time of the performance thereof ; and therefore haue I interferted the defcription of the artificiall part, which only fpeakes *M. Inago Iones.* ~ 80

TETHYS
FESTIVALL.

Wherein Tethys Qveene of the Ocean, and wife of
Neptune, attended with thirteene Nymphs of
feuerall Riuers, is reprefented in this manner.

IRST the Queenes Maieftie in the
figure of *Tethys*. The Ladies in the
fhape of Nimphes, prefiding feuerall
/ Riuers appropriate either to their
dignitie, Signiories, or places of 10
birth.

    1. *Whereof the firft was the Ladie
Elizabeths grace, reprefenting the Nymph of
Thames.*
  2. *The Ladie Arbella, the Nymph of Trent.*
  3. *The Counteffe of Arundell, the Nymph of Arun.*

l: 5,'In margin 'Tethys mater Nympharum & fluuiorum': l. 9, Mis-
printed 'appropriately': l. 16, In margin 'Arun, a Riuer that runs by
Arundell Caftle.'

4. *The Countesse of Darbie, the Nymph of Darwent.*
5. *The Countesse of Essex, the Nymph of Lee.*
6. *The Countesse of Dorcet, the Nymph of Ayr.*
7. *The Countesse of Mongommerie, the Nymph of* 20 *Severn.*
8. *The Vicountesse of Haddington, the Nymph of Rother.*
9. *The Ladie* Elizabeth Gray, *the Nymph of Medway.*

Thefe foure Riuers are in Monmouthfhire.
The Ladie Elizabeth Guilford, *the Nymph of Dulesse.*
The Ladie Katherine Peeter, *the Nymph of Olwy.*
The Ladie Winter, *the Nymph of Wy.*
The Ladie Winfor, *the Nymph of Vske.*   30

The difcription of the firft Scene.

ON the Trauers which ferued as a curtaine for the firft Scene, was figured a darke cloude, interior with certaine fparkling ftarres, which, at the found of a loud mufick, being inftantly drawne, the scene was difcouered with thefe adornements : Firft, on eyther fide ftood a great ftatue of twelue foot high, reprefenting *Neptune* and *Nereus.* *Neptune* holding a Trident, with an Anchor made to it, and this Mot, *His artibus :* that is, *Regendo, & retinendo,* alluding to this / verfe of 40 *Virgill, He tibi erunt artes, &c. Nereus* holding out a golden fifh in a net, with this word *Induftria :* The reafon whereof is deliuered after, in the fpeech vttered

In margin—l. 17, 'Darwent, a riuer that runs through Darbie': l. 18, 'Lee, the riuer that bounds Effex': l. 19, ' Ayr, a Riuer that runs nere Skipton, where this Lady was borne ' : l. 20, 'Seuerne, rifes in Mongommery fhire ': l. 22, 'Rother, a riuer in Suffex ': l. 24, 'Medway, a riuer in Kent ': l. 33, Mifprinted ' interfer.'

by *Triton.* Thefe Sea-gods ftood on pedeftals, and were al of gold. Behinde them were two pillafters, on which hung compartments, with other deuifes : and thefe bore vp a rich Freeze, wherein were figures of tenne foote long, of flouds, and Nymphes, with a number of naked children, dallying with a draperie, which they feemed to holde vp, that the Scene might 50 be feene, and the ends thereof fell downe in foldes by the pillafters. In the midft was a compartment, with this infcription, *Tethyos Epinicia,* TETHYS feafts of triumph. This was fupported with two winged boyes, and all the worke was done with that force and boldneffe on the gold and filuer, as the figures feemed round and not painted.

The Scene it felfe was a Port or Hauen, with Bul-workes at the entrance, and the figure of a Caftle commanding a fortified towne : within this Port were 60 many Ships, fmall and great, feeming to be at Anchor, fome neerer, and fome further off, according to pro-fpeĉtiue : beyond all appeared the Horifon, or ter-mination of the Sea ; which feemed to mooue with a gentle gale, and many Sayles, lying fome to come into the Port, and others paffing out. From this Scene iffued *Zephirus,* with eight Naydes, Nymphs of foun-taines, and two *Tritons* fent from *Tethys* to giue notice of intendement, which was the Ante-mafke or firft fhew. The Duke of Yorke prefented *Zephirus,* in a 70 fhort robe of greene fatin imbrodered with golden flowers, with / a round wing made of lawnes on wyers,

---

1. 69, In margin—' *The figure of Zephirus might aptly difcharge this repre-fentation in refpect that meffages are of winde,* and verba dicuntur alara, *winged wordes : befides it is a character of youth, and of the Spring.*'

and hung down in labels. Behind his ſhoulders two
ſiluer wings. On his head a Garland of flowers con-
ſiſting of all colours, and on one Arme which was out
bare, he wore a bracelet of gold ſet with rich ſtones.
Eight little Ladies neere of his Stature, repreſented the
Naydes, and were attired in light robes adorned with
flowers, their haire hanging down, and wauing with
Garlands of water ornaments on their heads.

The Tritons wore ſkin-coates of watchet Taffata
(lightned with ſiluer) to ſhew the Muſcles of their
bodies. From the waſte almoſt to the knee were finnes
of ſiluer in the manner of baſes: a mantle of Sea-
greene, laced and fringed with golde, tyed with a knot
vppon one ſhoulder, and falling down in foldes behinde,
was faſtened to the contrary ſide : on their heads
garlands of Sedge, with trumpets of writhen ſhels in
their hand : Buſkins of ſea-greene laid with ſiluer lace.
Theſe perſons thus attired, entred with this ſong of
foure parts, and a muſicke of twelue Lutes.

Youth of the Spring, milde Zephirus *blow faire,*
  And breath the ioyfull ayre,
Which Tethys *wiſhes may attend this day ;*
  Who comes her ſelfe to pay
  The vowes her heart preſents,
  To theſe faire complements.

Breath out new flowers, which yet were neuer knowne
  Vnto the Spring, nor blown
Before this time, to bewtifie the earth ;
  And | as this day giues birth
  Vnto new types of State,
  So. let it bliſſe create.

Beare Tethys *meſſage to the Ocean King,*
 Say how ſhe ioyes to bring
Delight vnto his Ilands and his Seas ;
  And tell Meliades
  The of-ſpring of his b[l]ood,
  How ſhe applaudes his good.

The ſong ended, *Triton,* on the behalfe of *Zephirus,* 110
deliuers *Tethys* meſſage with her Preſents (which was
a Trident to the King, and a rich ſword and ſkarfe to
the Prince of Wales) in theſe wordes :—

From that intelligence which moues the Sphere
Of circling waues (the mightie Tethys, *Queene*
Of Nymphes and riuers, who will ſtraight appeare,
And in a humane Character be ſeene)
We haue in charge to ſay, that euen as Seas
And lands, are grac'd by men of worth and might,
So they returne their fauours ; and in theſe 120
Exalting of the good ſeeme to delight.
Which ſhe, in glory, lately viſiting
The ſweete, and pleaſant Shores of Cambria, found
By an vnuſuall, and moſt forward Spring
Of comfort, wherewith all things did abound,
For ioy of the Inueſtiture at hand
Of their new Prince ; whoſe Rites, with acts renownd,
Were here to be ſolemniz'd on this Strand :
And therefore ſtreight reſolues t'adorne the day
With her al-gracing preſence, and the traine 130
Of | ſome choice Nymphs, ſhe pleaſ'd to call away
From ſeuerall Riuers which they entertaine.
And firſt the louely Nymphe of ſtately Thames

(The darling of the Ocean) fummond is :
Then thofe of Trent *and* Aruns *gracefull ftreames,*
Then Darwent *next with cleare-wau'd worthineffe.*
The beauteous Nymph of Chryftall-ftreaming Lee
Giues next attendance : then the Nymph of Ayr
With modeft motion makes her fweete repaire.
The Nymph of Seuerne *follows in degree,*   140
With ample ftreames of grace : and next to her
The cheerefull Nymph of Rother *doth appeare*
With comely Medway, *th'ornament of* Kent :
And then foure goodly Nymphes that beautifie
Cambers *faire fhores, and all that Continent*
The graces of cleere Vfke, Olwy, Duleffe, Wy.

   All thefe within the goodly fpacious Bay
Of manifold inharboring Milford *meete ;*
The happy Port of Vnion, which gaue way
To that great Hero HENRY, *and his fleete,*   150
To make the bleft coniunction that begat
O greater, and more glorious far then that.

   From hence fhe fends her deare lou'd Zephirus,
To breath out her affection and her zeale
To you great Monarch of Oceanus,
And to prefent this Trident as the feale
And enfigne of her loue and of your right.

   And therewithall fhe wils him, greete the Lord
And Prince of th'Iles (the hope and the delight,
Of all the Northerne Nations) with this fword   160
That fhe vnto Aftræa *facred found,*
And not to be vnfheath'd but on iuft ground.
Herewith, fayes fhe, deliuer him from mee
This fkarffe, the zone of Loue and Amitie,
T'ingird the fame ; wherein he may furuay,

Infigur'd all the fpacious Emperie
That he is borne vnto another day.
Which, tell him, will be world enough to yeeld
All | workes of glory euer can be wrought.
Let him not paſſe the circle of that field,   170
But thinke Alcides *pillars are the knot;*
For there will be within the large extent
Of theſe my waues, and watry Gouernment
More treaſure, and more certaine riches got
Then all the Indies *to* Iberus *brought;*
For Nereus *will by induſtry vnfold*
A Chimicke fecret, and turne fiſh to gold,
    This charge ſhe gaue, and lookes with ſuch a cheere
As did her comfort and delight bewray,
Like cleere Aurora *when ſhe doth appeare*   180
In brighteſt roabes to make a glorious day.

The Speech ended, the Naydes daunce about *Zephirus*
and then withdraw them aſide; when ſuddenly, at
the ſound of a loud and fuller muſique, *Tethys* with
her Nymphes appeares, with another Scene, which
I will likewiſe deſcribe in the language of their Archi-
tector who contriued it, and ſpeakes in his owne meſtier
to ſuch as are vnderſtaders & louers of that deſign.
Firſt at the opening of the heauens appeared 3 circles
of lights and glaſſes, one with[in] another, and came 190
downe in a ſtraight motion fiue foote, and then began
to mooue circularly: which lights and motion ſo
occupied the eyes of the ſpectators, that the manner
of altering the Scene was ſcarcely diſcerned: for in
a moment the whole face.of it was changed, the Port
vaniſhed, and *Tethys* with her Nymphes appeared in

their feuerall Cauerns glorioufly adorned. This Scene
was comparted into 5 Neeces, whereof that in the
middeft had fome flender pillowes of whole round, and
were made of moderne architecture in regard of roome : 200
thefe were of burnifht gold, and bare vp the returnes of
an Architraue, Freeze, and Cornifh of the fame worke :
on/ which, vpon eyther fide was a Plinth, directly ouer
the pillers, & on them were placed for finifhings, two
Dolphins of filuer, with their tailes wreathed together,
which fupported ouall vafes of gold.

Betweene the two pillers on eyther fide were great
ornaments of relieuo : the Bafement were two huge
Whales of filuer.   Aboue in an action mounting were
two Sea-horfes, and aboue them, on each fide of *Tethys* 210
feat was placed a great Trident.   The feate or Throne
it felfe was raifed fixe fteps, and all couered with fuch
an artificiall ftuffe, as feemed richer by candle, then any
cloth of gold.   The refts for her armes were two Cheru-
bines of gold : ouer her head was a great fkallop of
filuer, from which hung the foldes of this rich drapery.

Aboue the Skallop, and round about the fides was
a refplendent freeze of iewell glaffes or lights, which
fhewed like Diamonds, Rubies, Saphires, Emeralds, and
fuch like.   220

The part which returned from the two Plinthes
that bare vp the Dolphines, was circular, and made a
hollowneffe ouer *Tethys* head, and on this circle were
4 great Chartufes of gold, which bore vp a round
bowle of filuer, in manner of a fountaine, with mafk-
heads of gold, out of which ran an artificiall water.
On the middeft of this was a triangular bafement

          l. 199, ▬ Niches.   l. 200, ═ Pillars.

formed of fcrowles & leaues, and then a ˅rich Vayle
adorned with flutings, and inchafed worke, with a
freeze of fifhes, and a battaile of Tritons, out of whofe 230
mouthes, fprang water into the Bowle vnderneath. On
the top of this was a round globe of gold full of holes,
out of which iffued abondance of water, fome falling
into the receipt below, fome into the Ovall vafe, borne
vp by the Dolphines ; and indeed there was no place
in this great Aqua / tick throne, that was not filled with
the fprinckling of thefe two naturall feeming waters.
The Neeces wherein the Ladies fate, were foure, with
Pillafters of gold, mingled with ruftick ftones fhewing
like a minerall̃ to make it more rocke, and Cauern-like, 240
varying from that of *Tethys* throne. Equally with
the heads of the Pillars was an Architraue of the
fame work : aboue was a circular frontifpiece, which
rofe equall with the Bowle of the fountaine fore-
difcribed. On the ruftick frontifpice lay two great
figures in Rileue, which feemed to beare vp a Garland
of Sea-weeds : to which from two antick Candleftickes
which ftood ouer the Pillafters, were hanging Sibells of
gold. And thefe were the finifhings of the top of the
two Neeces next to that of *Tethys*. 250
 In the fpace betweene the frontifpice and the Archi-
traue, ftood a great Concaue fhel, wherein was the
head of a Sea-god, and on either fide the fhell to fill
vp the roome, two great mafk heads in perfile. The
other two Neeces which were outermoft, were likewife
borne vp with Pillafters of gold, and for variation had
fquare frontifpices, and againft the ftreight Architraue of
the other was an Arch. All thefe were mingled with
ruftick, as before.

In the middle betweene the frontifpice & the Arch, 260
was a bowle or fountaine made of foure great fkallops,
borne vp by a great mafke head, which had likewife
foure afpects, and lying vpon this Arch (to fill vp the
Concaues) were two figures turned halfe into fifhes :
thefe with their heads held vp the fides of the
Bowle : aboue this were three great Cherubines heads,
fpouting water into the Bowle.   On the middeft of the
fquare frontifpice ftood a great vafe adorned.   The /
reft of the ornaments confifted of mafke-heads, fpout-
ing water, fwannes, feftons of maritime weedes, great 270
fhels, and fuch like ; and all this whole Scene was
filled with the fplendor of gold and filuer : onely fome
beautifull colours behinde to diftinguifh them, and to
fet off the reft.

The whole worke came into the forme of a halfe
round : there fate three Ladies in each Neece, which
made fixe of a fide : the Queene in middeft, and the
Lady *Elizabeth* at her feete.   •

Now concerning their habite : firft their head-tire
was compofed of fhels and corrall, and from a great 280
Muriake fhell in forme of the creft of an helme,
hung a thin wauing vaile.   Their vpper garments
had the bodies of fky-colored taffataes for lightnes, all
embroidered with maritime inuention : then had they a
kinde of halfe fkirts of cloth of filuer imbrodered with
golde, all the groũd work cut out for lightnes, which
hung down ful, & cut in points : vnderneath that, came
bafes (of the fame as their bodies) beneath their knee.
The long fkirt was wrought with lace, waued round
about like a Riuer, and on the bankes fedge and Sea- 290
weedes, all of gold.   Their fhouders were all imbrodered

with the worke of the fhort fkirt of cloth of filuer, and
had cypreffe fpangled, ruffed out, and fell in a ruffe
aboue the Elbow.   The vnder fleeues were all im-
brodered as the bodies: their fhoes were of Satin, richly
imbrodered, with the worke of the fhort fkirt.

In this habite they defcended out of their Cauernes
one after another, and fo marched vp with winding
meanders like a Riuer, till they came to the Tree of
victory ; which was a Bay erected at the right fide of 300
the ftate, vpon a little mount there raifed ; where they
offer their / feuerall flowers in golden vrnes which they
bare in their hands : whilft a foft mufique of twelue
Lutes and twelue voyces, which entertained the tune,
expreft as a Chorus, their action in this manner.

> *Was euer howre brought more delight*
> > *To mortall fight,*
> *Then this, wherein faire* Tethys *daignes to fhew*
> > *Her, and her Nymphes arow*
> > *In glory bright ?*   310
> *See how they bring their flowers,*
> > *From out their watry bowers,*
> > *To decke* Apollos *Tree,*
> > *The tree of victory.*
> *About whofe verdant bowes,*
> *They Sacrifice their vowes,*
> > *And wifh an euerlafting fpring*
> > *Of glory, to the Ocean King.*

This fonge and ceremony ended, they fall into their
firft daunce, after which *Tethys* withdrawes and repofes 320
her vpon the Mount vnder the tree of victory, enter-
tain'd with Mufique and this Song.

> *If ioy had other figure*
> > *Then foundes, and wordes, and motion,*
> *To intimate the meafure,*
> > *And height of our deuotion ;*
> > *This day it had beene fhow'd.*
> > *But what it can, it doth performe,*
> *Since nature hath beftowd*
> > *No other letter,*   330
> > *To expreffe it better,*
> > *Then in this forme ;*
> *Our motions, foundes, and wordes,*
> > *Tun'd to accordes ;*
> *Muft fhew the well-fet partes,*
> *Of our affeƈtions and our harts.*

After / this *Tethys* rifes, and with her Nymphes performes her fecond daunce, and then repofes her againe vpon the Mount, entertaind with another fonge.   340

> *Are they fhadowes that we fee ?*
> *And can fhadowes pleafure giue ?*
> *Pleafures onely fhadowes bee*
> *Caft by bodies we conceiue,*
> *And are made the thinges we deeme,*
> *In thofe figures which they feeme.*
> *But thefe pleafures vanifh faft,*
> *Which by fhadowes are expreft :*
> *Pleafures are not, if they laft,*
> *In their paffing, is their beft.*   350
> *Glory is moft bright and gay*
> *In a flafh, and fo away.*

Feed apace then greedy eyes
On the wonder you behold.
Take it fodaine as it flies
Though you take it not to hold:
When your eyes haue done their part,
Thought muft length it in the hart.

After this Songe *Tethys* againe rifes, and with her
Nymphes, taketh out the Lordes to daunce their 360
Meafures, Corantos and Galliardes ; which done, they
fall into their third and retyring daunce, wherewith they
returne againe into their feuerall Cauernes, and fodainely
vanifh.   When to auoid the confufion which vfually
attendeth the defolue of thefe fhewes ; and when all
was thought to be finifht, followed another entertain-
ment, and was a third fhew no leffe delightfull then the
reft, whofe introduction was thus.

Zephirus marching a certaine fpace after *Tethys*
and her Nymphes, attended with his Tritons, a fodaine 370
flafh of lightning caufes them to ftay, and *Triton*
deliuereth this fpeech.

Behold, | the Poft of heauen, bright Mercury
Is fent to fommon and recall againe,
Imperiall Tethys *with her company,*
Vnto her watry Manfion in the maine :
And fhift thefe formes, wherein her power did daigne
T'inueft her felfe and hers, and to reftore
Them to themfelues, whofe beauteous fhapes they wore.

And   then   bowing   himfelfe   towardes   the   State, 380
craueth their ftay, and prepareth them, to the expecta-

tion of a returne of the Queene and her Ladies in their
formes, with thefe wordes.

> *And now bright Starre the Guidon of this ftate,*
> *And you great Peeres the ornaments of power,*
> *With all thefe glittering troupes that haue the fate,*
> *To be fpeftators of this bleffed houre.*
> *Be pleafed to fit a while, and you fhall fee*
> *A transformation of farre more delight,*
> *And apter drawne to nature, then can be*   390
> *Difcrib'd in an imaginary fight.*

Triton hauing ended his fpeech, *Mercury* moſt
artificially, and in an exquifite poſture defcends, and
fommons the Duke of Yorke, and fix yong Noble-
men to attend him, and bring backe the Queene and
her Ladies in their owne forme, direfting him to the
place where to finde them ; with this fpeech.

> *Faire branch of power, in whofe fweete feature here*˙
> *Milde* Zephirus *a figure did prefent*
> *Of youth and of the fpring-time of the yeare ;*   400
> *I fommon you, and fix of high defcent*
> *T'attend on you (as hopefull worthyes borne*
> *To fhield the Honour and the cleare Renowne*
> *Of Ladies) that you prefently returne*
> *And/bring backe thofe, in whofe faire fhapes were fhowne*
> *The late-feene Nymphes in figures of their owne ;*
> *Whom you fhall finde hard by within a groue*
> *And Garden of the fpring addreſt to Ioue.*

Hereupon the Duke of Yorke with his attendants
departing to performe this feruice, the lowde Mufique 410

foundes, and fodainely appeares the Queenes Maiefty in a moft pleafant and artificiall Groue ; which was the third Scene, and from thence they march vp to the King conducted by the Duke of Yorke, and the Noblemen, in a very ftately manner.

And in all thefe fhewes, this is to be noted, that there were none of inferiour fort, mixed amongft thefe great Perfonages of State and Honour (as vfually there haue beene) but all was performed by themfelues with a due referuation of their dignity. And for thofe two 420 which did Perfonate the Tritons, they were Gentlemen knowne of good worth and refpect. The introducing of Pages with torches, might haue added more fplendor, but yet they would haue peftred the roome ; which the feafon would not well permit.

And thus haue I deliuered the whole forme of this fhew, and expofe it to the cenfure of thofe who make it their beft fhow, to feeme to know: with this Poftfcript.

Prætulerim fcriptor delirus inerfque videri 430
Dum mea delectant mala me, vel denique fallant,
Quam fapere & ringi.

S. D./

VI.

HYMENS TRIUMPH.
1615

NOTE.

The original edition of 'Hymens Triumph' was published in 1615. The title-page is as follows :—

HYMENS TRI-
VMPH.

√

A Paſtorall Tragicomædie.

Preſented at the Queenes Court in the Strand at
her Maieſties magnificent entertainement of the
Kings moſt excellent Maieſtie, being at
the Nuptials of the Lord
Roxborough.

By Samvel Daniel.

Hinc . Lvcem . Pocvla . Sacra.

LONDON

Imprinted for *Francis Conſtable*, and are to bee ſold
at his ſhop in Pauls Church-yard at the ſigne
of the white Lyon. 1615 [12°].

A beautiful exemplar is in the British Museum (C. 39. a. 41). Our text
(4to, 1623) has only slight variations in orthography. It corrects the
'errata' noted at end of [1] (except one which it mis-corrects by 'lowe-
heſſe' for [1] 'loueneſſe' corrected by the Author into 'loneneſſe.' At
l. 30 (p. 336) I have altered 'ſave' into 'ſafe,' and l. 44 (*ibid.*) 'thinks'
into 'things'—and so elsewhere obvious misprints are corrected. Opposite
is title-page of our exemplar and text. **G.**

HYMENS

TRIVMPH.

A Paſtorall Tragicomædie.

Preſented at the Queenes Court in the
Strand, at her Maieſties magnificent enter-
tainement of the Kings moſt excellent
Maieſty, being at the Nuptials of the
Lord *Roxborough.*

By SAMVEL DANIEL.

LONDON,
Printed by NICHOLAS OKES for
SIMON WATERSON.
1623.

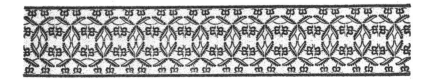

TO THE MOST EXCEL-
lent Maiefty of the Higheft-borne
Princeffe, ANNE *of Denmarke*, *Queene*
of England, Scotland, France,
and Ireland.

Ere, what your facred influence begat
    (Moft lou'd, and moft refpected
    Maiefty)
    With humble heart, and hand, I
    confecrate
    Vnto the glory of your memory :
    As being a piece of that folemnity,   10
    Which your Magnificence did cele-
    brate
  In hallowing of thofe roofes (you rear'd of late)
  With fires and chearefull hofpitality ;
Whereby, and by your fplendent Worthines,
  Your name fhall longer liue then fhall your walls :
For, that faire ftructure goodneffe finifhes,
  Beares off all change of times, and neuer falls.
  And that is it hath let you in fo farre
  Into the heart of *England* as you are.

And worthily ; for neuer yet was Queene   20
    That more a peoples loue haue merited
By all good graces, and by hauing beene
    The meanes our State ſtands faſt eſtabliſhed
And bleſt by your bleſt wombe : who are this day
    The higheſt-borne Queene of *Europe*, and alone
Haue brought this land more bleſſings euery way,
    Then all the daughters of ſtrange Kings haue done,
For, / we by you no claimes, no quarrells haue,
    No factions, no betraying of affaires :
You do not ſpend our blood, nor ſtates, but ſaue :   30
    You ſtrength vs by alliance, and your haires.
Not like thoſe fatall marriages of *France*,
    For whom this Kingdome hath ſo dearely paid,
Which onely our afflictions did aduance :
    And brought vs farre more miſeries, then aid.
Renowned *Denmarke*, that haſt furniſhed
    The world with Princes, how much do we owe
To thee for this great good thou didſt beſtow,
Whereby we are both bleſt, and honoured ?
    Thou didſt not ſo much hurt vs heretofore,   40
But now thou haſt rewarded vs farre more.
    But what do I on this high ſubiect fall
    Here, in the front of this low Paſtorall ?
This a more graue, and ſpacious roome requires
To ſhew your glory, and my deepe deſires.

Your Maieſties moſt

Humble Seruant,

SAM. DANIEL. 48

The Prologue.

Hymen oppoſed by *Auarice, Enuy,* and *Iealouſie,*
the diſturbers of quiet marriage, *firſt enters.*

Hymen.

*I*N *this diſguiſe and Paſtorall attire,*
  Without my ſaffron robe, without my torch,
Or other enſignes of my duty :
I Hymen *am come hither ſecretly,*
To make Arcadia *ſee a worke of glory,*
That ſhall deſerue an euerlaſting ſtory.   10
  Here, ſhall I bring you two the moſt entire
And conſtant louers that were euer ſeene,
From out the greateſt ſuffrings of anoy
That fortune could inflict, to their full ioy :
Wherein no wild, no rude, no antique ſport,
But tender paſſions, motions ſoft, and graue,
The ſtill ſpectators muſt expect to haue.
  For, theſe are onely Cynthias *recreatiues*
Made vnto Phœbus, *and are feminine ;*
And therefore muſt be gentle like to her,   20
Whoſe ſweet affections mildely mooue and ſtirre.

And here, with this white wand, will I effect
As much, as with my flaming torch of Loue :
And with the power thereof, affections mooue
In these faire nymphes, and shepheards round about.

   Enuy. *Stay* Hymen, *stay ; you shall not haue the day*
Of this great glory, as you make account :
We will herein, as we were euer wont,
Oppose you in the matches you addresse,
And vndermine them with disturbances.   30

   Hym. *Now, do thy worst, base* Enuy, *thou canst do,*
Thou shalt not disappoint my purposes.

   Auarice. *Then will I,* Hymen, *in despite of thee,*
I will make Parents crosse desires of loue,
With those respects of wealth, as shall dissolue
The strongest knots of kindest faithfulnesse.

   Hym. *Hence, greedy* Auarice ; *I know thou art*
A hagge, that do'st bewitch the mindes of men :
Yet shalt thou haue no [part] at all herein.

   Ieal. *Then will I,* Hymen, *do thou what thou canst ;* 40
I will steale closely into linked hearts ;
And shake their veines with cold distrustfulnesse ;
And euer keepe them waking in their feares,
With spirits, which their imagination reares.

   Hym. *Disquiet* Iealousie, *vile fury, thou*
That art the ougly monster of the mind,
Auant, be gone ! thou shalt haue nought to do
In this faire worke of ours, nor euermore
Canst enter there, where honour keepes the doore.

   And therefore hideous furies, get you hence,   50
This place is sacred to integrity,
And cleane desires : your sight most loathsome is
Vnto so well dispos'd a company.

Therefore be gone, I charge you by my powre,
We muſt haue nothing in Arcadia, *ſowre.*
    Enuy. Hymen, *thou canſt not chaſe vs ſo away,*
For, looke how long as thou mak'ſt marriages,
So long will we produce incumbrances.
And we will in the ſame diſguiſe, as thou,
Mixe vs amongſt the ſhepheards, that we may   60
Effect our worke the better, being vnknowne ;
For, ills ſhew other faces then their owne.

The Speakers.

THIRSIS.

PALÆMON, friend to *Thirfis*.

CLARINDO, SILUIA difguifed, the beloued of *Thirfis*, fuppofed to be flaine by wild beafts.

CLORIS, a Nymph whom *Clarindo* ferued, and in loue with *Thirfis*.

PHILLIS, in loue with *Clarindo*.

MONTANUS, in loue with *Phillis*.

LYDIA, Nurfe to *Phillis*.

DORCAS. ⎫
SILUANUS. ⎬ Forrefters.

MEDORUS, father to *Siluia*.

CHARINUS, father to *Thirfis*.

     Chorus of Shepheards.

ACTVS. I. SCENA. I.

Thirſis.   Palæmon.

O to be reft of all the ioyes of life,
How is it poſſible *Palæmon*, I
Should euer more a thought retaine
Of the leaſt comfort vpon earth
    againe?
No, I would hate this heart, that
    hath receiu'd   [come
So deepe a wound, if it ſhould euer
To be recur'd, or would permit a roome
To let in any other thing then griefe.   10
    Pal. But *Thirſis* you muſt tell me what is the cauſe ?
    Thi. Thinke but what cauſe I haue ; when hauing
        paſſ'd
The heates, the colds, the trembling agonies
Of feares, and hopes, and all the ſtrange aſſaults
Of paſſion, that a tender heart could feele
In the attempt, and purſuite of his loue :
And then to be vndone, when all was done ;

'o perifh in the hauen, after all
'hofe Ocean fuffrings, and euen then to haue
Iy hopefull Nuptiall bed, turn'd to a graue.   20
   Pal. Good *Thirfis* by what meanes, I pray thee tell.
   Thi. Tell thee? alas *Palæmon*, how can I tell
ınd liue? doeft thou not fee thefe fields haue loft
'heir glory, fince that time *Siluia* was loft?
'*iluia*, that onely deckt, that onely made
lrcadia fhine; *Siluia* who was (ah woe the while)
o miferable rent from off the world,
o rapt away, as that no figne of her,
ſo peece was left to tell vs by what meanes:
aue onely this poore remnant of her vaile,   30
ıll torne, and this deere locke of her rent haire;
ſhich holy reliques here I keepe with me,
'he fad memorialls of her difmall fate.
ſho fure deuoured was vpon the fhore
y rauenous beafts, as fhe was walking there
ılone, it feemes; perhaps in feeking me,
r els retir'd to meditate apart
he ftory of our loues, and heauy fmart.
   Pal. This is no newes, you tell, of *Siluias* death.
hat was long fince: why fhould you waile her now? 40
   Thi. Long fince *Palæmon?* thinke you any length
f time can euer haue a powre to make
 heart of flefh not mourne, not grieue, not pine?
ıat knows, that feels, that thinks as much as mine.
   Pal. But *Thirfis*, you know how her father meant
ɔ match her with *Alexis*, and a day
ɔ celebrate the nuptials was prefixt.
   Thi. True, he had fuch a purpofe, but in vaine,
ɔ oh it was beft knowne vnto vs twaine.

And hence it grew that gaue vs both our feares,　　50
That made our meeting ftealth, our parting teares.
Hence was it, that with many a fecret wile,
We rob'd our lookes th'onlookers to beguile.
This was the caufe, oh miferable caufe,
That made her by her felfe to ftray alone,
Which els God knows, fhe neuer fhould haue done.
For had our liberty as open beene,
As was our loues, *Siluia* had not beene feene
VVithout her *Thirfis*, neuer had we gone
But hand in hand, nor euer had mifchance　　60
Tooke vs afunder ; fhe had alwayes had
My body interpof'd betwixt all harmes
And her.　But ah we had our liberty
Layd faft in prifon when our loues were free.
　　Pal. But how knowft thou her loue was fuch to
　　　　thee ?
　　Thi. How do I know the Sun, the day from night ?
　　Pal. Womens affections do like flafhes proue,
They oft fhew paffion when they feele fmall loue.
　　Thi. Ah do not fo prophane that precious fexe,
Which I muft euer reuerence for her fake,　　70
Who was the glory of her kind ; whofe heart
In all her actions fo tranfparant was
As I might fee it cleere and wholy mine,
Alwayes obferuing truth in one right line.
　　How oft hath fhe beene vrg'd by fathers threats,
By friends perfwafions, and *Alexis* fighs,
And teares and prayers, to admit his loue,
Yet neuer could be wonne ! how oft haue I
Beheld the braueft heardfmen of thefe plaines,
(As what braue heardfman was there in the plaines 80

III.　　　　　　　　　　　　　　22

Of all *Arcadia*, that had not his heart
Warm'd with her beames) to feeke to win her loue !
  Ah I remember well (and how can I
But euer more remember well) when firft
Our flame began, when fcarce we knew what was
The flame we felt, when as we fate and figh'd
And look'd vpon each other, and conceiu'd
Not what we ayld ; yet fomething we did ayle,
And yet were well, and yet we were not well ;
And what was our difeafe we could not tell.   90
Then would we kiffe, then figh, then looke : and thus
In that firft garden of our fimpleneffe
We fpent our child-hood : but when yeeres began
To reape the fruite of knowledge ; ah how then
Would fhe with grauer looks, with fweet ftern brow
Check my prefumption and my forwardnes ;
Yet ftill would giue me flowers, ftil would me fhew
What fhe would haue me, yet not haue me know.
  Pal. Alas with what poore Coyne are louers paid,
And taken with the fmalleft bayte is laid ?   100
  Thi. And when in fport with other company,
Of Nimphes and fhepheards we haue met abroade
How would fhe fteale a looke : and watch mine eye
Which way it went ? and when at Barley breake
It came vnto my turne to refcue her,
With what an earneft, fwift, and nimble pace
Would her affection make her feet to run,
Nor farther run then to my hand ? her race
Had no ftop but my bofome, where no end.
And when we were to breake againe, how late   110
And loath her trembling hand wold part with mine,
And with how flow a pace would fhe fet forth

To meet the'ncountring party, who contends
T'attaine her, fcarce affording him her fingers ends?
   Pal. Fie *Thirfis*, with what fond remembrances
Doeft thou thefe idle paffions entertaine?
For fhame, leaue off to waft your youth in vaine,
And feede on fhadowes: make your choice anew.
You other Nimphes fhall find, no doubt will be
As louely, and as faire, and fweete as fhe.   120
   Thi. As faire and fweete as fhe? *Palæmon* peace:
Ah what can pictures be vnto the life?
What fweetnes can be found in Images?
Which all Nimphes els befides her feemes to me.
She only was a reall creature, fhe,
VVhofe memory muft take vp all of me.
Should I another loue, then muft I haue,
Another heart, for this is full of her,
And euermore fhall be: here is fhe drawne
At length, and whole, and more, this table is   130
A ftory, and is all of her; and all
Wrought in the liuelieft colours of my blood;
And can there be a roome for others heere?
Should I disfigure fuch a peece, and blot
The perfectft workmanfhip that loue euer wrought?
Palæmon no, ah no, it coft too deere,
It muft remaine intire whilft life remaines,
The monument of her and of my paines.
   Pal. Thou maieft be fuch a fond Idolater
To die for loue; though that were very ftrange.   140
Loue hath few Saints, but many confeffors.
And time no doubt will raze out all thefe notes,
And leaue a roome at length for other thoughts.
   Thi. Yes, when there is no fpring, no tree, no groue

In all *Arcadia* to record our loue :
And tell me where we were (the time we were)
How we did meete together, what we faid,
Where we did ioy, and where we fat difmai'd ;
And then I may forget her, not before.
Till then I muft remember one fo deere,   150
When euery thing I fee tells me of her.
And you deere Reliques of that martred Saint,
My heart adores, you the perpetuall bookes
Whereon when teares permit, mine·eyes ftill looks :
Ah you were with her laft, and till my laft
You muft remaine with me ; you were referu'd
To tell me fhe was left, but yet alas,
You cannot tell me how : I would you could :
   White fpotleffe vaile, cleane, like her womanhood,
Which whilome couerdft the moft louely face   160
That euer eye beheld.   VVas there no meffage fent
From her by thee ?   Ah yes, there feemes it was ;
Here is a *T* made with her blood, as if
Shee would haue written, *Thirfis,* I am flaine
In feeking thee ; fure fo it fhould haue beene,
And fo I reade it, and fhall euer fo.
   And thou fweet remnant of the faireft haire,
That euer wau'd with winde !   Ah thee I found
When her I hop'd to finde, wrapt in a round,
Like to an *O,* the chara&ter of woe ;   170
As if to fay, *O Thirfis,* I die thine.
This much you tell me yet, dumbe meffengers,
Of her laft minde ; and what you cannot tell
That I muft thinke, which is the moft extreame
Of wofulneffe, that any heart can thinke.
   Pal. There is no dealing with this man, I fee,

This humour muſt be let to ſpend it ſelfe
Vnto a leſſer ſubſtance, ere that we
Can any way apply a remedy.
But I lament his caſe, and ſo I know   180
Do all that ſee him in this wofull plight :
And therefore will I leaue him to himſelfe,
For ſorrow that is full, hates others ſight.

   Thir. Come boy, whilſt I contemplate theſe remaines
Of my loſt loue, vnder this myrtle tree,
Record the dolefull'ſt ſong, the ſighingſt notes,
That muſicke hath to entertaine bad thoughts.
Let it be all at flats my boy, all graue,
The tone that beſt befits the griefe I haue.

The Song.   190

Had ſorrow euer fitter place
To act his part,
Then is my heart,
Where it takes vp all the ſpace ?
Where is no veine
To entertaine
A thought that weares another face.
Nor will I ſorrow euer haue,
Therein to be,
But onely thee,   200
To whom I full poſſeſſion gaue :
Thou in thy name
Muſt holde the ſame,
Vntill thou bring it to the graue.

   Thir. So boy, now leaue me to my ſelfe, that I
May be alone to griefe, entire to miſery.

    l. 205, ' *Pal.*' wrongly prefixed here in 4to of 1623.

SCEN. II.

Cloris.   *Clarindo.*

NOw gentle boy *Clarindo*, haſt thou brought
   My flockes into the field ?   210
Cla. Miſtris I haue.
Clo. And haſt thou told them ?
Cla. Yes.
Clo. And are there all ?
Cla. All.
Clo. And haſt thou left them ſafe my boy ?
Cla. Safe.
Clo. Then whilſt they feede, *Clarindo*, I muſt vſe
Thy ſeruice in a ſerious buſineſſe ;
But thou muſt doe it well my boy.   220
Cla. The beſt I can.
Clo. Do'ſt thou know *Thirſis ?*
Cla. Yes.
Clo. But know'ſt him well ?
Cla. I haue good reaſon to know *Thirſis* well.
Clo. What reaſon boy ?
Cla. I oft haue ſeene the man.
Clo. Why then he knowes thee too ?
Cla. Yes I ſuppoſe, vnleſſe he hath forgotten me
     of late.
Clo. But hath he heard thee ſing my boy ?   230
Cla. He hath.
Clo. Then doubtles he doth well remember thee.
Well, vnto him thou muſt a meſſage do
From thy ſad miſtres *Cloris* ; but thou muſt
Doe it exactly well, with thy beſt grace,
Beſt choice of language, and beſt countenance.

I know thou canſt doe well, and haſt a ſpeech
And faſhion pleaſing to performe the ſame.
Nor can I haue a fitter meſſenger
In this imployment then thy ſelfe my boy.   240
For ſure me thinkes, noting thy forme and grace,
That thou haſt much of *Siluia* in thy face:
Which if he ſhall perceiue as well as I,
Sure, he will giue thee audience willinglie.
And for her ſake, if not for mine, heare out
Thy meſſage; for he ſtill (though ſhe be dead)
Holds ſparkles of her vnextinguiſhèd.
And that is death to me: for though ſometimes
Siluia and I moſt deere companions were,
Yet when I ſaw he did ſo much preferre   250
Her before me, I deadly hated her;
And was not ſorry for her death, and yet
Was ſorry ſhe ſhould come to ſuch a death.
    But to the purpoſe: goe to *Thirſis*, boy:
Say, thou art *Cloris* ſeruant, ſent to be
The meſſenger of her diſtreſſèd teares:
Who languiſhes for him, and neuer ſhall
Haue comfort more, vnleſſe he giue it her.
    Cla. I will.
    Clo. Nay but ſtay boy, ther's ſomething elſe: 260
Tell him, his cruelty makes me vndoe
My modeſty, and to put on that part
Which appertaines to him, that is to wooe:
And to diſgrace my Sexe, to ſhew my heart,
Which no man elſe could haue had powre to doe.
And that vnleſſe he doe reſtore me backe
Vnto my ſelfe, by his like loue to me,
I cannot liue.

Cla. All this I'le tell him too.

Clo. Nay but ſtay boy, there is yet more :⠀⠀⠀⠀270
Tell him, it will no honour be to him,
When euer it ſhall come to be made knowne,
That he hath beene her death that was his owne.
And how his loue hath fatall beene to two
Diſtreſſèd Nymphes.

Cla.⠀⠀⠀⠀⠀⠀This will I tell him too.

Clo. Nay but ſtay boy, wilt thou ſay nothing elſe?
As of thy ſelfe, to waken vp his loue ?
Thou mayſt ſay ſomething which I may not ſay,
And tell him how thou holdſt me full as faire,⠀⠀280
Yea and more faire, more louely, more compleate
Then euer *Siluia* was ; more wiſe, more ſtai'd :
How ſhee was but a light and wauering maid.

Cla. Nay there I leaue you, that I cannot ſay.

Clo. What ſayſt thou boy ?

Cla.⠀⠀⠀⠀⠀⠀⠀Nothing, but that I will
Endeauour all I can to worke his loue.⠀⠀⠀⠀•

Clo. Doe good my boy : but thou muſt yet adde more,
As from thy ſelfe, and ſay, what an vnkind
And barbarous part it is to ſuffer thus⠀⠀⠀⠀290
So beauteous and ſo rare a Nymph to pine
And periſh for his loue ; and ſuch a one,
As if ſhee would haue ſtoop'd to others flame,
Hath had the gallantſt heardſmen of theſe fields
Fall at her feete : all which ſhe hath deſpiſ'd,
Hauing her heart before by thee ſurpriz'd ;
And now doth nothing elſe, but ſit and mourne,
Speake *Thirſis*, weepe *Thirſis*, ſigh *Thirſis*, and
Sleepe *Thirſis* when ſhe ſleepes, which is but rare.
Beſides, good boy thou muſt not ſticke to ſweare,⠀300

Thou oft haſt ſeene me ſowne, and ſinke to ground
In theſe deepe paſſions, wherein I abound.
For ſomething thou maiſt ſay beyond the truth,
By reaſon of my loue, and of thy youth :
    Doe, good *Clarindo* ſweare, and vow thus much.
    But do'ſt thou now remember all I ſay,
Do'ſt thou forget no parcell of my ſpeech,
Shall I repeate the ſame againe to thee ?
Or els wilt thou rehearſe it vnto mee ?
That I may know thou haſt it perfeᴄt, boy.   310
    Cla. It ſhall not need : be ſure I will report,
What you enioyne me, in moſt earneſt ſort.
    Clo. Ah doe good boy.   Although I feare it will,
Auaile me little : for I doubt his heart
Is repoſſeſſèd with another loue.
    Cla. Another loue ?   Who may that be, I pray ?
    Clo. With *Amarillis*, I haue heard : for they
'Tis thought, will in the end make vp a match.
    Cla. With *Amarillis* ?   Well, yet will I goe,
And try his humour whether it be ſo ?   320
    Clo. Goe good *Clarindo*, but thou muſt not faile
To worke effeᴄtually for my auaile.
And doe not ſtay, returne with ſpeed good boy,
My paſſions are to great, t'indure delay.

ACT. I. SCEN. III.

Clarindo ſolus.

*T*Hirſis in loue with *Amarillis* ? then
    In what a caſe am I ? what doth auaile,
This altred habite, that belies my Sexe ?
What boots it t'haue eſcap'd from Pirats hands   330

And with fuch wiles to haue deceiu'd their wills,
If I returne to fall on worfer ills?
In loue with *Amarillis?* is that fo?
Is *Siluia* then forgot? that hath endur'd
So much for him? doe all thefe miferies
(Cauf'd by his meanes) deferue no better hire?
VVas it the greateft comfort of my life,
To haue return'd, that I might comfort him?
And am I welcom'd thus? ah did mine eyes
Take neuer reft, after I was arriu'd   340
Till I had feene him, though vnknowne to him?
Being hidden thus, and couer'd with difguife
Of mafculine attire, to temporize
Vntill *Alexis* mariage day be paft,
VVhich fhortly as I heare will be: and which
VVould free me wholly from my fathers feare:
VVho if he knew I were return'd, would yet
Vndoe I doubt that match, to match me there;
Which would be more then all my fuffrings were.
   Indeed me thought when I beheld the face   350
Of my deere *Thirfis*, I beheld a face
Confounded all with paffion, which did much
Afflict my heart: but yet I little thought
It could haue beene for any others loue.
I did fuppofe the memory of me,
And of my rapture, had poffeft him fo,
As made him fhew that countenance of woe.
And much adoe had I then to forbeare
From cafting me into his armes, and yeild
What comfort my poore felfe could yeild, but that 360
I thought our ioyes would not haue bin complete,
But might haue yeilded vs anoyes as great,

Vnleffe I could come wholly his, and cleer'd
From all thofe former dangers which we fear'd :
Which now a little ftay (though any ftay
Be death to me) would wholly take away.

 And therefore I refolu'd my felfe to beare
This burthen of our fufferings yet a while,
And to become a feruant in this guife,
To her I would haue fcornèd otherwife :   370
And be at all commands, to goe, and come,
To trudge into the fields, early, and late ;
Which though I know, it mifbecomes my ftate,
Yet it becomes my fortune, which is that,
Not *Phillis*, whom I ferue : but fince I ferue,
I will doe what I doe moft faithfully.

 But *Thirfis*, is it poffible that thou
Shouldft fo forget me, and forgoe thy vow ?
Or is it but a flying vaine report,
That flanders thine affeftion in this fort ?   380
It may be fo, and God grant it be fo :
I fhall foone finde if thou be falfe or no :
But ah here comes my Fury, I muft flie.

ACT. I. SCEN. IIII.

Phillis. *Clarindo.*

A H cruell youth, whither away fo faft ?
  Cla. Good *Phillis* do not ftay me, I haue haft.
 Phi. What haft fhoudft thou haue but to comfort me,
Who hath no other comfort but in thee ?
 Cla. Alas thou do'ft but trouble me in vaine, 390
I cannot helpe thee : t'is not in my powre.

Phil. Not in thy powre *Clarindo?* ah if thou
Hadſt any thing of manlines, thou wouldſt.

Cla. But if I haue not, what doth it auaile
In this ſort to torment thy ſelfe and me?
And therefore pre-thee *Phillis*, let me goe.

Phil. Ah whither canſt thou go, where thou ſhalt be
More deerely lou'd and cheriſht then with me?

Cla. But that my purpoſe cannot ſatisfie,
I muſt be gone, there is no remedie.   400

Phi. O cruell youth, will thy heart nothing moue?
Shew me yet pittie, if thou ſhew not loue.

Cla. Beleeue me *Phillis* I doe pittie thee;
And more, lament thy error, ſo farewell.

Phi. And art thou gone hard-hearted youth? haſt thou
Thus diſappointed my deſires, and let
My ſhame t'afflict me worſer then my loue?
Now in what caſe am I, that neither can
Recall my modeſtie, nor thee againe?

Ah were it now to do againe, my paſſions ſhould 410
Haue ſmothred me to death, before I would
Haue ſhew'd the ſmalleſt ſparkle of my flame:
But it is done, and I am now vndone.

Ah hadſt thou beene a man, and had that part
Of vnderſtanding of a womans heart,
My words had beene vnborne, onely mine eies
Had beene a tongue enough to one were wiſe.
But this it is, to loue a boy, whoſe yeares
Conceiues not his owne good, nor weighes my teares:
But this diſgrace I iuſtly haue deſeru'd.   420

SCEN. V.

Lidia. *Phillis.*

SO *Phillis* haue you, and y'are rightly feru'd.
  Haue you difdain'd the gallanft Forrefters,
And braueft heardfmen all *Arcadia* hath,
And now in loue with one is not a man?
Affure your felfe this is a iuft reuenge
Loue takes, for your mifprifion of his powre.
I told you often there would come a time,
When you would fure be plagu'd for fuch a crime: 430
But you would laugh at me, as one you thought
Conceiu'd not of what mettall you were wrought.
  Is this you, who would wonder any nimphes
Could euer be fo foolifh as to loue?
Who is fo foolifh now?   •
  Phil.   Peace *Lidia*, peace,
Adde not more griefe t'a heart that hath too much:
Do not infult vpon her mifery,
VVhofe flame, God wot, needs water, and not oyle.
Thou feeft I am vndone, caught in the toyle
Of an intangling mifchiefe: tell me how   440
I may recouer, and vnwinde me now.
  Lid. That doth require more time; we wil apart
Confult thereof, be you but rul'd by me,
And you fhall finde, I, yet, will fet you free.   *Exeunt.*

  The fong of the firft Chorus.
  Loue is a fickneffe full of woes,
    All remedies refufing:
  A plant that with moft cutting growes,
    Moft barren with beft vfing.
        Why fo?   450

More we enioy it, more it dyes,
If not enioy'd, it fighing cries,
  Hey ho.
Loue is a torment of the minde,
 A tempeft euerlafting ;
And Ioue hath made it of a kinde,
 Not well, nor full nor fafting.
  Why fo ?
More we enioy it, more it dies
If not enioyd, it fighing cries,   460
  Hey ho.

ACT. II. SCEN. I.

Siluanus. Dorcas. Montanus.

IN what a meáne regard are we now held,
 We aĉtiue and laborious forrefters ?
Who though our liuing rurall be and rough,
Yet heretofore were we for valour priz'd,
And well efteem'd in all good companies :
Nor would the daintieft nymphs that vallyes haunt
Or fields inhabite, euer haue defpif'd   470
Our filuane fongs, nor yet our plaine difcourfe ;
But gracefully accepted of our fkill,
And often of our loues, when they haue feené
How faithfull and how conftant we haue beene.
 Dor. It's true *Siluanus,* but you fee the times
Are altred now, and they fo dainty growne,
By being ador'd, and woo'd, and followed fo
Of thofe vnfinowed amorous heardfmen, who
By reafon of their rich and mighty flockes,
Supply their pleafures with that plenteoufneffe,   480

As they difdaine our plainneffe, and do fcorne
Our company, as men rude and ill borne.
 Sil. Well, fo they doe ; but *Dorcas* if you marke
How oft they doe mifcarry in their loue,
And how difloyall thefe fine heardfmen prooue ;
You fhall perceiue how their aboundant ftore
Payes not their expectation, nor defires.
Witneffe thefe groues wherein they oft deplore
The miferable paffions they fuftaine ;
And how perfidious, wayward, and vnkinde,   490
They finde their loues to be ; which we, who are
The eyes, and eares of woods, oft fee and heare.
For hither to thefe groues they muft refort,
And here one wayles apart the vfage hard
Of her difordred, wilde, and wilfull mate :
There mournes another her vnhappy ftate,
Held euer in reftraint, and in fufpect :
Another to her trufty confident,
Laments how fhe is matcht to fuch a one
As cannot giue a woman her content.   500
Another grieues how fhee hath got a foole,
Whofe bed, although fhe loath, fhe muft endure.
And thus they all vnhappy by that meanes
Which they accompt would bring all happineffe ;
Moft wealthely are plagu'd, with rich diftreffe.
 Dor. And fo they are, but yet this was not wont
To be the fafhion here ; there was a time
Before *Arcadia* came to be difeaf'd
With thefe corrupted humours reigning now,
That choife was made of vertue and defert,   510
Without refpect of any other endes :
When loue was onely mafter of their hearts,

And rul'd alone : when ſimple thoughts produc'd
Plaine honeſt deedes, and euery one contends
To haue his fame to follow his deſerts,
And not his ſhewes ; to be the ſame he was,
Not ſeem'd to be : and then were no ſuch parts
Of falſe deceiuings plaid, as now we ſee.
  But after that accurſèd greedineſſe
Of wealth began to enter and poſſeſſe   520
The hearts of men, integritie was loſt,
And with it they themſelues, for neuer more
Came they to be in their owne powre againe.
That Tyrant vanquiſht them, made them all ſlaues,
That brought baſe ſeruitude into the world,
Which elſe had neuer bin ; that onely made
Them to endure all whatſoeuer weights
Powre could deuiſe to lay vpon their necke.
For rather then they would not haue, they would not be
But miſerable.   So that no deuice   530
Needes elſe to keepe them vnder, they themſelues
Will beare farre more then they are made ; themſelues
VVill adde vnto their fetters, rather then
They would not be, or held to be great men.
  Sil. Then *Dorcas,* how much more are we to prize
Our meane eſtate, which they ſo much deſpiſe ?
Conſidering that we doe enioy thereby,
The deareſt thing in nature, *Liberty.*   .
And are not tortur'd with thoſe hopes and feares,—
Th'affliction layd on ſuperfluities,—   540
VVhich make them to obſcure, and ſerue the times :
But are content with what the earth, the woods
And riuers neere doe readily afforde
And therewithall furniſh our homely borde.

Thofe vnbought cates pleafe our vnlearned throats
That vnderftand not dainties, euen as well
As all their delicates, which doe but ftuffe
And not fuftaine the ftomacke : and indeede
A wel obferuing belly doth make much
For liberty ; for hee that can but liue,   550
Although with rootes, and haue no hopes, is free
Without the verge of any fou'rainty ;
And is a Lord at home, commands the day
As his till night, and then repofes him
At his owne houres ; thinkes on no ftratagem
But how to take his game, hath no defigne
To croffe next day ; no plots to vndermine.
   Dor. But why *Montanus* do you looke fo fad ?
What is the caufe your minde is not as free
As your eftate ? what, haue you had of late   560
Some coy repulfe of your difdainfull nymph,
To whom loue hath fubdu'd you ? who indeede
Our onely mafter is, and no Lord elfe
But he, hath any power to vexe vs here ;
Which had he not, we too too happy were.
   Mon. In troth I muft confeffe, when now you two
Found me in yonder thicket, I had loft
My felfe, by hauing feene that which I would
I had not had thefe eyes to fee ; and iudge
If I great reafon haue not to complaine :   570
You fee I am a man, though not fo gay
And delicate clad, as are your fine
And amorous dainty heardfmen, yet a man ;
And that not bafe, not vn-allyde to *Pan* ;
And of a fpirit doth not degenerate
From my robuftious manly anceftours,

III.   2

Being neuer foild in any wraftling game,
But ftill haue borne away the chiefeft prize
In euery braue and actiue exercife.
Yet notwithftanding that difdainfull mayd,   580
Prowd *Phillis*, doth defpife me and my loue,
And will not daigne fo much as heare me fpeake,
But doth abiure, forfooth, the thought of loue.
    Yet fhall I tell you (yet afham'd to tell ;)
This coy vnlouing foule, I faw ere while
Soliciting a youth, a fmooth fac'd boy,
Whom in her armes fhe held (as feem'd to me,
Being clofely bufht a prety diftance off,)
Againft his will ; and with ftrange paffion vrg'd
His ftay, who feem'd, ftruggled to get away ;   590
And yet fhe ftaid him, yet intreates his ftay.
    At which ftrange fight, imagine I that ftood
Spectatour, how confoundedly I ftood,
And hardly could forbeare from running in
To claime for mine, if euer loue had right,
Thofe her imbraces caft away in fight :
But ftaying to behold the end, I ftaid
Too long ; the boy gets loofe, her felfe retires,
And you came in ; but if I liue, that boy
Shall dearely pay for his misfortune, that   600
He was beloued of her, of whom I would
Haue none on earth beloued, but my felfe.
    Dor. That were to bite the ftone, a thing vniuft,
To punifh him for her conceiued luft.
    Mon. Tufh, many in this world we fee are
            caught,
And fuffer for misfortune, not their fault.
    Sil. But that would not become your manlines,

Montanus, it were fhame for valiant men
To doe vnworthily.

Mon. Speake not of that, *Siluanus*, if my rage 610
Irregular be made, it muft worke like effects.

Dor. Thefe are but billowes, tumbling after ftormes,
They laft not long ; come let fome exercife
Diuert that humour, and conuert your thoughts
To know your felfe ; fcorne her who fcorneth you ;
Idolatrize not fo that Sexe, but hold
A man of ftrawe more then a wife of gold. *Exeunt.*

ACT. II. SCEN. II.

Lidia. Phillis.

YOu muft not *Phillis*, be fo fenfible 620
Of thefe fmall touches which your paffion makes.

Phi. Small touches *Lidia*, do you count them fmall ?
Can there vnto a woman worfe befall
Then hath to me ? what ? haue not I loft all
That is moft deare to vs, loue and my fame ?
Is there a third thing *Lidia* you can name
That is fo precious as to match with thefe ?

Lid. Now filly girle, how fondly do you talke ?
How haue you loft your fame ; what for a few
Ill fauour'd louing words, vttred in ieaft 630
Vnto a foolifh youth ? Cannot you fay
You did but to make triall how you could,
If fuch a peeuifh qualme of paffion fhould
(As neuer fhall) oppreffe your tender heart,
Frame your conceit to fpeake, to looke, to figh
Like to a heart-ftrooke louer ; and that you
Perceiuing him to be a bafhfull youth,
Thought to put fpirit in him, and make you fport.

Phi. Ah *Lidia*, but he faw I did not fport,
He faw my teares, and more : what fhall I fay ?   640
He faw too much, and that which neuer man
Shall euer fee againe whil'ft I haue breath.

   Lid. Are you fo fimple as you make your felfe ?
What did he fee ? a counterfeited fhew
Of paffion, which you may, if you were wife,
Make him as eafily to vnbeleeue,
As what he neuer faw ; and thinke his eyes
Confpir'd his vnderftanding to deceiue.

How many women, thinke you, being efpide
In neerer-touching cafes by mifchance,   650
Haue yet not onely fac'd their louers downe
For what they faw, but brought them to beleeue
They had not feene the thing which they had feene,
Yea and t' fweare it too ; and to condemne
Themfelues ? fuch meanes can wit deuife
To make mens mindes vncredit their owne eies.

   And therefore let not fuch a toy as this
Difeafe your thoughts : and for your loffe of loue,
It is as much as nothing.   I would turne
A paffion vpon that fhould ouerturne   660
It cleane, and that is wrath ; one heate
Expels another.   I would make my thoughts of
   fkorne
To be in height fo much aboue my loue,
As they fhould eafe and pleafe me more by farre.
I would difdaine to caft a looke that way
Where he fhould ftand, vnleffe it were in fkorne,
Or thinke a thought of him, but how to worke
Him all difgrace that poffibly I could.

   Phi. That *Lidia* can I neuer doe, let him

Do what he will to me : report my fhame,   670
And vaunt his fortune, and my weakneffe blame.

    Lid. Nay as for that, he fhall be fo well charmd
Ere I haue done, as you fhall feare no tales.

    Phi. Ah *Lidia*, could that be without his harme,
How bleffed fhould I be : But fee where comes
My great tormentor, that rude Forrefter.
Good *Lidia* let vs flie, I hate his fight
Next to the ill I fuffer : let vs flie,
We fhall be troubled with him wofully.

    Lid. Content you *Phillis*, ftay and heare him   680
        fpeake :
We may make vfe of him more then you thinke.

    Phil. What vfe can of fo groffe a peece be made ?

    Lid. The better vfe be fure, for being groffe :
Your fubtler fpirits full of their fineffes,
Serue their owne turnes in others bufineffes.

ACT. II. SCEN. III.

Montanus.   *Lidia.*   *Phillis.*

VV Hat pleafure can I take to chafe wild beafts,
    When I my felfe am chac'd more egarly
By mine owne paffions, and can finde no reft ?   690
Let them who haue their heart at libertie,
Attend thofe fports. I cannot be from hence,
Where I receiu'd my hurt ; here muft I tread
The maze of my perplexed miferie.

    And here fee where fhee is the caufe of all !
And now, what fhall I doe ? what fhall I fay ?
How fhall I looke ? how ftand ? which vtter firft ?
My loue or wrath ? Alas I know not which.

Now were it not as good haue beene away,
As thus to come, and not tell what to fay ?   700
   Phil. See *Lidia* fee, how fauagely hee lookes !
Good let vs goe, I neuer fhall endure
To heare him bellow.
   Lid.   Prethee *Phillis* ftay
And giue him yet the hearing, in refpect
Hee loues you ; otherwife you fhew your felfe
A fauage more then hee.
   Phil.   Well, if I heare,
I will not anfwere him a word, you fhall reply :
And prethee *Lidia* doe, reply for mee.
   Lid. For that we fhall, *Phillis*, doe well enough
When he begins, who feemes is very long   710
To giue the onfet ; fure the man is much
Perplexed, or he ftudies what to fay.
   Phil. Good *Lidia* fee how he hath trickt himfelfe !
Now fure this gay frefh fuite as feemes to mee
Hangs like green Iuy on a rotten tree.   [goates :
   Lid. Some beafts do weare gray beards befide your
And beare with him, this fuit bewraies yong thoughts.
   Mon. Ah was it not enough to be oppreft
With that confounding paffion of my loue
And her difdaine, but that I muft be torne   720
With wrath and enuy too, and haue no veine
Free from the racke of fufferings, that I can
Nor fpeake nor thinke but moft diftractedly ?
   How fhall I now begin, that haue no way
To let out any paffion by it felfe,
But that they all will thruft together fo
As none will be expreffed as they ought ?
But fomething I muft fay now. I am here.

And be it what it will, loue, enuie, wrath,
Or all together in a comberment,   730
My words muſt be like me, perplext and rent ;
And ſo I'le to her.
    Phi.   *Lidia,* ſee he comes!
    Lid. He comes indeed, and as me thinkes doth ſhew
More trouble in his face by farre, then loue.
    Mon. Faire *Phillis,* and too faire for ſuch a one,
Vnleſſe you kinder were, or better then
I know you are : how much I haue endur'd
For you, although you ſcorne to know, I feele,
And did imagine, that in being a man
Who might deſerue regard, I ſhould haue bin   740
Prefer'd before a boy.   But well, I ſee
Your ſeeming and your being diſagree   [thus
    Phil. What *Lidia,* doth he brawle ? what meanes he
To ſpeake and looke in this ſtrange ſort on me ?
    Mon. Well modeſt *Phillis,* neuer looke ſo coy,
Theſe eyes beheld you dallying with a boy.
    Phil. Me with a boy, *Montanus* ? when ? where ? how ?
    Mon. To day, here, in moſt laſciuious ſort
    Lid. Ah, ha, he ſawe you *Phillis,* when
This morning you did ſtriue with *Cloris* boy   750
To haue your Garland, which he ſnatcht away,
And kept it from you by ſtrong force and might :
And you againe laid hold vpon the ſame,
And held it faſt vntill with much adoe,
He wrung it from your hands, and got away :
And this is that great matter which he ſaw.
    Now 'fye *Montanus* fye, are you ſo groſſe,
T'imagine ſuch a worthy Nymph as ſhee
Would be in loue with ſuch a youth as he ?

Why now you haue vndone your credit quite ;   760
You neuer can make her amends for this
So impious a furmife, nor euer can
Shee, as fhee reafon hath, but muft defpife
Your groffeneffe ; who fhould rather haue come in
And righted her, then fuffer fuch a one
To offer an indignity fo vile,
And you ftand prying in a bufh the while.
    Mon. What do I heare? what, am I not my felfe ?
How ? haue mine eyes double vndone me then ?
Firft feeing *Phillis* face, and now her fact,   770
Or elfe the fact I faw, I did not fee ?
And fince thou haft my vnderftanding wrong'd,
And traytour-like giuen falfe intelligence,
Whereby my iudgement comes to paffe amiffe.
And yet I thinke my fence was in the right :
And yet in this amaze I cannot tell,
But howfoere, I in an errour am,
In louing, or beleeuing, or in both.
And therefore *Phillis*, at thy feet I fall,
And pardon craue for this my groffe furmife.   780
    Lid. But this, *Montanus*, will not now fuffife,
You quite haue loft her, and your hopes and all.
    Mon. Good *Lidia* yet intreate her to relent,
And let her but command me any thing
That is within the power of man to do,
And you fhall finde *Montanus* will performe
More then a Gyant, and will ftead her more
Then all the Heardfmen in *Arcadia* can.
    Lid. Shee will command you nothing ; but I wifh
You would a little terrifie that boy   790
As he may neuer dare to vfe her name

But in all reuerence as is fit for her.
But doe not you examine him a word ;
For that were neither for your dignity,
Nor hers, that fuch a boy as he fhould ftand
And iuftifie himfelfe in fuch a cafe,
Who would but faine vntruths vnto your face.
And herein you fome feruice fhall performe,
As may perhaps make her to thinke on you.

 Mon. Alas, this is a worke fo farre, fo low   800
Beneath my worth, as I account it none ;
Were it t'incounter fome fierce mountaine beaft
Or Monfter, it were fomething fitting mee.
But yet this will I doe, and doe it home,
Affure you *Lidia* : as I liue I will.

 Phil. But yet I would not haue you hurt the youth,
For that were neither grace for you nor mee.

 Mon. That as my rage will tollerate muft be.

ACT II. SCEN. IV.

Cloris. Clarindo.   810

Eere comes my long expected meffenger,
 God grant the newes hee bring may make
  amends
For his long ftay ; and fure, I hope it will.
Me thinkes his face bewraies more iollytie
In his returning then in going hence.

 Cla. Well, all is well ; no *Amarillis* hath
Supplanted *Siluias* loue in *Thirfis* heart,
Nor any fhall : but fee where *Cloris* lookes
For what I fhall not bring her at this time.

Clo. Clarindo though my longing would be faine
Difpatch'd at once, and heare my doome pronoun
All in a word of either life or death,
Yet doe not tell it but by circumftance.
Tell me the manner vvhere, and how thou foundft
My *Thirfis*, what hee faid, how look'd, how far'd,
How he receiu'd my meffage, vfed thee;
And all in briefe, but yet be fure tell all.
 Cla. All will I tell, as neere as I can tell.
Firft after tedious fearching vp and downe,
I found him all alone, like a hurt Deare,
Got vnder couer in a fhadie groue,
Hard by a little chriftall purling fpring, ·
Which but one fullen note of murmur held;
And where no Sunne could fee him, where no eye
Might ouerlooke his lonely privacy;
There in a path of his owne making, trode
Bare as a common way, yet led no way
Beyond the turnes he made (which were but fhort)
With armes a croffe, his hat downe on his eyes
(As if thofe fhades yeelded not fhade ynough,
To darken them) he walkes with often ftops,
Vneuen pace, like motions to his thoughts.
 And when he heard me comming, for his eares
Were quicker watches then his eyes, it feem'd;
Hee fuddenly lookes vp, ftaies fuddenly,
And with a brow that told how much the fight
Of any interrupter troubled him,
Beheld me, without fpeaking any word,
As if expecting what I had to fay.
I finding him in this confuf'd difmay,
Who heretofore had feene him otherwife:

I muſt confeſſe, (for tell you all I muſt,)
A trembling paſſion ouerwhelmd my breaſt,
So that I likewiſe ſtood confuſ'd and dumbe
And onely lookt on him, as he on me.
In this ſtrange poſture like two ſtatues we
Remaind a while ; but with this difference ſet :
He bluſht, and I look'd pale ; my face did ſhew
Ioy to ſee him, his trouble to be ſeene.

    At length bethinking me for what I came,   860
What part I had to aċt, I rowzd my ſpirits,
And ſet my ſelfe to ſpeake ; although I wiſht
He would haue firſt begun ; and yet before
A word would iſſue, twiſe I bowd my knee,
Twice kiſt my hand; my aċtion ſo much was
More ready then my tongue : at laſt I told
Whoſe meſſenger I was, and how I came
To intimate the ſadde diſtreſſed caſe
Of an afflicted Nymph, whoſe onely helpe
Remaind in him : he when he heard the name   870
Of *Cloris*, turnes away his head, and ſhrinkes,
As if he grieued that you ſhould grieue for him.

    Clo. No, no, it troubled him to heare my name,
Which he deſpiſes ; is he ſo peruers
And wayward ſtill ? ah then I ſee no hope.
Clarindo, would to God thou hadſt not gone,
I could be, but as now, I am vndone.

    Cla. Haue patience Miſtres, and but heare the reſt.
When I perceiu'd his ſuffrings, with the touch
And ſodaine ſtop it gaue him, preſently   880
I layd on all the waights that motion might
Procure, and him beſought, adiur'd, invok'd,
By all the rights of Nature, pietie,

And manlines, to heare my meffage out.
Told him how much the matter did import
Your fafety and his fame.   How he was bound
In all humanity to right the fame.

   Clo. That vvas vvell done my boy, vvhat faid he then?

   Cla. Hee turnes about, and fixt his eyes on mee,
Content to giue his eares a quiet leaue,   890
To heare me ; vvhen I faild not to relate
All vvhat I had in charge ; and all he heares,
And lookes directly on me all the vvhile.

   Clo. I doubt he noted thee more then thy vvords ;
But now *Clarindo*, vvhat vvas his reply ?

   Cla. Thus.   Tell faire *Cloris*, my good boy, how that
I am not fo difnaturèd a man,
Or fo ill borne, to difefteeme her loue,
Or not to grieue, (as I proteft I doe)
That fhe fhould fo afflict her felfe for mee.   900
But——

   Clo.   Ah now comes that bitter vvord of But.
Which makes all nothing, that vvas faid before.
That fmooths and vvounds, that ftroakes and dafhes
Then flat denyals, or a plaine difgrace.   [more
But tell me yet vvhat followed on that *But* ?

   Cla. Tell her (faid hee) that I defire fhee would
Redeeme her felfe at any price fhee could,
And neuer let her thinke on mee ; vvho am
But euen the barke, and outfide of a man,
That trades not vvith the liuing, neither can   910
Nor euer vvill keepe other company
Then vvith the dead.   My *Siluias* memory
Is all that I muft euer liue vvithall.
With that his teares, vvhich likewife forced mine,

Set me againe vpon another racke
Of paffion fo, that of my felfe I fought
To comfort him the beft I could deuife.
And I befought him that he vvould not be
Tranfported thus ; but know that vvith the dead
He fhould no more conuerfe : and how his loue   920
Was liuing, that vvould giue him all content,
And vvas all his intire, and pure, and vvifht
To liue no longer then fhee fhould be fo.
When more I vvould haue faid, he fhooke his head
And vvild me fpeake no further at that time,
But leaue him to himfelfe, and to returne
Againe anone, and he vvould tell me more ;
Commending me for hauing done the part
Both of a true and mouing meffenger.
And fo I tooke my leaue, and came my vvay.   930
   Clo. Returne againe ? no, to what end,
If hee be [thus] conceited, and fo fond
To entertaine a fhadow ; I haue done,
And vvifh that I had neuer done fo much.
Shall I defcend below my felfe, to fend
To one is not himfelfe ? Let him alone
With his dead Image: you fhall goe no more.
Haue I here fram'd vvith all the art I could
This Garland deckt vvith all the various flowres
Arcadia yeelds, in hope hee vvould fend backe
Some comfort, that I might therwith haue crown'd 940
His loue, and vvitneff'd mine, in th'endles round
Of this faire ring, the Charaɗer of faith ?
   But now he fhall haue none of it, I rather vvill
Rend it in peeces, and difhatter all
Into a Chaos, like his formeles thoughts.

But yet thou faiſt hee vvild thee to returne,
And he vvould tell thee more.
 Cla.   Yes ſo hee ſaide.
 Clo. Perhaps thy vvords might yet ſo vvorke vvith
    him   950
As that hee takes this time to thinke on them,
And then I ſhould doe vvrong to keepe thee backe.
Well thou ſhalt goe, and carry him from mee
This Garland, vvorke it vvhat effeꞓt it vvill.
 But yet I know it vvill doe nothing. Stay
Thou ſhalt not goe, for ſure hee ſaid but that
To put thee off, that he might be alone
At his idolatrie, in vvorſhipping
A nothing, but his ſelfe made images.
But yet he may be vvearied with thoſe thoughts 960
As hauing worne them long, and end they muſt :
And this my meſſage comming in fit time,
And moouingly deliuered, may take hold :
He ſaid thou wert a moouing meſſenger.
Clarindo, did he not ?
 Cla.   Yes ſo he ſayd.
 Clo. Well, thou ſhalt goe ; and yet if any thought
Of me ſhould moue him, he knowes well my minde
(If not too well,) and where he may me finde.
Thou ſhalt not goe *Clarindo,* nor will I
Diſgrace me more with importunity :
And yet if ſuch a motion ſhould take fire,   970
And finde no matter ready, it would out,
And opportunities muſt not be flackt.
Clarindo, thou ſhalt go, and as thou goeſt,
Looke to my flocke, and ſo God ſpeed thee well.

SCEN. V.

Clarindo, alias Siluia folus.

VVEll, this imployment makes for my auaile,
    For hereby haue I meanes to fee my loue;
Who likewife fees me, though he fees me not;
Nor do I fee him as I would I did.   980
But I muft by fome meanes or other make
Him know I liue; and yet not fo as he
May know that I am I, for feare we might
Mifcary in our ioyes by ouer hafte.
But it is more then time his fuffrings were
Releeu'd in fome clofe fort; and that can I deuife
No way to doe, but by relating how
I heard of an efcape a nymph did make
From pirats lately, and was fafe return'd.
And fo to tell fome ftory that containes   990
Our fortunes and our loues, in other names;
And wifh him to expect the like euent;
    For I perceiue him very well content
To heare me fpeake; and fure he hath fome note,
Although fo darkly drawne, as that his eyes
Cannot exprefly reade it; yet it fhowes
Him fomething, which he rather feeles, then knowes.

The fong of the fecond Chorus.

Defire that is of things vngot,
   See what trauaile it procureth,   1000
   And how much the minde endureth,
To gaine what yet it gaineth not:
   For neuer was it paid,
   The charge defraide,
 According to the price of thought.

Charinus, the father of *Thirſis*.   *Palæmon.*

PAlæmon, you me thinkes might ſomething worke
　　With *Thirſis* my aggrieued ſonne, and found
His humour what it is : and why he thus　　　　1010
Afflicts himſelfe in ſolitarineſſe.
You two were wont to be moſt inward friends,
ᵛAnd glad I was to ſee it ; knowing you
To be a man well tempred, fit to ſort
With his raw youth ; can you do nothing now,
To win him from this vile captiuity
Of paſſion, that withholdes his from the world ?
　　Pal. In troth, *Charinus*, I haue oftentimes,
As one that ſuffred for his grieuances,
Aſſayd to finde a way into the cauſe　　　　1020
Of his ſo ſtrange diſmay ; and by all meanes
Aduiſ'd him make redemption of himſelfe,
And come to life againe, and be a man　　　　•
With men : but all ſerues not, I finde him lockt
Faſt to his will, alleadge I what I can.
　　Char. But will he not impart to you the cauſe ?
　　Pal. The cauſe is loue ; but it is ſuch a loue,
As is not to be had.
　　Cha.　　　　　　Not to be had ?
Palæmon, if his loue be regular,
Is there in all *Arcadia* any ſhe,　　　　1030
Whom his ability, his ſhape, and worth
May not attaine, he being my onely ſonne ?
　　Pal. She is not in *Arcadia* whom he loues,
Nor in the world, and yet he deerely loues.
　　Cha. How may that be, *Palæmon* ? tell me plaine.

Pal. Thus plainly ; he's in loue with a dead woman,
And that fo farre, as with the thought of her
Which hath fhut out all other, he alone
Liues, and abhorres to be, or feene, or knowne.

    Cha. What was this creature could poffeffe him fo ?

    Pal. Faire *Siluia*, old *Medorus* daughter, who   1041
Was two yeares paft reported to be flaine
By fauage beafts vpon our Country fhore.

    Cha. Is that his griefe ? alas, I rather thought
It appertain'd vnto anothers part
To wayle her death : *Alexis* fhould doe that,
To whom her father had difpofed her,
And fhe efteemed onely to be his.
Why fhould my fonne affliʃt him more for her,
Then doth *Alexis*, who this day doth wed   1050
Faire *Galatea*, and forgets the dead ?
And here the fhepheards come to celebrate
His ioyfull nuptials with all merriment ;
Which doth increafe my cares, confidering
The comforts other parents do receiue :
And therefore good *Palæmon* worke all meanes
You can to win him from his peeuifh will, ·
And draw him to thefe fhewes, to companies,
That others pleafures may inkindle his ;

    And tell him what a finne he doth commit,   1060
To wafte his youth in folitarineffe,
And take a courfe to end vs all in him.

    Pal. Affure your felfe *Charinus*, as I haue
So will I ftill imploy my vtmoft powre,
To faue him ; for me thinkes it pitty were,
So rare a peece of worth fhould fo be loft,

ACT. III. SCEN. II.

Charinus. *Medorus.*

MEdorus come, we two muſt ſit, and mourne 1076
Whilſt others reuell. We are not for ſports,
Or nuptiall ſhewes, which will but ſhew vs more
Our miſeries, in being both depriu'd
The comforts of our iſſue ; which might haue
(And was as like to haue) made our hearts
As ioyfull now, as others are in theirs.

Med. Indeed *Charinus*, I for my part haue
Iuſt cauſe to grieue amidſt theſe feſtiuals,
For they ſhould haue beene mine. This day I ſhould
Haue ſeene my daughter *Siluia* how ſhe would   1080
Haue womand it ; theſe rites had beene her grace,
And ſhe had ſat in *Galateas* place.
And now had warm'd my heart to ſee my blood
Preferu'd in her ; had ſhe not beene ſo rapt
And rent from off the liuing as ſhe was.
But your caſe is not paralell with mine ;
You haue a ſonne, *Charinus*, that doth liue,
And may one day to you like comforts giue.

Cha. Indeed I haue a ſonne ; but yet to ſay he
   liues,
I cannot ; for who liues not to the world,   1090
Nor to himſelfe, cannot be ſayd to liue
For euer ſince that you your daughter loſt,
I loſt my ſonne : for from that day he hath
Imbrak'd in ſhades and ſolitarineſſe,
Shut him ſelfe vp from light or company
Of any liuing : and as now I heard
By good *Palæmon*, vowes ſtill ſo to doe.

Med. And did your fonne, my daughter loue fo deare?
Now good *Charinus*, I muft grieue the more,
If more my heart could fuffer then it doth ;   1100
For now I feele the horrour of my deede,
In hauing croft the worthieft match on earth.
Now I perceiue why *Siluia* did refufe
To marry with *Alexis*, hauing made
A worthier choice ; which oh had I had grace
To haue forefeene; perhaps this difmall chance
Neuer had beene, and now they both had had
Ioy of their loues, and we the like of them.
    But ah my greedy eye, viewing the large
And fpacious fheep-walkes ioyning vnto mine,   1110
Whereof *Alexis* was poffeft, made me,
As worldlings doe, defire to marry grounds,
And not affections, which haue other bounds.
How oft haue I with threats, with promifes,
With all perfwafions, fought to win her minde
To fancy him, yet all would not preuaile !
How oft hath fhe againe vpon her knees
With teares befought me ; Oh deare father mine
Doe not inforce me to accept a man
I cannot fancy : rather take from me,   1120
The life you gaue me, then afflict it fo.
    Yet all this would not alter mine intent,
This was the man fhe muft affect or none.
But ah what finne was this to torture fo
A heart forevow'd vnto a better choice,.
Where goodneffe met in one the felfe fame point,
And vertues anfwer'd in an equall ioynt ?
Sure, fure, *Charinus*, for this finne of mine
The gods bereaft me of my child, and would

Not haue her be, to be without her heart,   1130
Nor me take ioy where I did none impart.
   Cha. Medorus, thus we fee mans wretchedneffe
That learnes his errours but by their fucceffe,
And when there is no remedie ; and now
VVe can but wifh it had beene otherwife.
   Med. And in that wifh *Charinus* we are rackt ;
But I remember now I often haue
Had fhadowes in my fleepe that figures bare
Of fome fuch liking twixt your childe and mine.
And this laft night a pleafing dreame I had   1140
(Though dreames of ioy makes wakers minds more fad)
Me thought my daughter *Siluia* was return'd
In moft ftrange fafhion, and vpon her knees
Craues my good will for *Thirfis*, otherwife
She would be gone againe and feene no more.
   I at the fight of my deare childe, was rapt
VVith that exceffe of ioy, as gaue no time
Either for me to anfwere her requeft,
Or leaue for fleepe to figure out the reft.
   Cha. Alas *Medorus*, dreames are vapours, which 1150
Ingendred with day thoughts, fall in the night
And vanifh with the morning ; are but made
Afflictions vnto man, to th'end he might
Not reft in reft, but toile both day and night.
   But fee here comes my folitarie fonne :
Let vs ftand clofe *Medorus* out of fight,
And note how he behaues himfelfe in this
Affliction, and diftreffed cafe of his.

SCEN. III

Thirſis ſolus. 1160

THis is the day, the day, the lamentable day
  Of my deſtruction, which the Sun hath twice
Returnd vnto my griefes, which keepe one courſe
Continually with it in motion like,
But that they neuer ſet : this day doth claime
Th'eſpeciall tribute of my ſighes and teares ;
Though, euery day I duely pay my teares
Vnto that ſoule which this day left the world.

  And yet I know not why ? me thought the Sun
Aroſe this day with farre more cheerefull raies, 1170
With brighter beames, then vſually it did,
As if it would bring ſomething of releaſe
Vnto my cares, or elſe my ſpirit hath had
Some manner of intelligence with hope,
Wherewith my heart is vnacquainted yet :
And that might cauſe mine eie with quicker ſence,
To note th'appearing of the eie of heauen ;
But ſomething ſure I feele which doth beare vp
The weight of ſorrow eaſier then before.

SCEN. IV.

Palæmon. Thirſis. 1180

WHat *Thirſis* ſtill in paſſion ? ſtill one man ?
  For ſhame ſhew not your ſelfe ſo weakely
So feebly ioynted, that you cannot beare   [ſet,
The fortunes of the world like other men.
Beleeue me *Thirſis* you much wrong your worth :
This is to be no man, to haue no powers.

Paſſions are womens parts, aĉtions ours;
I was in hope t'haue found you otherwiſe.
　Thir. How ? otherwiſe *Palæmon* ? do not you
Hold it to be a moſt heroicke thing　　　　　1190
To aĉt one man, and do that part exaĉt ?
Can there be in the world more worthineſſe
Then to be conſtant ? is there any thing
Shewes more a man? What, would you haue me change?
That were to haue me baſe, that were indeed
To ſhew a feeble heart, and weakely ſet.
　No no *Palæmon*, I ſhould thinke my ſelfe
The moſt vnworthy man of men, ſhould I
But let a thought into this heart of mine
That might diſturbe or ſhake my conſtancy.　　　1200
　And thinke *Palæmon* I haue combates too,
To be the man I am, being built of fleſh,
And hauing round about me traytors too
That ſeeke to vndermine my powres, and ſteale
Into my weakeneſſes, but that I keepe
Continuall watch and ward vpon my ſelfe,
Leaſt I ſhould be ſurpriz'd at vnawares
And taken from my vowes with other ſnares.
　And euen now at this inſtant I confeſſe,
Palæmon, I doe feele a certaine touch　　　1210
Of comfort, which I feare to entertaine ;
Leaſt it ſhould be ſome ſpie, ſent as a traine
To make diſcouery of what ſtrength I am.
　Pal. Ah worthy *Thirſis*, entertaine that ſpirit
What euer elſe thou doe : ſet all the doores
Of thine affeĉtions open thereunto.
　Thir. Palæmon no. Comfort and I haue beene
So long time ſtrangers, as that now I feare

To let it in, I know not how t'acquaint
My felfe therewith, being vfed to conuerfe   1220
With other humours, that affect me beft.
Nor doe I loue to haue mixt company
VVhereto I muft of force my felfe apply.
    Pal. But *Thirfis* thinke that this muft haue an end,
And more it would approoue your worth to make
The fame your worke, then time fhould make it his.
    Thir. End fure it muft *Palæmon,* but with me:
For fo I by the Oracle was told
That very day wherein I loft the day
And light of comfort that can neuer rife   1230
Againe to me : when I the faddeft man
That euer breath'd before thofe Altars fell,
And there befought to know what was become
Of my deare *Siluia,* whether dead, or how
Reaft from the world : but that I could not learne.
Yet thus much did that voice diuine returne :
Goe youth, referue thy felfe, the day will come
Thou fhalt be happy, and returne againe.
But when fhall be the day demanded I :
The day thou dyeft, replide the Oracle.   1240
    So that you fee, it will not be in thefe
But in th'Elizian fields, where I fhall ioy :
The day of death muft bring me happineffe.
    Pal. You may miftake the meaning of thofe words
Which is not knowne before it be fulfill'd.
Yeeld you to what the gods command, if not
Vnto your friends defires : referue your felfe
For better dayes, and thinke the Oracle
Is not vntrue, although not vnderftood.
    But howfoeuer, let it not be faid   1250

hat *Thirſis* being a man of ſo rare parts,
ɔ vnderſtanding and diſcreete, ſhould pine in loue
nd languiſh for a ſilly woman thus :
o be the fable of the vulgar, made
. ſcorne, and laught at, by inferiour wits.
  Thir. In loue *Palæmon* ? know you what you ſay
oe you eſteeme it light to be in loue ?
.ow haue I beene miſtaken in the choice
f ſuch a friend, as I held you to be,
hat ſeemes not, or elſe doth not vnderſtand   12
he nobleſt portion of humanity,
he worthieſt peece of nature ſet in man ?
h know that when you mention loue, you name
ſacred miſtery, a Deity,
ot vnderſtood of creatures built of mudde,
ut of the pureſt and refined clay
ʰereto th'eternall fires their ſpirits conuey.
nd for a woman, which you prize ſo low,
ike men that doe forget whence they are men ;
now her to be th'eſpeciall creature, made   12
ⁿ the Creator as the complement
f this great Architeꝗt the world ; to hold
ıe ſame together, which would otherwiſe
ıll all aſunder : and is natures chiefe
cegerent vpon earth, ſupplies her ſtate.
  And doe you hold it weakeneſſe then to loue ?
ıd loue ſo excellent a miracle
  is a woman ! ah then let mee
ll be ſo weake, ſtill let me loue and pine
  contemplation of that cleane, cleare ſoule,   12
at made mine ſee that nothing in the world
ſo ſupreamely beautifull as it.

Thinke not it was thofe colours white and red
Laid but on flefh, that could affe&t me fo.
But fomething elfe, which thought holds vnder
    locke
And hath no key of words to open it.
They are the fmalleft peeces of the minde
That paffe this narrow organ of the voyce.
The great remaine behinde in that vaft orbe
Of th'apprehenfion, and are neuer borne.   1290
    And therefore if your iudgement cannot reach
Vnto the vnderftanding of my Cafe,
You doe not well to put your felfe into
My Iury, to condemne me as you doe.
Let th'ignorant out of their dulneffe laugh
At thefe my fufferings, I will pitty them
To haue beene fo ill borne, fo mifcompof'd
As not to know vvhat thing it is to loue.
    And I to great *Apollo* here appeale
The foueraigne of the Mufes, and of all   1300
Well tun'd affe&tions, and to *Cinthia* bright,
And glorious Lady of cleere faithfulneffe;
Who from aboue looke down with blisfull beames
Vpon our humble groues, and ioy the hearts
Of all the world, to fee their mutuall loues;
They can iudge what worthineffe there is
In worthy loue. Therefore *Palæmon* peace,
Vnleffe you did know better what it were.
    And this be fure, when as that fire goes out
In man, he is the miferableft thing   1310
On earth, his day-light fets, and is all darke
And dull within; no motions of delight,
But all oppreft, lies ftruggling with the weight

Of worldly cares : and this olde *Damon* 'faies,
Who well had felt what loue was in his daies.
   Pal. Well *Thirfis*, well, how euer you do guilde
Your paffions, to indeere them to your felfe,
You neuer fhall induce me to beleeue,
That fickneffes can be of fuch effe&ct: :
And fo farewell, vntill you fhall be well.   1320

SCEN. V.

Medorus. Charinus.

O Gods, *Charinus*, what a man is this ?
    Who euer heard of fuch a conftancy ?
Had I but knowne him in enioying him,
As now I doe, too late in loofing him,
How bleft had beene mine age ! but ah I was
Vnworthy of fo great a bleffedneffe.
   Cha. You fee, *Medorus*, how no counfell can
Preuaile to turne the current of his will,   1330
To make it run in any other courfe
Then what it doth ; fo that I fee I muft
Efteeme him irreuocably loft.
   But harke, the fhepheards feftiuals begin,
Let vs from hence, where fadneffe were a fin.

     Here was prefented a rurall marriage, con-
        ducted with this Song.

    From the Temple to the Boord,
    From the Boord vnto the Bed,
     We conduct your maidenhead :   1340
    Wifhing Hymen *to affoord*
     All the pleafures that he can,
     Twixt a woman and a man.

ACT. IIII. SCEN. I.

Thirſis ſolus.

I Thought theſe ſimple woods, theſe gentle trees
   Would, in regard I am their daily gueſt,
And harbour vnderneath their ſhady roofes,
Not haue conſented to delude my griefes,
And mocke my miſeries with falſe reports :   1350
But now I ſee they will afflict me too.
   For as I came by yonder ſpreading Beech
Which often hath the Secretary beene
To my ſad thoughts, while I haue reſted me
(If loue had euer reſt) vnder his gentle ſhade,
I found incaru'd, and faire incaru'd, theſe words :
Thy Siluia, Thirſis, *liues ; and is return'd.*
Ah me, that any hand would thus adde ſcorne
Vnto affliction ; and a hand ſo faire
As this may ſeeme to be ; which were more fit,   1360
Me thinkes, for good, then to doe iniurie ;
For ſure no vertue ſhould be ill imploy'd.
   And which is more ; the name of *Siluia* was
Caru'd in the ſelfe ſame kind of Character
Which ſhe aliue did vſe, and wherewithall
Subſcrib'd her vowes to me, who knowes it beſt ;
Which ſhewes the fraud the more, and more the wrong.
Therefore you Stars of that high Court of Heauen,
Which doe reueale deceits, and puniſh them,
Let not this crime, to counterfeit a hand   1370
To couzin my deſires, eſcape the doome.
Nor let theſe riots of intruſion, made
Vpon my loneneſſe, by ſtrange company
Afflict me thus, but let me haue ſome reſt.

Come then, refrefher of all liuing things,
Soft fleepe, come gently, and take truce with thefe
Oppreffours, but come fimple and alone.
Without thefe Images of fantafie,
Which hurt me more then thou canft do me good :
Let me not fleepe, vnleffe I could fleepe all.   1380

SCEN. III.

Palæmon.   Thirfis.

ALas, he here hath laid him downe to reft,
    It were now finne his quiet to moleft ;
And God forbid I fhould ; I will retire
And leaue him, for I know his griefs require
This poore relieuement of a little fleepe.   [free ?
    Thir. What fpirit here haunts me? What no time
Ah, is it you *Palæmon?* would to God
You would forbeare me but a little while :   1390
You fhew your care of me too much in this,
Vnfeafonable loue fkarce kindneffe is.
    Pal. Good *Thirfis,* I am forry I fhould giue
The leaft occafion of difeafe to you ;
I will be gone and leaue you to your reft.
    Thir. Doe good *Palæmon,* go your way, farewell ;
And yet *Palæmon* ftay, perhaps you may
By charmes you haue, caufe fleepe to clofe mine eyes ;
For you were wont, I doe remember well,
To fing me Sonnets, which in paffion I   1400
Compofed in my happier dayes, when as
Her beames inflam'd my fpirits, which now are fet.
And if you can remember it, I pray
Sing me the fong, which thus begins: Eyes hide my loue,

Which I did write vpon the earneſt charge
Shee gaue vnto me, to conceale our loue.

The Song.

Eyes hide my loue, and doe not ſhew
To any but to her my notes,
Who onely doth that cipher know, 1410
Wherewith we paſſe our ſecret thoughts :
Belie your lookes in others ſight ;
And wrong your ſelues to doe her right.

Pal. So now hee ſleepes, or elſe doth ſeeme to ſleepe ;
But howſoeuer, I will not trouble him.

SCEN. III.

Clarindo.   Thirſis.

SEe where he lies, whom I ſo long to ſee ;
    Ah my deare *Thirſis*, take thy quiet reſt,
I know thou needſt it ; ſleepe thy fill, ſweet loue, 1420
Let nothing trouble thee ; be calme oh windes,
Be ſtill you heards, chirp not ſo loud ſweet birds,
Leſt you ſhould wake my loue : thou gentle banke
That thus are bleſt to beare ſo deare a weight,
Be ſoft vnto thoſe dainty lymmes of his ;
Plie tender graſſe, and render ſweet refreſh
Vnto his weary ſenſes, whilſt he reſts.
    Oh could I now but put of[f] this diſguiſe,
With thoſe reſpeĉts that fetter my deſire,
How cloſely would I neighbour that ſweet ſide ! 1430
But ſtay, he ſtirres ; I feare my heart hath brought
My feete too neare, and I haue wakened him.

Thir. It will not be, fleepe is no friend of mine,
Or fuch a friend, as leaues a man, vvhen moft
He needes him.　See a new affault : vvho now?
Ah tis the boy that vvere vvith me erewhiles,
That gentle boy ; I am content to fpeake
With him, he fpeakes fo pretily, fo fweet,
And vvith fo good refpeƈtiue modefty :
And much refembles one I knew once vvell :　　1440
Come hither gentle boy, vvhat haft thou there ?

Cla. A token fent you from the Nymph I ferue.

Thi. Keepe it my boy, and weare it on thy
　　　head.　　　　　　　　　　　　　　　.

Cla. The gods forbid, that I, a feruant, fhould
Weare on my head, that vvhich my Miftreffe hath
Prepar'd for yours : Sir, I befeech you vrge
No more a thing fo ill becomming me.

Thi. Nay fure I thinke, it better vvill become
Thy head then mine ; and therefore boy, thou muft
Needes put it on.　　　　　　　　　　1450

Cla.　　　　　　I truft your loneneffe hath not fo
Vnciuil'd you, to force a meffenger
To doe againft good manners, and his vvill.

Thi. No, good my boy, but I intreate thee now
Let me but put it on, hold ftill thy head,
It fhall not be thy aƈt, but onely mine :
Let it alone good boy, for if thou faw'ft
How vvell it did become thee, fure thou vvouldft.
Now, canft thou fing my boy fome gentle fong ?

Cla. I cannot fing, but I could vveepe.　　1460

Thi.　　　　　　　　　　　Weepe; why ?

Cla. Becaufe I am not as I wifh to be.

Thi. Why fo are none ; be not difpleaf'd for this ;

And if you cannot fing; tell me fome tale
To paffe the time.
    Cla. That can I doe, did I but know what kinde
Of tale you lik't.
    Thi. No merry tale my boy, nor yet too fad,
But mixed, like the tragicke Comedies.
    Cla. Then fuch a tale I haue, and a true tale,   1470
Beleeue me Sir, although not written yet
In any booke; but fure it will, I know :
Some gentle fhepheard, moou'd with paffion, muft
Record it to the vvorld, and vvell it vvill
Become the vvorld to vnderftand the fame.
And this it is : There vvas fometimes a Nymph,
Ifulia nam'd, and an *Arcadian* borne ;
Faire can I not auouch fhee vvas, but chaft,
And honeft fure, as the euent vvill prooue ;
Whofe mother dying, left her very young   1480
Vnto her fathers charge, vvho carefully
Did breed her vp, vntill fhee came to yeares
Of vvomanhood, and then prouides a match
Both rich, and young, and fit enough for her.
    But fhee, vvho to another fhepheard had
Call'd *Sirthis*, vow'd her loue, as vnto one
Her heart efteem'd more vvorthy of her loue,
Could not by all her fathers meanes be vvrought
To leaue her choice ; and to forget her vow.   1489
    Thi. No more could my deare *Siluia* be from me.
    Cla. Which caufed much affliction to them both,
    Thi. And fo the felfe fame caufe did vnto vs.
    Cla. This Nymph one day, furcharg'd vvith loue & griefe,
Which commonly (the more the pitty) dwell
As Inmates both together, vvalking forth

With other Maydes to fifh vpon the fhoare ;
Eftrayes apart, and leaues her company ;
To entertaine her felfe vvith her owne thoughts :
And vvanders on fo farre, and out of fight,
As fhee at length vvas fuddenly furpriz'd   1500
By Pyrats, vvho lay lurking vnderneath
Thofe hollow rocks, expecting there fome prize.
And notwithftanding all her pitious cryes,
Intreaty, teares, and prayers, thofe fierce men
Rent haire, and vaile, and carried her by force
Into their fhip, vvhich in a little Creeke
Hard by, at Anckor lay, and prefently hoyf'd faile,
And fo away.
 Thi. Rent haire and vaile? and fo
Both haire and vaile of *Siluia*, I found rent,
Which heere I keepe with mee. But now alas   1510
What did fhee ? what became of her my boy ?
 Cla. When fhee was thus infhipp'd, and woefully
Had caft her eyes about to view that hell
Of horrour, whereunto fhee was fo fuddenly
Implung'd, fhee fpies a woman fitting with a child
Sucking her breaft ; which was the Captaines wife.
To her fhee creepes, downe at her feet fhee lyes ;
O woman, if that name of woman may
Moue you to pitty, pitty a poore maid,
The moft diftreffed foule that euer breath'd ;   1520
And faue me from the hands of thefe fierce men,
Let me not be defil'd, and made vncleane,
Deare woman now : and I will be to you
The faithfull'ft flaue that euer Miftreffe feru'd ;
Neuer poore foule fhall be more dutifull,
To doe what euer you command, then I.

No toile will I refufe ; fo that I may
Keepe this poore body cleane and vndeflowr'd,
Which is all I will euer feeke.   For know
It is not feare of death layes me thus low,   1530
But of that ftaine will make my death to blufh.
   Thi. What, would not all this moue a womans heart?
   Cla. All this would nothing mooue the womans heart,
Whom yet fhee would not leaue, but ftill befought ;
Oh woman, by that Infant at your breaft,
And by the paines it coft you in the birth,
Saue me, as euer you defire to haue
Your babe to ioy and profper in the world ;
Which will the better profper fure, if you
Shall mercy fhew, which is with mercy paid.   1540
   Then kiffes fhee her feet, then kiffes too
The Infants feet : and oh fweet babe (faid fhee)
Could'ft thou but to thy mother fpeake for me,
And craue her to haue pitty on my cafe ;
Thou might'ft perhaps preuaile with her fo much,
Although I cannot ; child, ah could'ft thou fpeake !
   The Infant, whether by her touching it
Or by inftinᵭ of nature, feeing her weepe,
Lookes earneftly vpon her, and then lookes
Vpon the mother, then on her againe,   1550
And then it. cryes, and then on either lookes ∶
Which fhee perceiuing, bleffed child, faid fhee,
Although thou canft not fpeake, yet do'ft thou cry
Vnto thy mother for me.   Heare thy child
Deare mother, it's for me it cryes,
It's all the fpeech it hath : accept thofe cryes,
Saue me at his requeft from being defilde ;
Let pitty mooue thee, that thus mooues thy childe.

III.   25

The woman, though by birth and cuftome rude,—
Yet hauing veynes of nature, could not bee   1560
But peircible,—did feele at length the point
Of pitty, enter fo, as out gufht teares,
(Not vfuall to fterne eyes) and fhee befought
Her hufband to beftow on her that prize,
With fafegard of her body at her will.
    The Captaine feeing his wife, the childe, the nymph,
All crying to him in this pitious fort;
Felt his rough nature fhaken too, and grants
His wiues requeft, and feales his grant with teares;
And fo they wept all foure for company :   1570
And fome beholders ftood not with dry eyes;
Such paffion wrought the paffion of their prize.
    Thi. In troth my boy, and euen thy telling it
Mooues me likewife, thou dooft fo feelingly
Report the fame, as if thou hadft beene by.
But I imagine now how this poore nymph
When fhee receiu'd that doome, was comforted ?
    Cla. Sir, neuer was there pardon, that did take
Condemned from the blocke, more ioyfull then
This graunt to her.   For all her mifery   1580
Seem'd nothing to the comfort fhee receiu'd,
By being thus faued from impurity :
And from the womans feet fhee would not part,
Nor truft her hand to be without fome hold
Of her, or of the child, fo long as fhee remain'd
Within the fhip ; which in few dayes arriues
At *Alexandria*, whence thefe Pirats were ;
And there this woefull maide for two yeares fpace
Did ferue, and truly ferue this Captaines wife,
Who would not loofe the benefit of her   1590

Attendance for her profit otherwife.
But daring not in fuch a place as that
To truft her felfe in womans habite, crau'd
That fhe might be appareld like a boy :
And fo fhee was, and as a boy fhee feru'd.

Thi. And two yeares tis, fince I my *Siluia* loft.

Cla. At two yeares end, her Miftreffe fends her forth
Vnto the Port for fome commodities,
Which whilft fhee fought for, going vp and down
Shee heard fome Merchant men of *Corinth* talke, 1600
Who fpake that language the *Arcadians* did,
And were next neighbours of one continent.

To them all wrapt with paffion, down fhe kneeles,
Tels them fhee was a poore diftreffed boy,
Borne in *Arcadia*, and by Pirats tooke
And made a flaue in *Egypt*, and befought
Them, as they fathers were of children, or
Did hold their natiue countrey deare, they would
Take pitty on her, and relieue her youth
From that fad feruitude wherein fhee liu'd : 1610
For vvhich fhee hop'd that fhee had friends aliue
VVould thanke them one day, and reward them too ;
If not, yet that fhee knew the Heauens vvould doe.
The Merchants moou'd with pitty of her cafe,
Being ready to depart, tooke her vvith them,
And landed her vpon her countrey coaft.
Where vvhen fhee found her felfe, fhee proftrate falls,
Kiffes the ground, thankes giues vnto the gods;
Thankes them vvho had beene her deliuerers.

And on fhee trudges through the defart woods, 1620
Climes ouer craggy rockes, and mountaines fteepe,
Wades thorough riuers, ftruggles thorough bogs,

Suſtained onely by the force of loue ;
Vntill ſhee came vnto the natiue plaines,
Vnto the fields, vvhere firſt ſhee drew her breath.
　　There lifts ſhee vp her eyes, ſalutes the ayre,
Salutes the trees, the buſhes, flowres, and all :
And oh deare *Sirthis*, heere I am, ſaid ſhee,
Heere, notwithſtanding all my miſeries :
I am the ſame I was to thee ; a pure,　　　　　1630
A chaſt, and ſpotleſſe maide : oh that I may
Finde thee the man, thou didſt profeſſe to be.
　　Thi. Or elſe no man, for boy who truly loues,
Muſt euer ſo ; that dye will neuer out :
And who but would loue truly ſuch a ſoule ?
　　Cla. But now, the better to haue notice how
The ſtate of things then ſtood, and not in haſte
To caſt her ſelfe on new incumbrances,
Shee kept her habite ſtill, and put her ſelfe
To ſerue a nymph, of whom ſhee had made choice 1640
Till time vvere fitting to reueale her ſelfe.
　　Thi. This may be *Siluias* caſe ; this may be ſhee ;
But it is not : let mee conſider vvell :
The teller, and the circumſtance agree.

SCEN. III.

Montanus.　Thirſis.　Chorus.

A H ſirrha, haue I found you ? are you heere .
　　You princock boy ? & with your garland on ?
Doth this attire become your peeuiſh head ;
Come, I muſt teach you better manners, boy.　　1650
　　He ſtabs Clarindo *and daſhes off his garland.*

So *Phillis*, I haue done my tafke, and heere
I bring the Trophey to confirme the fame.

 Thi. Ah monfter man, vile wretch, what haft thou done?
Alas, in what a ftrait am I ingaged heere?
If I purfue reuenge, I leaue to faue.
Helpe, helpe, you gentle fwaines, if any now be neare,
Helpe, helpe: ah harke, euen Eccho helpes me cry helpe.

 Cho. What meanes this outcry? fure fome fauage beaft
Difturbs our heards, or elfe fome Wolfe hath feaz'd 1660
Vpon a Lambe.

 Thi.   A worfe thing then a Wolfe
More bloody then a beaft, hath murthered here
A gentler creature then a Lambe : therefore
Good fwaines purfue, purfue the homicide.
That ougly wretch, *Montanus*, who hath ftab'd
This filly creature heere, at vnawares.

 Cho. Montanus? why, we met him but euen now,
Deckt with a garland, grumbling to himfelfe ;
We will attach that villaine prefently :
Come firs, make hafte, and let vs after him. 1670

SCEN. IIII.

Palæmon. *Thirfis.*

A Las, what accident is here falne out ?
 My deare friend *Thirfis*, how comes this to paffe?
 Thi. That monfter man *Montanus*, heere hath ftab'd
A harmleffe youth, in meffage fent to me.
Now good *Palæmon* helpe me hold him vp,
And fee if that we can recouer him.

 Pal. It may be *Thirfis*, more his feare then hurt :
Stay him a while, and I will hafte and fend 1680

For *Lamia*, who with oyntments, oyles and herbes
If any helpe remaine, will helpe him fure.
    Thi. Do good *Palæmon*, make what haft you may,
Seeke out for helpe, and be not long away.
Alas fweet boy, that thou fhould'ft euer haue
So hard misfortune, comming vnto me,
And end thy tale with this fad tragedy ;
That tale which well refembled *Siluias* cafe,
Which thou refembleft ; for fuch browes had fhe,
Such a proportion'd face, and fuch a necke.   1690
    What haue we here, the mole of *Siluia* too ?
What and her breafts? what? and her haire? what all?
All *Siluia* ? yes, all *Siluia*, and all dead.
And art thou thus return'd againe to me ?
Art thou thy felfe, that ftrange deliuered nymph ?
And didft thou come to tell me thine efcape
From death to die before me ? had I not
Enough to doe, to wayle reported harmes
But thou muft come to bleed within my armes ?
Was not one death fufficient for my griefes   1700
But that thou muft die twice ? why thou wert dead
To me before. Why ? muft thou dye againe ?
Ah, better had it beene ftill to be loft
Then thus to haue beene found ; yet better found
Though thus, then fo loft as was thought before.
For howfoeuer, now 1 haue thee yet
Though in the faddeft fafhion that may be.
Yet *Siluia* now I haue thee, and will I
No more for euer part with thee againe :
And we this benefit fhall haue thereby,   1710
Though fate would not permit vs both to haue
One bed, yet *Siluia* we fhall haue one graue.

And that is fomething, and much more then I
Expected euer could haue come to paffe.
　And fure the gods but onely fent thee thus
To fetch me ; and to take me hence with thee ;
And *Siluia* fo thou fhalt.　I ready am
T'accompany thy foule, and that with fpeed.
The ftrings I feele, are all diffolu'd, that hold
This woefull heart, referu'd it feemes for this,　　1720
And well referu'd, for this fo deare an end.

SCEN. V.

Chorus.　Palæmon.

SO, we haue tooke the villaine, and him bound
　　Faft to an Oake, as rugged as himfelfe.
And there he ftares and gapes in th'ayre, and raues
Like a wilde beaft that's taken in the toyle :
And fo he fhall remaine, till time we fee
What will become of this his fauage act.
　Cheere *Thirfis*, *Lamia* will come prefently　　1730
And bring the beft preferuatiues fhe hath.
What now ?　Who lyes difcouered heere ?　Ay me,
A woman dead ?　Is this that boy transform'd ?
Why, this is *Siluia*.　O good *Thirfis* how
Comes this to paffe ?　Friend *Thirfis*, *Thirfis* fpeake.
Good *Thirfis* tell me.　Out alas he fownes,
As well as fhe, and both feeme gone alike.
　Come gentle heardfmen, come and carry them
To yonder fheepe-cote quickly, that we may
(If poffible) recouer them againe.　　1740
If not, performe thofe rites that appertaine
Vnto fo rare a couple.　Come my friends, make haft.

The fourth Song of the Chorus.

Qu. *Were euer chaſt and honeſt hearts*
     Expoſ'd vnto ſo great diſtreſſes?
Anſ. *Yes : they that act the worthieſt parts,*
     Moſt commonly haue worſt ſucceſſes.
Great fortunes follow not the beſt,
It's vertue that is moſt diſtreſt.

Then fortune why doe we admire   1750
     The glory of thy great exceſſes ?
Since by thee what men acquire,
     Thy worke and not their worths expreſſes.
Nor doſt thou raiſe them for their good :
But t'haue their illes more vnderſtood.

ACT. V. SCEN. I.

Chorus.   Palæmon.

Did euer yet *Arcadia* heare before
     Of two ſo worthy louers, as we find
Thirſis and *Siluia* were ? or euer had   1760
Cleare truth, and ſimple conſtant honeſty,
So lamentable an euent as this ?
But heere comes foorth *Palæmon*, we ſhall now
Learne all of him, what hath beene done within.
  Pal. Goe *Pollio*, ſummon all th'*Arcadia* youth
Heere, round about, and will them to prepare
To celebrate with all delights they can
This ioyfull houre, that hath reſtor'd to vs
The worthieſt paire of hearts that euer were.
  Will them to ſhew the height of muſiques art, 1770

And all the ftraines of cunning they can fhew ::
That we may make thefe rockes and hilles about,
Ring with the Eccho of redoubled notes.
 And will *Charinus* and *Medorus* too,
The aged parents of this worthy paire,
To come with fpeed, whofe ioy, good foules, wil be
More then their fpeed ; and yet their fpeed I know,
Will be beyond th'allowance of their yeares,
When they fhall vnderftand this happy newes.
 And fummon likewife all the traine of nymphes 1780
That glorifie our plaines, and all that can
Giue honour to this day.
Goe *Pollio* haft away, and as you go
Vnbind *Montanus* that rude fauage fwaine :
And though he be vnworthy to be here,
Yet let him come.   He hath beene in his dayes
Held a good fellow, howfoeuer now
His rage and loue tranfported him in this.
 Cho. Palæmon, we are glad to fee you thus
Delightfull, now we hope there is good newes.   1790
 Pal. Good newes my friends, and I will tell it you.
Siluia and *Thirfis* being to my cottage brought,
The fkilfull *Lamia* comes and fearcht the wound
Which *Siluia* had receiu'd of this rude fwaine,
And finding it not deadly, fhe applide
Thofe remedies fhe knew of beft effeft.
And binds it vp, and powres into her mouth
Such cordiall waters as reuiue the fpirits :
And fo much wrought, as fhe at length perceiu'd
Life was not quite gone out, but lay oppreft.   1800
 With like endeauours we on *Thirfis* worke,
And miniftred like Cordials vnto him :

At length we might heare *Siluia* fetch a groane,
And therewithall *Thirfis* perceiu'd to moue,
Then *Thirfis* fet a groane, and *Siluia* mou'd
As if their liues were made both of one peece.
Whereat we ioyd, and then remou'd and fet
Each before other and held vp their heads, [cheekes :
And chaf'd their temples, rub'd and ftroak'd their
   Wherewith firft *Siluia* caft vp her dimme eyes, 1810
And prefently did *Thirfis* lift vp his.
And then againe they both together figh'd,
And each on other fixt an vnfeeing eye :
For yet t'was fcarfe the twylight of their new
Returning day, out of the night of death.
And though they faw, they did not yet perceiue
Each other, and yet both turn'd to one point
As toucht alike, and held their lookes direct.
At length we might perceiue, as life began
T'appeare ; and make the morning in their eyes, 1820
Their beames were cleerer, and their opener lookes
Did fhew as if they tooke fome little note   •
Of each the other : yet not fo as they
Could thorowly difcerne who themfelues were.
   And then we tooke and ioyn'd their hands in one
And held them fo a while, vntill we fealt
How euen each others touch, the motion gaue.
Vnto their feeling, and they trembling wrung
Their hands together, and fo held them lockt :
Lookt ftill vpon each other, but no words at all. 1830
   Then we call'd out to *Thirfis, Thirfis* looke,
It is thy *Siluia* thou here holdft, fhe is
Return'd, reuiu'd and fafe.   *Siluia*, behold thou haft
Thy *Thirfis*, and fhalt euer haue him thine.

Then did we fet them both vpon their feete
And there they ftood in act, euen as before
Looking vpon each other, hand in hand:
At laft we faw a blufhing red appeare
In both their cheekes, which fenfe fent as a lampe
To light their vnderftanding.   And forthwith   1840
The teares gufht forth their eyes, which hindred them
A while from feeing each other, till they had
Cleared them againe.   And then as if new wak'd
From out a fearefull dreame, they ftand and doubt
Whether they were awake indeed, or elfe
Still in a dreame, diftrufting their owne eyes.
Their long indured miferies, would not
Let them beleeue their fudden happineffe,
Although they faw it: till with much adoe
They had confirm'd their credit, and had kift   1850
Each other and imbrac'd, and kift againe,
And yet ftill dumbe: their ioy now feem'd to be
Too bufie with their thoughts, t'allow them words.

    And then they walkt a little, then ftood ftill,
Then walkt againe, and ftill held other faft
As if they fear'd, they fhould be loft againe.

    And when at laft they fpake, it was but thus,
O *Siluia*, and O *Thirfis*, and there ftopt.

    We, left our fight and prefence (being there
So many) hinder might the paffage of   1860
Their modeft, fimple, and vnpractif'd loue,
Came all our way, and onely *Lamia* left;
Whofe fpirit, and that fufficient fkill fhe hath
Will ferue no doubt, to fee they fhall doe well.

    Cho. Well may they do deere couple, who haue thus
Grac'd our *Arcadia* with their faithfulneffe.

SCEN. II.

Phillis.   Lidia.   Cloris.

V V Hat fhall we now do *Lidia* ? now am I
Vtterly fham'd : this youth turn'd woman is.
Clarindo, Siluia is become ; how now ?   1871
Can I for euer looke on her againe ?
Or come in any company for fhame ?
Now muft I needs be made a common ieaft
And laughing ftocke to euery one that fhall
But heare how groffely I behau'd my felfe.

Lid. Faith *Phillis* as it is falne out, your cafe
Is very crazy, and to make it whole
There is no way but euen to laugh it out,
And fet as good a face, as you can doe   1880
Vpon the matter, and fay thus : How you
Knew well enough it was no man whom you
Affeﬆed fo, who neuer could loue man
Nor euer would, and that by meere inftinﬆ
And fimpathy of Sexe, you fancied him :
So put it off, and turne it to a ieaft.

Phi. That fhall I neuer do, but euer blufh
Either, to thinke what fhe will thinke of me,
Who did bewray my felfe fo foolifhly.

Lid. Are you here *Cloris* ? you are bleft to day 1890
For being miftres vnto fuch a boy :
You may reioyce that euer this fell out.

Clo. Reioyce ? ah *Lidia*, neuer was there nymph
Had more occafion to be fad then I,
For I am quite vndone and fham'd hereby.
For I imploy'd this my fuppofed boy
In meffage vnto *Thirfis*, whom I lou'd

I muſt confeſſe, more dearely then my life :
And told him all the ſecrets of my heart.
And therefore with what face can euer I   1900
Looke vpon them that know thus much by me ?
No *Lidia*, I will now take *Thirſis* courſe :
Hide me for euer in theſe deſert woods,
And neuer come in company againe ;
They ſhall not laugh at me in their great ioyes.
    Lid. But *Cloris*, I would laugh with them, were I as
        you.
And howſoeuer felt my ſelfe within,
Yet would I ſeeme be otherwiſe without.
Cannot you ſay, that you knew well enough
How it was *Siluia* that you intertain'd,   1910
Although you would not ſeeme to take ſuch note ;
And thereupon imploy'd her in that ſort
To *Thirſis*, knowing who it was would giue
To him the greateſt comfort vpon earth,
    And thus faire Nymphes you fitly may excuſe
Theſe ſimple flips, and know that they ſhall ſtill
Haue croſſes with their piles, who thus do play
Their fortunes with their loues, as you two did;
But you muſt frame your countenance thereto
And looke with other faces then your owne.   1920
As many elſe do here, who in their parts ·
Set ſhining lookes vpon their cloudy hearts.
And let vs mixe vs with this company
That here appeares with mirth and iollity.

The Song of the fifth Chorus.

Who euer ſaw ſo faire a ſight,
Loue and vertue met aright :

And that wonder Conſtancy,
 Like a Comet to the eye
Seldome euer ſeene ſo bright?   1930
 Sound out aloud ſo rare a thing,
 That all the Hilles and Vales may ring.

Looke Louers looke, with paſſion ſee,
If that any ſuch there bee :
 As there cannot but be ſuch
 Who doe feele that noble touch
In this glorious company,
 Sound out aloud, &c.

FINIS.   1939

END OF VOL. III.

Printed by Hazell, Watson, and Viney, Ld., London ana Aylesbury.

ERRATUM-NOTE

The line-marking in 'Philotas' (p. 155) inadvertently loses ten lines by repetition of 1450 ; and (p. 169) leaps from line 1900 [1890] to 2000—thus gaining ninety lines thenceforward. The student will please 'take a note' of this.